THE LAST ENGLISHMAN

A 2,640-Mile Hiking Adventure on the
Pacific Crest Trail

KEITH FOSKETT

The Last Englishman

By Keith Foskett

www.keithfoskett.com

ISBN: 978-1480169111

Cover photo by Josh 'Pockets' Myers - trekkingphotography.com

In memory of my Nan

Contents

Acknowledgements

Writing a book and attempting a thru-hike are similar in many ways. They are both long journeys involving some heartache, lots of persistence and patience. Both require little steps to reach a far-distant goal, covering a little ground each day until eventually the finish is in sight. However, a writer has many allies fighting with him to make that journey a little smoother, and it's a pleasure to be able to give them credit here.

Apart from acknowledging individuals who helped me with the actual writing, I also need to express gratitude to those who put up with my unsociable lifestyle but are proud, I hope, of what I have become. Thanks therefore to:

Mum and Dad, for their continued support and understanding of my raging wanderlust since I first realised it was too strong to resist (not that I ever wanted to). Ideally, from their point of view, I'd be married with two kids and a solid job, but I think they've accepted that this is what I'm happy doing.

My sister Tracey and nephews Thomas and Liam, whom I don't get to see often enough.

For work on the book:

My editors Ingrid and Adam Cranfield, who again have taken a raw rock and honed it into a far more polished stone. I will remember where the apostrophes go in the next book, I promise.

I enlisted the voluntary help of a few proofreaders who deserve recognition: Katie Bryant, Big Foot, Tradja, Chris Partridge, Mumfa, Obs the Blobs, Sugar Moma and Amy Lou.

Spencer Vignes, Rosie Fuller of Adventure Travel magazine, Ingrid Cranfield, Chris Townsend, Jennifer Pharr Davis, Andrew Skurka and Kimberlie Dame for supplying endorsements.

Those who helped out with the words of wisdom at the beginning of each chapter – Charlie 'Hojo' Mead, Michael Thomas 'Lion King' Daniel, Mahmood 'Cedar Elk' Mokhayesh, Patti 'Sugar Moma' Kulesz, Shane 'Jester' O'Donnell, John 'Tradja' Drollette, David 'Walker Texas Ranger' Allen, Jennifer Pharr Davies, Patrick 'Wideangle' Pöndl, Ned Tibbits, Jake Nead, Nick 'The Brit' De Bairacli Levy, Monty 'Warner Springs Monty' Tam, and Dave 'Upchuck' Ferber.

Jennifer Pharr Davies and Andrew Skurka for permission to use their quotes.

Josh 'Rockets' Myers for the photo on the front cover and all his photographic work on the website.

All the trail angels en route who took time out to help the thru-hikers and smooth their passage.

Alex Johnson for at least trying to get me a discounted flight.

Uncle Tony, Aunty Jillian, Rudy, Hayley and all my relatives over in the US for feeding me, giving me somewhere to stay, running me on errands and generally acting as a first-class HQ.

The countless drivers who picked up a dirty, smelly hiker and went out of their way to take me to a shower.

My hike may not have even happened had it not been for

the generosity of my sponsors, who ask nothing except for a little recognition:

Shane Ohly at Inov-8, Niels Overgaard Blok at Backpackinglight.dk, Richard Codgbrook at Smartwool, Francesca Sanchez at Olympus, Aimee Gasparre at Nalgene, Rand Lindsley at Trail Designs, Jake Bennett at Numa Sport Optics, Road Java at Stickpic, Erik Asorson at Blackwoods Press for the Pacific Crest Trail Atlas and Seamus at Sportkilt.

Not least, my heartfelt thanks go to all the thru-hikers I met. You are very much a part of my Pacific Crest Trail memories, as well as honorary members of Hiker Trash! I feel privileged both to have met you and to continue to know you:

Dicentra, Space Blanket, Kara, Gabe, Mojave, Cheeks, Ben, Mad Hatter, Upchuck, Wyoming, Bob, Logic, Stumbling Norwegian, Sugar Moma, Dinosaur, Swayze, Hojo, Jess, Tradja, Burnie, Alex, Elk,

Charmin, Grey Fox, Spiller, Flashlight, Vadar, Pyjamas, Pigpen, Pony, Your Mom, Yvo, Lo, Bones, Borders, Professor, Vicki, Dennis, Jake, Scorpion, Trooper, Steve Climber, Turbo, Stanimal, Big Foot, Wideangle, Tomer, Littlebit, Walker Texas Ranger, Flannel, Chad, Justin, Flyboxer, Indie, Answerman, Humming Bird, Flashback, Grinder, Uncle Gary, Stax, Black Gum, Ursa Major, Pockets (aka Rockets), Brains, Jolly Green Giant, Dan, Splizzard, Chrissie, Dodge, Mr Green, Dozer, Jack Straw, The Pro from Dover, Spartan, Wreckless, Crow, Dundee, Karma, Detective Bubbles, No Pain and finally the Brits - Chris and Nick.

And, lastly, an apology if I have missed anyone out. If that's you, please let me know, but in the meantime consider yourself thanked.

Chapter 1

Escaping Volcanoes

There's no sense in dreaming small, moderation is for monks.
Charlie 'HoJo' Mead

F ew things in life are certain. I can tell you the Pope is
Catholic, NASA did fake the moon landings and that
Tottenham Hotspur is the greatest football team ever
to grace the playing field. What's also certain is I don't like
cold weather and I get grouchy when it's too hot. I have an
aversion to rain, and if there is the slightest chance of
snowfall, I head south. Getting dirty makes me
uncomfortable, and I become grumpy if I haven't enough to
eat. Sleeping well in tents doesn't come naturally, and I get
scared in the woods after dark too.

Hardly impressive credentials to hike the 2,640 miles
that make up America's Pacific Crest Trail, otherwise known
as the PCT. So why attempt it? It was a question asked many
times before, during and after my hike, and later on in this
book, I promise I'll tell you.

Before I describe why, allow me to explain what. The
PCT is arguably the greatest long-distance hiking trail on

Earth. It's not the longest, but the PCT isn't merely about length; it's also about variety. Starting under a searing Californian sun just south of a small cluster of houses called Campo near the Mexican border, it winds its way north (and indeed east, west and frustratingly even south). Continuing through scorching desert, the magnificent Sierra Nevada Mountains, the volcanic landscapes of Oregon and Washington, and the northern Cascade mountains, it finishes at the Canadian border.

The route was first explored in the 1930s by members of the YMCA. Once its feasibility became clear, Clinton Clarke and Warren Rogers lobbied the federal government. Because of the sheer amount of work involved, they had to settle for several disconnected trails that already existed. During the ensuing years, hikers and equestrians worked to link these routes together and fill in the gaps. It was designated a scenic trail by Congress in 1968 and subsequently dedicated in 1993.

A thru-hike of the PCT means trying to complete its entirety in one attempt. 40 per cent who start drop out in the first month alone. As the months pass, the numbers dwindle further, until we're left with those who complete the challenge. Some sources claim 85 per cent don't finish. Take it on and there is a very real chance you won't make it.

I need to enlighten you to the pitfalls and dangers because you could try it, so it would be remiss of me if I didn't tell you what this entails.

First, more people have climbed Mount Everest than have hiked the PCT. That suggests it is easier to climb the world's highest mountain. A thru-hike means negotiating over sixty major passes. Think about that for a second. Most of us haven't even been up a mountain pass. At best, it involves at least a day's hard walking with an early start and a late finish. You'll probably get wet, may get cold and spend most of the day cursing for even trying. So, try doing it sixty times – and that's just the 'major' passes, not all of them.

If you like quality and choice in your diet, then make the most of it before you go. You can still have the variety, but dehydrated food is most common because it's light. You can't just visit the supermarket for your usual shop of fresh meat, fruit, veg and packaged goods. Dried food reigns; get used to it.

Your load weight restricts taking alcohol. Indeed, most hikers don't take any drink at all; it's too heavy. Forget your six-pack of beer and bottles of Chardonnay. If you must, settle with spirits like whisky or rum that come in smaller and lighter sizes, needing less to produce the desired effect. We rarely left town with a bottle, given that we had to carry it.

Inseparable from your bathroom cabinet? Make do with a toothbrush and toothpaste, toilet paper and maybe a small piece of soap. It's pointless taking anything else. You won't be able to wash your hair in the wild and deodorant is begging for forgiveness midway through the first morning; you'll stink whether you spray or not.

Attempting a thru-hike of the PCT is no holiday; it is a physical and psychological minefield. OK, 95 per cent of the time it's just a case of putting one foot in front of the other, but the remaining 5 per cent can beat you into submission. In truth, if you make it, or manage a credible attempt, the most amazing experience of your life awaits you.

And, dear prospective thru-hiker, that experience is mind-blowing.

So, negatives aside, let's look at the positives. The draw of being able to spend several months in the great outdoors, and indeed pristine wilderness, is what lures most people to the trail. Leave your mundane job, kiss your bills goodbye and appreciate life at its simplest. Trail life educates you. It becomes obvious that we don't need most of our luxuries, we can live without shopping, TV becomes a distant memory, and realising how uncomplicated life can be is an absolute revelation.

You rise when it feels right, crawl out of your tent, rub your eyes and establish a rough location. Sit with a coffee and a bowl of oats. The only sounds are those that nature has laid on: birdsong, the rustling of the pines as a gentle breeze weaves through them and possibly the nearby tinkle and babble of a creek. No alarm clock, TV, or traffic.

I became detached – gladly separated from the life that I had become accustomed to. Detachment on the trail is a good thing. It imparts an understanding and a yearning to learn more about the outdoors. At times I wanted to be back in civilisation for a day or so, but in the main I relished being lucky enough to have witnessed the wilderness at its most pristine for a duration that most people will only ever dream of.

Human beings have spent the vast majority of their existence in the wild. Towns and cities are a relatively recent concept and, although they feel secure, we don't belong there. They are not our natural surroundings. You will realise quickly that the outdoors is where we were nurtured, spent our infancy and were raised. It is embedded in us.

There's camaraderie on the trail that you won't find anywhere else. Don't be deterred attempting this hike on your own; there are many others, a lot of them soloing. You'll meet like-minded people you can walk with and make friends for life. On the other hand, if you value your independence, spend time alone as well.

I was raised to appreciate the outdoors and walking; it's always been part of my make-up. I have photos of my sister and me in the countryside when I was just a toddler: I was literally learning to walk before I could properly walk. Other activities come and go, but heading out into the green open spaces is second nature to me. I don't question it.

The anticipation of throwing my gear into a backpack for the weekend and venturing out curls my mouth into a smile. Escaping the annoyances of everyday life and instead discovering the energising, invigorating quality of the countryside makes me complete and content. The restless rush and needless stresses of the working week are left behind.

I have explored many interests in my life by studying, training and taking part in them. If they are not for me, I move on. Some activities come naturally, requiring little effort and offering so much enjoyment that they seem made for me.

I work to earn enough money to satisfy my wandering tendencies. I receive different reactions to my lifestyle. People think I'm weird, which I find flattering. The rest respond with either interest or envy.

I do not subscribe to the idea that life is about school, then breaking my back to progress in a career, having two kids, accepting the standard two to four weeks' yearly holiday and handing over my hard-earned cash to fund a pension annuity that the financial company swing in their favour. It's just not for me.

I have a recurring dream in which I am 85 years old, sitting in my living room, swaying back and forth in a rocking chair, and studying the newspaper. I pause, look up and think of the adventures I could have experienced and say, "Shit, I should have done that." That scenario will not happen in real life.

So, a weekend camping recharges my batteries. A week, maybe two, provides an opportunity to get lost in the outdoors and completely relax. Occasionally, though, every two or three years, my yearning for something more rewarding starts to gnaw at me. If I was a normal chap, I'd ignore these feelings, but I'm not, so I don't. I sit up and take notice. I get excited about the prospect of what I could do. At any given moment, I'm contemplating numerous ideas: cycling around the world, taking a year out to explore the canals of Great Britain on a boat, restoring a camper van and travelling through Europe for the summer or – and this idea always takes centre stage – walking a crazy distance through a part of the world that beckons.

The PCT grabbed my attention five years before I hiked it. I had completed a thousand-mile walk through France and Spain known as El Camino de Santiago, and the long-distance hiking experience had taken root. As with most challenges, we finish one and then try to surpass it. In walking terms, this usually means increasing the mileage.

Apart from the duration and difficulty of the PCT, the other factor nibbling away at my sanity was its location, and my longing for the remote wild places. I love walking in the UK, but it lacks large areas of backcountry – and, although it can, with planning, offer routes of insane length, I couldn't have both distance and wilderness.

The three most renowned long-distance routes in the world are in North America. The Appalachian Trail (2,181 miles), the Pacific Crest Trail (2,640 miles) and the Continental Divide Trail (3,100 miles) are fine objectives for any serious long-distance hiker. Completing all three means becoming a 'Triple Crowner'.

There is no standard order of finishing these masterpieces, but most attempts start with the AT because it is the shortest, progress to the PCT and finish with the CDT. To me, not known for my conformity, the PCT appealed primarily because of its climate. You could possibly walk its entirety and never get rained on, although you will definitely experience extremes of heat and cold. I discounted the AT because of its reputation for high precipitation and I didn't want to follow the trend and do it first. The CDT is a serious undertaking. It's obviously long, still not completely finished and it's likely that, in spite of the scores of walkers who tackle the route each year, you could go for days without seeing a soul. I wouldn't have minded this, but I felt the PCT was a more well-worn trail in terms of the numbers attempting it, which could aid logistical planning. PCT towns are well accustomed to strange-looking people with backpacks, weird-looking footwear, crusty hair, soiled clothes and potentially lethal body odour aimlessly wandering around, muttering either 'food' or 'shower'. They always welcomed us.

Having made the decision to go a year in advance, I had spent the time playing an anxious waiting game. I needed those 12 months to nurture a healthier bank balance and, although I didn't realise it at first, to plan. This amount of time sounds excessive, but I was surprised at how much preparation went into organising such an expedition.

Most evenings I spent glued to my PC trying to find equipment sponsors, start a blog of my trip and arrange flights, medical insurance, gear and logistics. I formed kit lists, looking at each item, noting weights, durability, reliability and recommendations. Basically, I turned into a gear nerd.

Finally, as D-Day dawned, I had packed and was checking final details when a radio newsreader caught my ear.

'Flights are being cancelled from the UK due to a volcanic eruption in Iceland.'

I turned up the volume. The reports were sketchy at best, and for five days preceding my flight no-one in the UK, including the airlines, seemed to know what the hell was happening. The TV news either showed a plume of white ash rising from Eyjafjallajökull or pictures of Gordon Brown trying to become Prime Minister. I remember posting on my blog:

> Volcano – What volcano?
> This is clearly a conspiracy theory. The English Tourist Board has dreamt this up to prevent us from flying to foreign destinations, thus forcing people to holiday in the UK. It's very frustrating, and I was going to write to my MP about it, but he's out all the time. Something to do with an election?

Eventually, I received an email from the airline saying the flight had been cancelled. Now I was getting annoyed.

Events were conspiring against me to end my hike before it had even begun. What was the hurry to get to California? It was the ADZPCTKO, standing for Annual Day Zero Pacific Crest Trail Kick Off.

Lake Morena campground, a short drive from the southern terminus of the PCT, hosts the ADZPCTKO and is the destination for most of the year's thru-hikers, section hikers, previous hikers, organisers, equipment manufacturers and all manner of general misfits. It usually takes place around the end of April, generally considered the ideal time to start the hike, considering receding snow levels in the High Sierra, and getting to Canada before the winter grips. No way in hell was I missing it.

The media reports advised that the dust cloud causing the problem to aircraft did not affect airports in southern Europe. Rome, Madrid, Athens and others were throwing up 747s like they were going out of fashion. I decided to get to Madrid.

I checked train timetables on the internet, in particular Eurostar, and watched, amazed, as seats disappeared every time I refreshed the page. An urgent decision was needed, so I made a reservation to leave that evening. The rest of the afternoon entailed running around the house saying goodbyes on the phone, spilling coffee on the carpet, looking at my packing list and tripping over my sleeping bag.

I arrived in Paris at 9pm and took stock. I needed to get to Madrid overland and fly to San Diego via my Uncle Tony and Aunty Jillian's place near San Francisco – my 'HQ' for the hike. The Gare du Nord station was strangely tranquil. Coffee machines hissed from a couple of snack bars. Damp footprints from the rain wove in from the entrance and gradually faded, the loudspeaker crackled occasionally and a cleaning machine hummed from a distant corner. I went outside for air and sheltered under a shop front. Paris was alive, humid and noisy. As I returned inside, the cacophony ceased abruptly as though I had closed the door of a crowded bar.

An attendant told me I needed to get to Gare de Lyon where the Madrid trains left from. I cringed when he advised taking the underground. London Underground I can handle, but the Paris Métro is notoriously confusing, and the instructions were in French.

A suspicious-looking character loitered by the ticket machine, watching travellers and occasionally attempting conversation. It transpired he'd made it his business to help those unfortunate souls, like me, decipher the train system and work the screen display. Within two minutes he'd provided a welcome tutorial on finding the correct route. He didn't ask for payment nor indicate that he expected it, but I passed him a couple of Euros and a grateful 'Merci'.

The Gare de Lyon was deserted, save a few homeless; and I ambled round a stark terminal, a prison of cold, lifeless white tiles which seemed like a sanatorium. I decided against a hotel on the grounds of cost, plus I needed to be at the ticket office when it opened in case half the population of Europe had also decided to buy tickets to Madrid. Unsavoury looking characters peered at me from behind pillars, so I decided against sleeping on a bench. For eight hours I tried to amuse myself, waiting for 6am, when I hoped to be able to secure onward transit. Eventually, I gave in to my drooping eyelids and curled up on the floor by a row of fourteen glass windows displaying 'Fermé' signs. I managed to get four hours' sleep, despite a hard floor half-crippling my left side.

I woke to the hum of chatter, cracked open my left eye and peered out at a student wearing, somewhat appropriately, a red T-shirt with the slogan 'All is not lost' contrasting in yellow across her chest. She was giggling at me – and for good reason. As I opened the other eye, I realised I'd been lovingly spooning my rucksack while sleeping, and a long string of drool stretched from my mouth to my shoulder.

As I queued, the omens looked bleak. Vendors shook their heads gravely and, although I spoke no French, I could see the disappointment from the pained expressions of those queuing. I inched forward to window number seven and held my breath.

"Bonjour, madame," I stuttered anxiously. "Avez-vous une ticket to Madrid please? I mean, sivous plaît."

She smiled shyly, displaying one tooth with an alarming slant trying to break free from the others, and pushed a pair of rebellious orange spectacles back up her nose.

"Please, I speak enough English to help you. Probably a little better than your French?"

It sounded like a question but her tone suggested otherwise, so I just smiled.

"Madrid is no problem; the next train is at ten," she advised.

I dropped my money on the counter in a rush to pay her before she either changed her mind or gave the ticket to someone else. Relieved, I made a beeline for the coffee shop.

After a long day sitting on trains watching green countryside flash by, I eventually hit Madrid at 1am the following morning. I felt confused by the deserted airport. I had expected hordes of people who had followed the same logic to get here, but it was not so. A solitary woman sat at a help desk, glad of someone to talk to. Most of the airline desks, she told me, opened at 6am, and she suggested I either wait until then or go to an internet terminal and try to book a ticket. Not wanting to take any chances, as my progress had been smooth, I went online but got irritated with the slow and erratic booking system.

A chap called Adonis was sitting nearby with his laptop.

"You need help?" he asked.

"I have to book a flight to the States for today. This connection speed is killing me," I replied, just on the verge of kicking the machine.

"I can do the searching for you," he offered.

I paused, cautious as always of anyone offering me something I haven't requested, especially while travelling. If successful, it would entail taking my credit card details. I decided to let him have a go and see what happened when it came to the booking stage.

For an hour we sat against a vending machine. Adonis couldn't have been more helpful. His hands floated over the keyboard so quickly I got tired just watching.

My original flight was extremely cheap, a favour from a friend who worked for one of the airlines. I winced when most of the opportunities for flights departing that morning were four times as much, but there was nothing I could do.

After we had whittled it down to one choice, Adonis explained that he would erase the browsing history and left me for a minute while I entered my credit card details. He then showed me he had done what he had promised. I took him to McDonald's, the only place open, and told him to eat whatever he wanted. The poor guy devoured three hamburgers, fries, a milkshake and an apple pie as if he hadn't eaten for days. He thanked me profusely and wandered off to help someone else book a flight to Amsterdam.

Smiling contentedly, I felt the plane lurch as it hit Californian tarmac and the tyres squealed a welcome confirmation that finally, 54 hours after leaving England, my destination was within striking distance. At least I was in the right country.

A bleary-eyed Uncle Tony missed me at Arrivals, as I did him, but we found each other and used the hour's drive to catch up. I had last seen him ten years earlier when I had spent a few months bumming around America. Arriving at his house, I went straight to bed and slept solidly for eleven hours, emerging refreshed to hugs from Aunty Jillian and introductions to their grandchildren, Rudy and Hayley.

Several parcels were waiting for me, containing gear I'd ordered, and I spent the day organising final logistics. A shop for the first week's food was trial and error, as I could only guess the quantities. A ritual I'd repeat many times over the next few months followed, removing all excess packaging and decanting the contents into Ziploc bags, discarding an astonishing amount of cardboard and plastic in the process. This not only cut a little weight, but it also saved carrying unnecessary trash. After a few weeks on the trail, I tired of this because it wasted precious time on my rest days.

That evening Tony and Rudy dropped me off at the San Jose Greyhound station for the final leg to San Diego and the ADZPCTKO, four days after leaving England. I was tired and not looking forward to an overnight bus ride, but I was proud of the determination I'd shown getting this far. Persistence and a stubborn refusal to quit were traits I was to nurture during my time on the trail, and I needed to.

The most difficult part of the PCT, and indeed any extended adventure, is making the choice to attempt it in the first place. The second hardest is the waiting. Once you've committed to both, it becomes surprisingly obvious that commitment should have been made a long time ago. The apprehension you felt making such a big decision suddenly seems insignificant, and your goal appears clear and lucid.

Make the choice, and everything falls into place.

Chapter 2
The Five-Minute Hobble

The time you spend out here is worth more than the time it takes, so take your time.
Michael Thomas 'Lion King' Daniel

I walked aimlessly out of the San Diego Greyhound station, unsure of my next step. It was 5.30am; beams of sunlight from a cloudless blue sky sliced and ricocheted around glass buildings. A cluster of birds took flight, soaring skyward, swerving and changing direction as if calculating the best bearing. A street cleaner stopped and cupped his hands to light a cigarette, illuminating his face as he leant on his broom. Startled by a shop door rattling open, I watched a businessman hurry out, trying to balance a briefcase, laptop, coffee and bagel, and he promptly dropped the coffee. Like me, the city was struggling to wake up, scruffy but full of potential.

I rubbed my eyes, tired from the overnight bus ride from San Jose, and searched for possible onward transport options to Lake Morena. Being Sunday and early morning, buses and other services were non-existent.

A driver was leaning against his cab with folded arms on the roof, resting his chin on his hands. He looked bored and lost in thought.

"Hi," I offered, becoming distracted by the smell of coffee from a nearby café. "I need a ride to Lake Morena."

"Where?" he asked, looking bemused and scratching his head while a cigarette hovered hesitantly near his mouth.

"Lake Morena. It's east on the main highway out of town."

"Donny!" he called over to his mate. "You know some place called" – he turned back to me – "what was it again?"

"Lake Morena," I reminded him. I had a familiar feeling of unease in the pit of my stomach that bubbles up when events don't bode well.

"Where?" replied Donny.

"Lake Morena," I answered louder so they both caught my reply. "It's about 30 miles east of town on the main highway."

"Haven't heard of it, but I'll try the satnav. We can get you there."

"How much?" I asked. Wise from my travels, I'd learned to agree on a price before accepting a service, especially with taxis.

"Thirty miles you say? A hundred bucks."

Previous experience had also taught me not to accept the first offer.

"How does $60 cash sound?"

They both discussed the situation as I longed to taste the espresso a woman had passed by with, leaving waves of coffee aromas lingering.

"We can take you there for $80 cash," Donny finally settled on.

"Fine, let's go. Give me five minutes to grab a coffee."

We headed east on the 94. Donny slouched on the driver's seat, one hand on the wheel, the other switching between a breakfast burrito and a soda. The highway was quiet as we left the city but gridlocked on the other side. Glum-faced commuters stuck in the jam peered round vehicles in front to see what the holdup was. I didn't envy them – despondent people with another day at work ahead of them – but I realised that just two weeks earlier I had been one of them, gazing out of my car on the dull and frustrating commute. This was my first inkling I was leaving the fast pace of life behind and winding down for the backcountry.

"How far did you say this place was?" Donny asked, his narrowed eyes in the mirror suggesting distrust.

"I think it's 30 miles, but I'm not sure."

"Well, we're on 35 now and I haven't seen the turn-off yet."

I grimaced as I saw the fare hit $120 but remembered our agreement.

"You mean that turn-off there?" I replied, smiling as I pointed to a blurred sign displaying 'Lake Morena'.

"Oh, shit," Donny said and then cursed again as he dropped the last part of his burrito on his trousers. "I got another five miles before I can turn around."

Thirty minutes later we pulled up at the Lake Morena campsite.

"$225 please," he said. I detected a slight sneer.

"You must be having a laugh or something! We agreed on $80."

"Yeah, but it was more mileage than you said. Man, I gotta charge you or I'm in trouble with the office."

"Don't feed me a line, Donny," I said, that feeling creeping back into the pit of my stomach. "We settled on $80; a deal is a deal where I come from and we shook on it. You're the bloody cab driver with the satnav here – why are you asking me the mileage? You can sing for the other $145." I handed him four twenty-dollar bills, which he counted.

"I gotta charge you as the metre says," he said. "Pay or your backpack stays in the trunk."

I cursed myself silently for not keeping my stuff with me. After five minutes of arguing, we settled on $120 and Donny roared off in a cloud of gravel.

The ADZPCTKO is held at the Lake Morena campground towards the end of April each year. The entire event is devoted to the registration, entertainment, feeding and watering of many potential thru-hikers, plus others associated with the PCT.

The place was buzzing and crammed to bursting point. Tents jammed into plots too small for them, guy lines acted as trip-wires, and marshals milled around. The atmosphere was one of anticipation and excitement. Strangers said hi and smiled at me. I felt at ease straight away.

I made my way towards the registration area, taking it all in. Some volunteers who had previously hiked the trail had returned to give something back. Many toiled in the food preparation areas, peeling potatoes, lighting barbecues and chopping vegetables. Gear manufacturers set up their stalls, placing tantalising merchandise on view. New sleeping bags hung from canopies and the latest tents lined up in rows from the tallest to the smallest. Boxes lay everywhere waiting to be unpacked.

"Hi, good morning," said the woman at the checking-in tent. "Have you registered?"

"Yes," I replied. "My name is Keith Foskett."

"Oh, we dispense with formalities here! What's your trail name?"

"Sorry, it's Fozzie."

Over the next few months, I'd hardly use my real name. Everyone on the PCT goes by their trail name. It's usually pinned on you by other hikers and reflects how you look, what you have done or how you act. Each has a story behind it, often humorous in nature, and if you're offered one it normally has to be accepted, although not all of them are. I had registered with the nickname that stretched back to my school days, loosely derived from my surname. This was partly because I was fond of it and also because I didn't want any bizarre suggestions such as 'Irregular Banana', 'Radical Curtains', 'Shits Skyward' or 'Shave your arse and walk backwards' directed my way. You can understand my eagerness to nip this one in the bud.

"OK, Fozzie, I have you down for a camp spot, and you're from England. There's only a handful of English here this year," she said, checking the long list of names.

Handing me a name badge, she insisted I pin it on my shirt and then gave me the much sought-after hiker bandana. The PCT class of 2002 started the bestowing of the bandana, making the first design available to hikers in 2003, and the tradition continues every year. It sports the same layout each time, namely a map of the route with major place names, the year and the phrases 'Hiker to Town' and 'Hiker to Trail' printed boldly near the edges, useful when hitching a ride. The only change each season was the colour of the material. I cringed when she handed me the latest incarnation in a rather fetching shade of pink.

There was so much going on, I didn't know where to turn. The smell of bacon floated over, and I made a beeline for the food stalls. One of the many advantages of being a thru-hiking virgin at the kick-off is we eat for free. Hungry souls formed an orderly line, licking their lips in anticipation and practicing for the next few months, trying to increase calorie intake to catch up with their energy expenditure. I took more coffee than I needed and slurped it up, in between mouthfuls of scrambled egg, tomatoes and bacon, while conversing with the organisers.

I found my tent space squeezed between three others who had nabbed more than their fair share of grass, and began setting up what was to be home for the next couple of nights.

"Hey, this plot was for a hiker who isn't showing after all, so you can set up here if you like." John, one of the volunteers gestured to a far more spacious section. His expression suggested I should take it before someone else did.

"Thanks, I'd have struggled to get in there." I shook his hand and we exchanged a few pleasantries.

One item of gear I'd failed to obtain before leaving was a backpack. Logic and experience suggests this piece of equipment is vital to try on before you buy, but I hadn't found a suitable model back home. The volume was either too big or small, they were uncomfortable, many were too heavy or just poor quality. During my research, I'd heard good reports about a company called ÜLA. I needed a light pack but with a built-in frame to stiffen the whole unit. Many packs shed the frame to save weight, resulting in a limp sack that dangles off the shoulders like a half-full bag of potatoes.

ÜLA's proprietor, Chris McMaster, had politely declined my sponsorship request.

"I don't need the advertising, Fozzie. Most hikers this year have my packs."

He was right; his familiar models were all over the campground. He had, however, asked me to go and see him, as he had made the trip to set up a stall.

"Chris, Fozzie from…"

"Fozzie!" He interjected and started laughing. "This guy sends me email after email from England wanting a freebie," he said, motioning others to look my way. "You're a persistent guy, Fozzie. You get the pack OK?"

"Yeah, fine, thanks. It fits well. I mentioned I'd come over to meet you and get that expert fitting you offered."

"Sure, hoist her up and let's take a look." He studied the pack and me for a while, suggesting I lift the hip belt up a touch. We talked and as I left I said, chuckling, "I still want the next one for free, though!"

I woke the following morning realising my thru-hike was starting. Opening one eye and peering out through a slit in my sleeping bag, a dim light struggled to illuminate California. It was freezing, ice crystals clung to the roof of my little haven and the ground outside sparkled white with a crisp frost; not the temperature I had associated with the southern USA. Escaping the confines of a warm sleeping bag and getting into cold clothing is not one of my favourite experiences and I shivered, slid on my hiking gear and got out of the tent. Flapping my arms and jumping, I tried to warm up.

"I definitely don't recommend this."

I looked over at the guy: yes, he was talking to me, his face contorted into an expression of sheer disgust.

"Don't recommend what?" I asked.

"Well, I thought I'd save time and washing up by mixing coffee in with the oats. It tastes like shit."

A few hikers were awake, and the steam from boiling water atop cooking stoves looked like smoky chimneys in an industrial landscape. People cocooned in hats and gloves stood around waiting for coffee to brew while chatting and smiling at the prospect of their first day on the PCT. Green footprints meandered where shoes had broken the white, frosty crust. I'd never seen so many excited expressions. The atmosphere was so thick with intoxicating enthusiasm I could smell it.

Lake Morena looked glorious, saving its best for the day. Blanketed by a weak mist, which gently parted like theatre curtains by a gentle breeze. I glimpsed pockets of clear air and sunlight bouncing off the water as Morena slowly unwrapped itself.

The start point at the Mexican border lay a few miles south, and several visitors to the kick-off were laying on transport. I jumped into Shrek's car with Gabe and Cara, who I'd met the day before. The familiar sight of the PCT monument appeared, flanked by an imposing black steel fence separating us from Mexico. It was a view I had seen countless times during my research. A few hikers were leaving; some took photos for posterity. We did the same, handing our cameras to Trailbird, who obligingly clicked away for us.

It's an old adage but one of my favourites: It's better to have tried and failed than never to have tried at all. I admire everyone who commits to an adventure and those that don't make it. I watched others set off and wondered how many might drop out. Four or five out of every ten potential starters quit in the first month alone and even more wouldn't last the distance. I glanced at Cara and Gabe, who both looked confident. Were they wondering the same about me? Averages dictated that two of us wouldn't finish. As it transpired, in the ensuing weeks both of them unfortunately joined those drop-out statistics.

The morning chill soon surrendered to a magnificent day, the norm for California. The sky was a flawless blue; wind occasionally ruffled my hair, and before long I had replaced my jacket with shorts and a T-shirt as sweat trickled down my back. We found our own pace that first day, sometimes walking with others or on our own. Space Blanket and Dicentra joined me, and we idly chatted away the twenty miles back to Lake Morena, itself situated right on the trail. The abundance of plants surprised me. Desert stretched for the first 700 miles, although not the typical sand dunes and searing heat you might imagine. It was known as chaparral, consisting of waist-high scrubby vegetation clinging on to a mix of grit and rock, which gave a satisfying crunch underfoot. Yuccas towered over me, their flowers a thousand dangling white bells. Over time I learned those flowers were edible and regularly grabbed a handful to supplement my dried provisions. They provided a refreshing crispness in the mouth and tasted of lettuce. I made my way through sections of lush pasture that moistened my legs from the lingering dew. Memories of England returned as I pulled off pieces of rye grass and threw them like darts.

Gabe and I stopped under a low tree for lunch, trying to squeeze back in the shade, Dicentra soon joined us. She'd tucked her long hair under a green sun hat as white rimmed sunglasses perched on the brim. The dust gaiters on her shoes were a colourful fabric, and I'd seen her modelling them to admirers earlier. She was happy-go-lucky, smiled a lot and made frequent arm gestures when excited about a topic, her favourite being nutrition. I learned she had written a book extolling the tricks, virtues and delights of eating healthily on the trail. This book, One Pan Wonders, was proving a success with those who were looking for something more exciting than the usual supermarket offerings. I thought I was doing well stuffing tuna and tomato in a tortilla until saliva started trickling from the corner of my mouth as I noticed her preparing lunch. Gabe's eyes too were twitching enviously in her direction. She placed three tortillas on her lap and prepared the fillings. Rehydrating fried beans with water, she added fresh avocado and topped it off with taco sauce.

I did my best to look envious and hungry, Gabe was doing splendidly too, but Dicentra merely made us a tortilla each without blinking an eye and smiled.

"I'm happy to make you one," she said.

Walking on my own for most of the afternoon, I stopped at Hauser Creek for water. The desert had received abundant rainfall over the winter and I had several opportunities each day to restock, which in the temperatures was a godsend. A hiker called Motor joined me as I filtered a couple of litres for the remaining five miles. She asked if I had seen any snakes, which I hadn't, and went on to tell me she had encountered three already.

"How many?! Where?" I enquired, gulping.

"Well, the last one was only 10 minutes back up the trail. It slithered off as I rounded a corner. It was a rattler for sure, saw its tail."

I grimaced. I have a phobia of snakes and bears – hardly ideal for the PCT, which boasts healthy numbers of both. I inherited my anxiety from my father, whom I've witnessed executing six-foot jumps in fright on sighting a grass snake, one of our completely harmless native English species.

"You know, there's a simple way of dealing with snakes," Motor said.

"I'm all ears."

"Well, you have to make sure you're walking with two others and you're not the last in line."

"Uh-huh."

"Well, the first person wakes the rattler up. The second pisses it off and the third gets bitten."

"Right, thanks for that," I said dryly, raising my eyebrows to let her know I'd hoped for better.

For a few weeks I walked in perpetual fear of Crotalus atrox, the western diamond-backed rattlesnake. Even the name sounds formidable, but it scared me because it ticked all the right boxes – or, rather, the wrong boxes. First, it grew to crazy sizes. Second, its poison was nasty, although not lethal if one received medical attention. Mainly it frightened me because it just looked terrifying. I'm not suggesting any snake comes across as exactly 'cuddly', but the rattler's eyes are evil. Its brows slant diagonally from a high point on the outside of the eye to the lower centre, giving a relentlessly pissed off expression.

I'd received a lot of snake advice, mainly that I wouldn't see any, which always makes me nervous because it's a sure-fire way of ensuring I will. Others told me it can only strike as far as its body length and I read that if you do get bitten, the best thing is to lie down! This priceless piece of wisdom originates from the Aborigines. The theory is it relaxes the victim, slows the heart rate, and hence delays the poison spreading through the bloodstream. I was sure my reaction to a rattler bite would be less subtle, more hopping about screaming I was going to die. Taking a nap on the ground wasn't an option. I'd read somewhere that the bite is rarely fatal and at worst victims experience excruciating pain, like liquid fire being pumped around the arteries. I didn't know if that piece of wisdom was intended as reassurance.

I was on rattler alert in prime reptile territory, which in California is everywhere except the local 7 Eleven. I'd scan up to 50 feet ahead, making visual and mental notes of anything resembling a snake. From a short distance, sticks scattering the trail could easily resemble one. I imagined myself sweeping the environment through the eyes of a Terminator machine: anything looking potentially dangerous flashed up in red with three warning beeps and margined to my left-hand vision for further investigation as I approached.

Natural debris spread everywhere, so my head beeped like an over-active microwave and my left field of vision spotted so many potentially lethal unknowns that it reduced to a hazy shade of crimson.

Once I had seen a few, I began evaluating and

understanding what little danger they posed. The positive thing with rattlers is they let you know their location by rattling and can be given a wide berth. I saw many during my hike and came to have a healthy respect for them, but I kept a mental record of both snakes, and false alarms.

Snake count: 1
False alarms: 27

I walked the final two hours back to Lake Morena on my own. Gabe and Dicentra were behind because I had increased my speed to arrive before darkness.

21 miles isn't a huge distance by thru-hiking standards. But for a first day, with a full pack and in high temperatures, those final miles lasted an eternity – albeit an enjoyable one. The temperature plummeted with the approach of another freezing night as the sinking sun painted stripes of shadow across the trail. With the last 3,000 foot-hill under my belt, I descended two miles back to camp just as dusk was falling, willing Lake Morena to appear before me. Finally, I saw countless headlamps moving like fireflies and the laughter and chatter of happy hikers.

At least 100 people cheered and gave a standing ovation as I crossed over the last dirt track into the campsite. Initially, I looked around expecting to see someone famous behind me, but then realised they were cheering me, just as they'd welcomed every successful hiker that first day. It honestly brought a tear to my eye and I bowed in appreciation, then raised my trekking poles above my head in salute.

As I stumbled in, Terrie Anderson greeted me. I was to

meet her later in my hike – she and her husband Joe open their house to hikers every year. Thrusting a gigantic plate of Mexican stew into my hand and a beer in the other, she kissed me on the cheek and said, "Sit, stay!"

We were in good spirits that evening thanks to food, drink and great company. I ate, rested, chatted and laughed for a couple of hours until, succumbing to tired limbs and too much ale, I wove my way through the rolling mist back to my tent.

Sliding into my sleeping bag and placing a weary head on my rolled-up jacket, I smiled, sighed contentedly and remembered that to become a Pacific Crest Trail thru-hiker, I just needed to repeat that first day … another 180 times.

I've never had problems with solitude and can happily spend a whole week or longer on my own. This obviously is a positive attribute for a thru-hiker. I hadn't expected to have company straight away, preferring to find my own feet. I planned on socialising in small bouts as I met different hikers, to figure out which ones I clicked with. So, it goes to show what a sterling bloke Gabe was that we ended up walking together for most of the first week.

We were both laid back and preferred taking it easy, so we had no problems agreeing when to rest, where to camp and how far to walk. On the final miles approaching Mt Laguna campground at 6,000 feet, we were taking lunch and comparing our food supplies. Hikers experiment a lot with recipes. We have to; our favourite stuff depletes quickly, leaving the less tempting options, which get livened up by mixing with something else. Gabe proudly offered me his simple concoction of a flour tortilla generously smeared with Nutella and scattered with banana chips, exclaiming, "Foz, it tastes just like a pastry!"

He declined my offer of a fair trade, turning his nose up at my tortilla with peanut butter, shaved parmesan and chocolate M&Ms. Can't say I blamed him.

Gabe was 26 and attempting the PCT to try something exciting before starting medical school. He hailed from Orange County and was keen to escape the hustle and grind of city life. Over six feet tall and well-built, he was someone you wouldn't pick an argument with. But if you did, he'd shrug it off and make a joke.

For the first week we concentrated on finding our feet. Our gear was bedding in and we were learning how to use it. We honed our skills in packing and unpacking, pitching tent, cooking, hygiene (or lack of it) and sourcing water. Searing heat meant this was one area we could not skimp on: either drink or dehydrate. Our maps indicated the water sources and thankfully most of them were flowing well. Gabe carried a gravity filter, which entailed filling a small bag, hanging it on a branch or something similar, where the fluid seeped through an attached hose and filter at the bottom. Other than lifting the bag, it required no effort; but it took longer than my equipment, which resembled a bicycle pump. Dipped in a stream, the handle pulled out to suck in water, then pressed in to expel clean water down a tube to my bottle.

I loathed the thing. After just one morning, we'd developed a powerful love-hate relationship. It kept clogging up, needing regular dismantling and unblocking. For every two litres I treated, I needed to backwash a further litre, which I soon found frustrating. There was Gabe, sitting and munching on snacks while his bag did all the work. He grinned as I crouched, elbows stretched out to my sides, exerting so much effort that my face looked as if it was about to explode. With the struggle required to filter one litre, I swear I'd sweated the same amount.

The gurgle and splutter of sweet, chilled water was wonderful to hear. Not only could we drink, but we could sit and rest too. To save weight, I filled a bottle and drank it straight away, feeling the cool liquid tumble down my throat. Then I'd take another litre to last an hour or two until the next creek. On one particularly hot day I worked my way through seven litres. You can imagine my filter frustration that day.

As we walked the final section to the Mount Laguna store, we saw several hikers sitting outside in the shade eating ice cream. Mojave and Cheeks, whom I was to see many times on my hike, told us the shop owner was warning of a fierce storm. After discussing the options, we decided to rent one of the nearby cabins. Mojave and Cheeks took the separate room, Gabe commandeered the main single bed, leaving me with the famous 'cot'. This American institution, common in motels, hotels and other establishments, is what we English refer to as a fold-away bed. It stores vertically and folds down, usually leaving an uncomfortable ridge in the middle. The hard frame sinks into your arms (so by morning my biceps had red indentations across them), the twanging springs keep you awake, and one particular model later in my hike even tried springing back upright every time I left it.

At 3am I parted the curtains and peered out at horizontal rain whipping debris through the parking lot. By the time we got up, the storm had subsided a little. The owner persuaded us to stay put until lunch when kinder conditions were due.

Gabe and I left shortly after midday and bumped into a steady stream of hikers backtracking to the store to dry out, some borderline hypothermic. We later learnt that before the first week had even finished, a few had decided enough was enough after the storm and quit their thru-hikes. With around 350 registered attempts that year, the PCT had already claimed nine hikers.

We continued through vicious wind gusts to the Penny Pines water supply, where Ben, glad of the company, joined us. Being constantly blown in all directions, we stumbled into the Pioneer Mail picnic area late afternoon and decided that we should camp – mainly on my insistence, because there were tables.

This may seem a strange reason for choosing a camping spot, and hardly embracing the wilderness experience, but benches were high on my checklist. After spending days sitting on the ground to eat with no backrest, and doing simple tasks such as journal writing, they were a bonus. Occasionally, families used them to have picnics or impromptu barbecues, and shared their food. I don't think I'll ever make a hard-core explorer to the planet's remoter parts if picnic tables are expedition pre-requisites.

We helped pitch each other's tents, two sitting on the canvas while the other pegged them out. We couldn't help noticing we'd camped just near a col, the wind funnelling through the hills with frightening ferocity. Mojave and

Cheeks arrived an hour later and retreated, wisely, back to a lower, more sheltered position to set up their camp.

The gale howled hauntingly for hours, shaking and billowing our tents. I peered out in the morning to take stock of the mayhem. Twigs and branches scattered the area and upturned trash cans spilled refuse. I laughed as I looked at Ben's tent: during the night, he'd cleverly anchored two of his guy lines to an adjacent table for stability. The warden arrived and surveyed the scene, taking off his hat with one hand and scratching his head with the other, amazed we were still alive. Camping wasn't allowed at picnic sites, but after we promised to pack up and be on our way quickly, he accepted that the circumstances were unusual. Mojave and Cheeks sauntered in, looking battered, explaining their tent got wrecked and they had to get a new one.

An English guy called the Mad Hatter soon joined us. I had seen him at the kick-off with an impressive top hat straight out of Alice in Wonderland, which he'd ditched as it kept blowing off. Having bought a house in Oregon, he was essentially walking home. Up to the point where we met him, he'd been with a guy called Upchuck and they shared a tent as he hadn't thought it necessary to bring his own, but a personality clash meant they'd separated.

"Upchuck is like herpes," he said, grinning. "I can deal with him but only in small doses."

At that precise moment, Upchuck came careering round the corner riding a runaway train. Mojave and Cheeks had to jump off trail as he ploughed straight through our group, with a feeble 'excuse me' and muttered something about a 40-mile day.

After the storm, the trail – strewn with pine needles and

32

cones – alternated between light-coloured dry sections and darker damp ones, which I called milk or plain chocolate paths. We dipped in and out of shade before returning to the chaparral as we descended. Gabe and I were suffering from blisters, which subsided as usual when we were walking but were excruciating for the first few minutes after we began again.

"It's called the five-minute hobble," I explained.

"Yeah," he replied. "So, this is how it feels to be ninety!"

I used to ponder how my body dealt with the onslaught. I conjured up an imaginary woman called Angela, who lived in my feet, sending signals up to the nerve centre HQ in my brain, run by Reginald.

"We've got problems here," Angela said. "I don't know what the hell is going on, but I'm dealing with three blisters, impact issues, muscle sprains and potential abrasion to the third toe of the right foot. You gotta send me backup; I can't hold it together much longer!"

"You idiot!" Reginald scolded. "There's six months of this! He's on another hiking adventure, isn't he? You think I don't have other complications up here? There's lower backache, neck sunburn, grit in the left eye, and if we don't take on board more water, we're in for some serious overtime tonight! I'm in desperate need of nutrients, and I can't get those from chicken ramen! Pray he stops in the fruit and veg aisle in the next supermarket. You'll just have to shore up the defences in the meantime and use what you've got! There's no resources! You hear me? No resources to work with!"

We hobbled to the Rodriguez Spur Road where a local called Wayne had set up some welcome hiker amenities. A table excited me, and even chairs. Solar showers provided an unexpected but sorely needed wash. The Mad Hatter camped in one of the shower tents and soon began to realise that the uneven ground and cramped space weren't boding well for a good night's sleep. He then spilled water on the floor, so he wasn't in the best of moods.

Gabe's blisters were troubling him. I sympathised; no matter what action or precautions I took, I usually suffered too. I had a few but was coping. Trying to lift his spirits, I kept reminding him that the first month on the trail was going to be the hardest, and blisters were inevitable, but he was despondent and withdrawn. Before we turned in, I urged him to get to the next town stop, Julian, and maybe take a day's rest. Good food and a warm bed usually worked wonders for morale.

"A life needs a purpose. A life without purpose is meaningless and a meaningless life has no purpose."

The Mad Hatter was lavishing profound quotes on me as we worked our way down from the hills towards Road 78, where we hoped to get a ride into the town of Julian. He was hankering after a hotel bed and I for the pie shops that I had heard so much about. Riding the switchbacks, I could feel the slight crunch of pastry in my mouth as the crust crumbled and my teeth sank into the sweetness of a cherry pie. I also needed meat, chips, ice cream, beer and coffee. Reginald, up in nerve centre HQ, was becoming stressed after realising the fruit and veg aisle wouldn't be a priority. I craved fat, and lots of it. We'd left Gabe tending to his blisters, and I worried about him.

We stumbled on our first water cache. These were maintained by locals and found in dry areas or long sections of trail with no water sources. This one set a high standard. There must have been 160 litres nestling on wooden shelving, along with several cool boxes harbouring Cokes and other soft drinks. We sat in the shade for thirty minutes and drank our fill.

Managing to get a quick ride with a local called Mandy to the town of Julian, it impressed me the moment I arrived. I needed only to restock on food and eat a couple of good meals. My walking was going well and progress seemed positive, so I wanted to take advantage and depart the same day. I left the Mad Hatter at the hotel and got a quick ride back to the trailhead to put in more miles as the sun began sinking.

Barely 50 feet up a 2,000 foot climb into the San Felipe Hills, I noticed someone waving at me. I didn't recognise her but reciprocated anyway.

"Hi," I said, finally reaching her.

She greeted me with, "I'm a bit freaked out. There's two Mexicans, and I'm sure they're following me. Every time I look round, they duck behind a bush. I'm walking on my own, and it's making me uncomfortable. Sorry, hi, I'm Brittany." We shook hands.

"I'm Fozzie. Look, it's getting dark," I said. "There are trees with cover from the road over there and a creek. If you like, we can set up camp there. I think Ben is just behind; he'll probably join us."

"I'd like that, thanks."

We intercepted him on the way. He was glad of the company again for the night, and we pitched tents. I hopped about on one leg by the creek while trying to wash one foot at a time.

"I killed a scorpion!" screamed Ben triumphantly.

So far, I had become fond of every single person I had walked with. Such a mix of characters but with a common love and respect for the outdoors. I nodded off with a contented smile and an ear cocked for lost Mexicans.

Journal entry:
The ADZPCTKO party was fantastic; lots of like-minded individuals exchanging advice. 350 or so thru-hikers registered this year, free food, amazing people and great fun.

I started at 7am on Sunday 25 April, at the Mexican border. I signed the register at the official start monument, took photos, paused for a moment to contemplate my adventure, and began walking north 2,640 miles.

The first three to four weeks is desert, although not as hot as I'd expected. For a thru-hiker, long sleeves, trousers, sun hat and a bandana over the neck are the norm. The PCT gains in elevation from 2,200 feet at the start to 6,000 in the Laguna mountains. Very few trees, but generous rainfall over the winter means there is greenery, including spring flowers.

Occasional shade to sit and rest is welcome, I feel the damp ground on my skin and smell its earthiness. There's more water than usual for this time of the year, but not much. Most of the sources are flowing; little creeks and streams of clear, sweet water gurgle past. I dunk my head or soak my bandana and squeeze it under my hat, to give some respite.

Within two hours Gabe and I received our first greeting from the resident rattlesnake population. We rounded a bend, and suddenly a rattler is coiled and ready to strike, tasting the air and shaking its tail. A few well-aimed sticks didn't move it, so we skirted around. Twenty minutes later – another one! Two snakes in as many hours. Now I've encountered them, though, I fear them less.

We climbed up to Mt Laguna at 6,000 feet, arriving late on Tuesday 27th April. Awe-inspiring panoramas all around, and it's only the first few days. There's the occasional small patch of snow, and we've been warned more is coming.

Physically I'm good. My old knee injury is OK, my right calf aches as usual, and I massage them each night. I have blisters already, piercing them every day with a needle, squeezing out the fluid and sterilising with alcohol. My face is dry, which I expected, my hair matted and I smell like a skunk.

I've yet to embrace the filth.

Chapter 3
The Art of Hitching a Ride

Spam: it's pure energy condensed to a slow vibration.
Mahmood 'Cedar Elk' Mokhayesh

Sweltering under the Californian sun, I started early, leaving Brittany and Ben sleeping. I loved the solitude, and continued to knock miles off the desert section. Unlike routes such as the Appalachian Trail, the PCT tackles hills by using switchbacks. The AT takes a direct approach, steep but straight up and over. I often pondered which I preferred. Switchbacks drive you insane: a two-mile up and over can double in distance with all the turns. Conversely, because the incline is kinder, the ascent is easier. I kept reminding myself of this, but it was still frustrating. After all, the route is still 2640 miles however many turns there are.

I surveyed the valley and saw green lines of meandering vegetation nestling near a creek for water. Minerals glistened and winked as I looked at the trail, infinite glistening eyes. Dead trees dotted the way, sun-bleached white and long since stripped of bark. Bare, stark branches towered over me, giant's hands clawing and grasping. Hummingbirds buzzed around my head, at times stopping a mere two feet from my face. Hovering miraculously, motionless, their iridescent plumage changing colour in a pearlescent blur. They scrutinised, eyeing me curiously. I was mesmerised and bewitched, awestruck at their sheer beauty. Never had I experienced a creature so innocent and harmless.

I passed the 100-mile mark, where someone had carefully laid out '100' in a neat stone pile. Most major mileage targets were signified this way, and I praised myself for making it this far. Just do that again twenty-six times, I thought, chuckling.

At another water cache I found hikers contorted and squeezed in any morsel of shade they could find. Bob was sitting under his umbrella and introduced himself, and I met Stumbling Norwegian, Sugar Moma, Dinosaur, and Swayze. As I sat and reversed, cheek by cheek on my bum, until I was under a low hanging bush, the conversation picked up from where it had left off.

"Did you go today?" Dinosaur asked Bob.

"Yeah," he replied, smirking.

"Are we already on the poo topic?" Sugar Moma asked.

"It would appear so." I joined in, feeling like my first day at school, wanting to be part of everything.

"How about you, Fozzie, you keepin' regular?"

"Very much so. I may miss a day, but that's to be expected with a lack of fruit and veg out here. M&Ms, jerky and cheese don't exactly assist the passage, you know? I crave fibre."

"I agree," Bob offered. "Nevertheless, a good colour, nice consistency?"

"Yeah, I don't have any complaints."

Apart from Julian, Warner Springs heralds the first main chance to rest and re-supply, and it's very near the actual trail. There's not much there except a gas station with some meagre rations to restock, a golf club serving a great breakfast and the actual holiday resort. PCT hikers benefit from discounted rooms, reduced further by pitching in with a few others to share the cost of a cabin. I had agreed en route to split with Brittany and Ben, and in anticipation of a rest day I'd left 13 miles to walk before I arrived. I often did this before a town stop. Arriving late means it's soon time for bed, and as most establishments chuck guests out mid-morning, you don't get much chance to enjoy the room in the morning either. At the latest I aimed to arrive at midday, but usually I'd camp an hour from town, arrive early and have the whole day to chill out.

After camping overnight in a dry stream bed at 5,000 feet, the PCT descended to 2,000 feet on the approach to Warner Springs. From a damp, misty and cold start, the trail welcomed me with open arms at the end of an extraordinary first week. I spent the day weaving through woodland, providing dappled shade, passed Eagle Rock and listened to the tinkle of the San Ysidro Creek as it kept me company. Trees merged into meadows bursting and overflowing with spring flowers in shades of lilac, blue, red, and pink. Vibrant orange poppies peered over tall grass. Mice peeked at me from their burrows; lizards ran for cover; rabbits hopped about happily.

After the cold, the wind, the aches, the blisters, and the

hunger, it felt as though I had proven myself over week one, and in return the PCT gave me a huge welcome hug.

I passed Hojo, Jess, and Tradja, admiring how they'd camped, 'cowboy-style', as the Americans call it, in a sleeping bag on the ground without a tent. With no need for a shelter, this saves time, but the real reward is gazing at mesmeric night skies as a breeze tickles your face. I regularly used this method back home in England but was reluctant out here because of the variety of wildlife that could bite, sting, claw, or just plain kill me. A flimsy piece of canvas isn't going to save you from a bear or mountain lion, but any camper knows that when inside that little haven, it feels impenetrable. There's something remarkably (if falsely) comforting being cocooned in a tent: you think you're safe from anything. I vowed to cowboy-camp more often regardless.

Hojo caught up as I checked in at the resort, and he accepted my offer of a spare place in the room. Ben and Brittany had already arrived, revelling in the opportunity to take a shower, lie on a bed and walk barefoot on a carpet. The room already revealed the staple thru-hiking food preferences as ice cream containers, Dorito packets, empty soda cans and cookie crumbs littered the lounge. Days off were all about ingesting fat and sugar.

The others left early the next morning, and I made the most of the golf club's great American breakfast with Tradja, Jess, Brittany, and Burnie.

"How would you like your eggs, sir?" the waiter asked.

I paused, unexpectedly flummoxed, and looked at everyone.

"How the hell do you order eggs over here?" I asked.

The table giggled.

"Fozzie, I'll give you the American breakfast tutorial," Tradja replied. "First, eggs. Sunny side up, they're just cooked on the bottom, tend to be somewhat raw on the top. Next, over easy. Flipped for a few seconds to cook the top. Finally, well done. As the name suggests, turned over until the yolk cooks through completely. Potatoes, either hash browns, which are shredded and cooked on a hot plate, or home fries, little cubes, sometimes with onion and garlic. Lastly, toast. You can have white, which is self-explanatory, wheat, which is the same as your brown bread, and rye, kinda like sourdough with rye seeds in it."

"Thanks very much," I said. The waiter hovered as I perused the menu.

"OK, two eggs over easy. Bacon, well done, hash browns, also well done and wheat toast with orange marmalade, if you have it. To drink I'll have orange juice, no ice, and coffee, strong, black and keep it coming."

There was silence and smiles around the table as heads nodded in approval, confirming my first successful American breakfast order.

I headed out at midday, taking advantage of the lower and flatter terrain. It was hotter away from the hills as the grass turned from greens to browns with summer approaching. Cheeks was resting under a tree and explained that Mojave had returned to Warner Springs to check if their new tent had arrived at the post office. I stopped and chatted with Alex from Scotland, although his accent was diluted with English private school overtones. He walked in a white collared shirt, soiled after days of grime and sweat. He had removed the hip belt from his pack to save weight, and astonishingly, his budget for the entire PCT was $600. I never found out if he made it.

I have the fondest memories of the camp spot that evening at Lost Valley Spring. Water was on hand, albeit half a mile down a side track. A small plateau commanded a worthy view over the lowlands as a blue sky merged into maturing reds and oranges. Stumbling Norwegian, Sugar Moma, Bob, Brittany, Elk, and Burnie were settling in, cooking or playing impromptu guitar. Giggles floated through the air, and aromas of mac and cheese, coffee, and chicken Ramen mingled with scents of young flowers and pine sap. Burnie was eyeing my hot sauce to spice up her dinner, and Elk was extolling the benefits of spam as he made inroads into his fourth Pop Tart. Early starts and early bedtimes, known as 'hiker midnight', meant we turned in at dark and got up at light. Most of us were therefore asleep by 9pm. The body adopts this natural sleep pattern immediately, seemingly aware, and grateful, to be in tune with nature. Darkness is for rest, daylight for smashing miles.

The food topic cropped up at breakfast. Porridge, as we English say, or oatmeal as the Americans call it, took pride of place. I go through phases with porridge: sometimes it turns my nose but at other times I can happily subsist on it for weeks. I researched our friendly grain and learnt to cook it for at least eight hours. I regularly did this at home although not, I hasten to add, every morning. I'd make a pot to keep in the fridge and reheat what I needed. The lengthy cooking time brings out the flavour, and the consistency is wonderful. Additions of raisins or other dried fruit, nuts, spices such as cinnamon, nutmeg and even chocolate had me experimenting and never forget a pinch of salt. I became an oataholic.

The trail limits your food options, but I usually settled on adding powdered milk to my oats, water obviously, sultanas and honey powder, which I found in a hiker box (I'll come to hiker boxes later). I mixed this up in the evening and let it steep overnight, which meant less cooking and a superior texture.

"They're a good respite from depression," claimed Cedar Elk (shortened by everyone to 'Elk'), watching my recipe as he cooked his.

"Does that explain why you're so freakin' happy all the time?" Brittany asked.

Pop Tarts were constantly debated. I'm no fan: there are too many ingredients for starters, which makes me suspicious; they're heavy; but mainly I thought they tasted horrible. Elk was converted, along with a few others, and he used to munch on a couple to solve the immediate hunger crisis before his main meal had cooked. Marshall Walker Lee referred to eating Pop Tarts as his 'morning ritual of self-loathing'.

The San Jacinto Mountains peeked at me every time I crested a high point, their flanks still dressed in snow. I'd acclimated to the temperatures quickly, and the heat wasn't affecting me greatly. As long as I concentrated on drinking at least half to one litre of water an hour, and covering any bare skin with clothing, I was OK. This made me sweat, but my thin wool layers remained comfortable. The ascents produced more perspiration as my body strained and my breathing rate increased. Wiping a hand over my forehead, a mixture of SPF50, sweat, sand, and grit grated against my brow.

I progressed towards my next stop and re-supply at Idyllwild, a regular haunt of hikers due to relatively good hitching opportunities on a busy road, a variety of eating establishments, a store, and gear shop. There was also a campsite with showers. I had camped near the highway on the approach to town with Hojo, Charmin, Stumbling Norwegian and Sugar Moma. Hojo and I stuck out our thumbs at 7.30am in the hope of getting a ride, a ritual I was to repeat many times over the following months.

Often there's no pattern or luck to a successful hitch, but I follow some basic tips picked up over the years to increase my chances. First, I place my pack by the roadside where it's visible. This advertises I'm a hiker and not an axe-wielding madman. A straight stretch of tarmac aids a driver's visibility, but preferably a short section so they can't pick up speed; a fast vehicle is less likely to stop. A layby, is handy so any potential rides can pull in, and standing 200 feet before it presents an opportunity for cars to get off the road quickly. If it's before a corner, even better as they have to slow down. Junctions are perfect spots as vehicles are stationary, the occupants faced with my well-honed helpless look.

My worst effort was later in my hike by the roadside outside Etna. It took three hours and I eventually resorted to beseeching a returning day-hiker by his parked car. The best? Reaching a dead-end road near Wrightwood, where cars had to turn around to go back down the hill. I approached, still on trail, as a car was doing just this and as

I stuck out my thumb, the driver came out of the manoeuvre and started to accelerate. She saw me, stopped, reached round and opened the door, which enabled me to get straight in her car without so much as breaking stride. It couldn't have been quicker or easier. Hitching with a woman increased my odds substantially, I guess drivers found solo men more intimidating.

Lastly, failing everything, do something stupid. I often jumped up and down, danced (not a pretty sight) or opened my umbrella and spun it round in front of me. This caught the driver's attention. Once I had that, I sought eye contact and smiled, looking resigned and sorry for myself.

After an hour with Hojo of dancing, umbrella spinning and enough smiling to make my jaw ache, I finally received a reciprocal smile from a young lady, and she took us both into town.

The campsite was excellent, and I set about my day-off routine. First, my body and the important task of removing dirt, grime, sweat, and odour. I cringed at the violent stench as I removed my shoes, leaving a stark sock line separating a white ankle from a brown mix of congealed dust on my lower legs. Gingerly peeling off my socks with two fingers and placing them with other laundry in a bag, I put on the only spare clothing I had that wasn't heading for the tumble drier: my waterproofs. You can always spot a thru-hiker in a launderette because they're waiting for the machine to run its course while dripping inside a Gore-Tex jacket and trousers. I liked to wash my clothes first because it meant I had something clean to wear when I emerged from the shower. While waiting, I'd read a magazine, lifting the lid out of curiosity to see how brown the water was. Water colour is a great indication of the length and severity of the past section, the harder the trail, the darker the suds. A quick tumble dry and off to the showers.

I'd never been so grateful for a wash. Watching a tawny-coloured murk swirl down the plug hole, I cherished the invigorating feeling of mutating from soiled to squeaky-clean.

I hadn't bothered shaving. Most of the males dispensed with this chore and, as the walk progressed, so did our beards. After a few months there were impressive clumps of hair adorning many chins. My ability to grow bristles is pathetic, I end up with a reasonable goatee merging into my cheeks, where it somewhat gives up. That said, further into the PCT, even I was proud of my beard. Impressive facial hair is a sure way to distinguish a bona fide thru-hiker.

Washed and laundered, I'd catch up with emails, update my blog, check my gear was OK, and replace, repair or upgrade if necessary. The main call, however, was food. American breakfasts are incredible affairs, and I salivated at the thought of them days before hitting town. Eggs, bacon, pancakes, hash browns, beans, mushrooms, sausages, patties, toast, and coffee. Drooling, I made my way over to the Red Kettle Cafe, teeming with hikers, where Elk and Brittany invited me to their table.

Elk was a true outdoorsman and completely at home in the wild. His plant and animal knowledge was exceptional, and he'd soon give me a first taste of rattlesnake. I aspired to match his enviable beard. He strode effortlessly along on two tree trunks for legs. Our conversations always made me laugh, often to the point of hysterics, thanks to the sheer preposterousness of his obscure angles on various subjects. If you look at the quote at the beginning of this chapter, you'll get the idea.

Brittany was married with a daughter and attempting a section of the PCT. Whenever I saw her, she smiled cheekily, as if she'd just pulled a prank I knew nothing about. I was immensely fond of her; her infectious cheer rubbed off on me, and she always lifted my day.

I returned to the campsite, pondering lunch options on the way, and found Burnie had set up her tent near to mine. With a gentle voice, slightly tinged with a squeak, when she laughed it made her sound like a seven-year-old witch, if you can imagine such a tone. I often tried to amuse her just so I could hear her giggle. Not to mention sinus problems, which meant she blew her nose regularly and loudly, making the strangest of noises.

I remember one particular night camped with a few others in the forest, and Burnie had gone off to pee.

"What the hell is that noise? Is that a moose?" I asked everyone, who were listening intently, trying to figure out what creature could produce such a bellowing. Closer it got, to the point where torches came out to illuminate the scene. Most of the camp fell about laughing as Burnie emerged from behind a bush with a handkerchief, post sneezing session, wondering why everyone was looking at her. After a few days, tired of carrying an endless supply of tissues, she started employing the method most of us used: holding one nostril shut with a finger and blowing hard to remove any debris from the other, and then repeating the other side. Americans refer to this as 'snot rocketing my boogers'.

Burnie was in her mid-twenties. She had the Appalachian Trail under her belt and the long-distance walking bug had taken hold. When using her petrol stove during the early days on the AT, she couldn't get the timing right and the burner kept going up in flames (MSR WhisperLite stove owners can surely relate to this). After melting the sleeve of her synthetic jacket, burning a hole in her wool hat and nearly incinerating Springer Mountain shelter, her trail name was born.

With me, she seemed hesitant and unsure at first; and for that reason, unfairly, I tended not to spend time with her, before realising I exhibited the same trait towards others. People often find me difficult to get to know and unapproachable. This is not something I do intentionally; I think it's a subconscious warning signal. The result is those who break my barriers are genuinely worth knowing. After we'd broken each other's, we got along famously.

"Apache Peak still has snow," she said, sounding concerned.

"Yes, I heard."

"I've mailed my ice axe and crampons up trail for the Sierras; I don't have them."

"Me too but there won't be much up there," I said, trying to reassure her. "Even if there is, I'm sure it's negotiable with care."

She still looked worried.

"Look, if you feel safer, we can team up and watch each other's backs."

"No, it's fine – I don't want to impose."

"Burnie, you're not imposing. If you want me to walk with you, it's not a problem, really."

"But I hike slow; I'll hold you up."

"Look, think about it. It makes sense. I leave tomorrow; offer's there if you want it."

In the morning she'd agreed, and we got an easy ride back to the trailhead taking full advantage of stationary cars at a junction, with my insistence she took the prominent position. Having barely started, we abruptly stopped, thanks to our first experience of PCT hospitality. Trail magic is the term used to describe an act of kindness or generosity – usually by the trailside or where it intersects a road. Invariably, it involves food and drink in abundance and somewhere to rest in the shade. It's often laid on by past thru-hikers who realise its value, having experienced the PCT themselves.

Meat spat on the grill, chilled drinks lined coolers, and various snacks spread over tables. I was introduced to Grey Fox, Spiller, Flashlight, Vader, and Pyjamas, all taking a well-earned break away from the sun.

Burnie and I fuelled up and continued, passing Upchuck sitting by a pile of beer cans on the trailside and smoking something that made him talk at speed about nothing in particular for ten minutes. We didn't stop long but leant on our trekking poles, pretending to be interested, and escaped as quickly as possible.

"What's he going to do?" Burnie asked afterwards. "Hallucinate his way to Canada?"

Burnie did hike slower than me, but remembering my reasons for taking on the PCT in the first place, namely to be completely open to events and circumstances, I didn't mind the relaxed pace. I would join others during the hike and rarely found someone who walked naturally at my pace, or I theirs. One had to adjust speed, or walk ahead and rest once in a while for them to catch up, which I gladly did with her. Having offered to accompany her, I had a duty to see her safely over Apache Peak – or at least the snow-bound sections – and it was equally reassuring to have her watch my back as well.

In any case, she was great company, in no hurry and had a relaxed aura that rubbed off on me. There were, again, rumours of storms and we were due to climb to 9,000 feet. On reaching Fobes Saddle (in the US a saddle is a pass or depression in a mountain range or ridge), we noticed a side trail marking a water source half a mile away and decided it would make a suitable early camp spot, mindful of the imminent storm. A quick reccy proved a good idea: there was indeed a flowing spring and space to pitch our tents, sheltered by trees 500 feet below the saddle. I remembered how Gabe and I had wisely chosen to shelter on Mount Laguna, and as the trail continued up to 9,000 feet I was keen to stay put.

We set up camp. It was still only 4pm, but the winds were increasing. The spring provided excellent water, and miner's lettuce grew in abundance. Also known as winter purslane, it was named after the Gold Rush miners who ate it to stave off scurvy. Brittany had shown me this edible plant a few days earlier; it was common in shade and damp areas. As the name suggests, it tastes like a salad leaf, and I filled up my pan, added grated parmesan, olive oil, and pepper for a tasty starter. Several people had warned me not to make a habit of eating too much because of its reputation of loosening one's movements. I double-checked I had enough toilet paper just in case.

By dusk, the storm raced over a mere hundred feet above. There was no rain, but sand blew everywhere, blasting everything in its path, including us. As each successive deafening blast ripped across the valley below, we braced ourselves for the impact. We retreated to our tents, where I spent most of the night unable to sleep until it abated around 2am. Frustrated by the lack of rest, I resorted to snacking after a raging hunger kicked in, and I worked my way through a large part of my supplies. Despite restocking in Idyllwild, I now needed to descend the Devil's Slide trail back to town to buy more food.

We climbed the next day, hoping to reach Saddle Junction by the Devil's Slide. The early morning heat melted the last remnants of snow clinging to branches, and I felt the occasional slap of meltwater on my head. Little puffs of dust erupted on the trail as droplets landed. Eventually, we rounded the north side of Apache Peak, renowned for colder conditions and lingering snow.

It was worse than I had anticipated but not impassable. Sections of the trail were still obscured by snow banks covering the steep hill, but there were plenty of dry parts as well. We progressed tentatively; one slip meant tumbling into the infinite Andreas Canyon Gorge which loomed menacingly below.

Post-holing was also a problem. The first hikers to walk over fresh snow on the PCT each year leave footprints for others to follow, assuming they are going in the right direction! We often followed these prints as the footing was firmer on the compressed snow. The problems start as the summer wears on and the snow melts, becoming unstable; hikers can break through the surface and a stray leg can hit the ground underneath. It usually results in nothing more than a graze, but bruises, sprains, breaks, and cuts are common. The worst scenario is when descending and an entire leg postholes. The momentum carries you forward while the limb stays in place, leading to horrible injuries.

We climbed and dipped relentlessly like leaves on a fluctuating breeze, gasping and sweating on the inclines, then pulling on extra clothing as we cooled going downhill. From Fobes Saddle to Saddle Junction, we tentatively made our way through six-foot snow drifts that littered the trail, progressing at just one mile an hour. I, too, had mailed my ice axe and spikes up to the start of the Sierra at Kennedy Meadows, so we gingerly tiptoed through, supported by our trekking poles.

By the time we reached the bottom of the Devil's Slide, it was getting dark and we still had an hour on the road to town, 12 miles having taken 11 hours. I stumbled into the same campsite again, too tired from effort and lack of sleep to even cook or shower, and fell immediately into a deep slumber.

Chapter 4

Blisters, Perfect Hot Sauce,
and the Silver Spoon

Hiking is my addiction. The PCT is my dealer.
Patti 'Sugar Moma' Kulesz

I hadn't seen Gabe for days, but at breakfast I heard he'd quit at the Rodriguez Spur Road. He emailed later, citing blisters as the problem but added he should have prepared more in terms of fitness and gear. 'I wasn't ready for a thru-hike, Fozzie,' it read.

The Red Kettle was buzzing. I sat with Brittany, Burnie, and Elk. Brittany, wearing an orange top with white trousers, bounced around to the piped music, looking like a lost buoy on choppy seas. She also had an alarming habit of smothering everything she ate with tomato ketchup, so her breakfast looked like she'd lost a limb in some freak accident.

I wasn't fond of ketchup, but I kept a condiments stash to spice up my trail food. Salt and pepper were staples, along with curry powder, cumin, oregano, and sugar. I'd developed a fondness for hot sauce, commonplace in American restaurants. It's uneconomical to buy these items because they're packaged in large sizes, so I used to obtain them in restaurants. I didn't class it as stealing, as I was eating there anyway, so my conscience was untroubled. Elk always said, 'Stolen condiments taste better.'

Once the server had brought my food, I unscrewed the salt and pepper shakers and poured some into my container. I also added to my sugar stocks and tipped hot sauce into a plastic bottle I kept purely for the condiment. This top-up lasted a week.

My favourite hot sauce was a brand called Cholula, but I also loved Tapatio, the ever-popular Tabasco and many other varieties. The further I progressed along the PCT, several brands found their way into my mix, which varied in taste from one week to the next. Sometimes sweet, then salty, occasionally fierce, other times mellow. I thought at some point, the different types would mingle perfectly and I'd have discovered my ideal, fiery condiment. When that happened a few weeks later, I realised the secret was lost forever, as I had only a rough idea of the contents and quantities in the bottle. I had reached hot sauce nirvana, but not for posterity.

The Red Kettle chatter centred on Fuller Ridge, which we'd cross that day. It was still snow bound and enjoyed a fierce reputation as the first difficult section. I got a ride back to the bottom of Devil's Slide, where a group had formed, all keen to have company and reassurance. Stumbling Norwegian, Sugar Moma, Burnie, and Pigpen (a new face) were checking equipment and preparing for the slog up the slide and then Fuller itself. Four day-hikers sporting beer bellies smiled, playfully mocking us as they passed on the way up, remarking that it was easier to walk with day packs than our loads bursting with several days' food. 20 minutes later, we caught up with them, lying on the trail in varying states of decay and pools of sweat, trying to catch their breath.

"It's also far easier to walk when you're fit," I remarked, winking as I passed.

"Touché!" they replied, laughing.

Pony, another new face, and Your Mom joined us as we steered our way over Fuller Ridge. Navigation proved difficult through the snow. With the trail buried and, at times, the actual PCT signs too, we hiked hesitantly. Occasionally, we picked up footprints, although they weren't any guarantee of the right track. On a ridge, we couldn't go far off course, so we kept near the top, involving GPS checking, scouting around and general discussion. Slips, slides, and falls were the order of the day as we picked a route through the white. Trying to grip the icy banks meant that our walking speed plummeted. Every step took time, fearful that at any moment our feet could whip from beneath us as if someone had pulled them sharply sideways.

Bringing up the rear of the pack, I watched horrified as Pony slipped and slid over the slope to our right, gaining momentum towards the steepening cliffs. Under other circumstances she could have self-arrested (plunged an ice axe into the snow to stop the slide). But we didn't have our axes, as we'd not expected snow this early in the hike. In a flash, Pigpen dived over the side and tried to catch her, arresting with his feet and any other part that could bring them to a halt. I wouldn't have attempted such a risky manoeuvre, but ignoring caution, he acted on impulse. Having only met him that morning, I already respected him. Pony was understandably shaken, and thankful.

I expect you may be shaking your head at this point because we were negotiating a snow ridge without ice axes, crampons or rope. In mountaineering terms, this is bad practice and I agree with you, but allow me to explain. If a thru-hiker carried every piece of equipment needed, we'd be struggling under a towering rucksack weighing 50 kilos and the inevitable injuries that would cause. Pack weight is extremely important. If we can hike a section with 100ml of stove fuel, then we risk it. When buying a jacket, the first thing we check is not whether it's waterproof but how much it weighs. One pair of socks is fine for a week because two pairs increase the weight (and they'd both stink anyway).

Lightening up is a series of small steps making an overall improvement. Carrying one shirt is indistinguishable from two, but several of these minor tweaks mean a lighter load. Buy the lightest gear possible that works, carry the least you're comfortable with and make minor sacrifices.

Failing that, learn the hard way. Every year, somewhere around Warner Springs, hikers throw stuff from their packs and mail it home, that is one busy mail office.

Fatigued although in good spirits, we arrived at Black Mountain Road. No one had remembered to fill up with water, and had it not been for Your Mom, Pigpen and Pony, who graciously offered to walk two miles back up the trail to collect some, we'd have gone thirsty and hungry.

I walked with Stumbling Norwegian down the endless switchbacks on Fuller Ridge's east side as the sky fired red and orange. We stopped to rest and seek shade under an overhanging rock that morning. I reached for my spork (a plastic eating utensil with a spoon one end and a fork the other), only to discover it had disintegrated into four pieces. Norwegian laughed at my forlorn expression as I realised I had nothing to scoop out my peanut butter.

"The spork devil has struck!" I exclaimed, showing him the remnants for verification.

"Don't worry, Fozzie, the trail will provide," he said reassuringly.

'The trail will provide' is a well-known expression in thru-hiking circles. Quite how the Stumbling Norwegian expected me to locate a spork, or indeed any cutlery at short notice in the Californian desert escaped me. I reached the bottom of Fuller Ridge on my own and navigated across a scorched, featureless flatland to a promised water cache under the Interstate 10 bridge. Marker poles in the sand every quarter mile guided me. I crossed dry creek beds, their surfaces etched and rippled from forgotten creeks. A huge gopher snake whipped out from beneath a bush, making me stop abruptly. Longer than I was tall, it flew across the terrain faster than any human could run.

I reached the bridge and water cache just as the local trail angel who looked after it arrived on his quad bike. Dr No stopped in front of me and, without even asking, opened the cooler strapped to his bike and handed me the coldest beer ever. As I accepted the bottle, a sliver of ice gently slid off the top and glided down the side, where it dripped onto my finger and melted.

"Thanks," I said. "Absolutely perfect timing."

"No problem, here to help," he replied.

We chatted for a while, and putting my trash in the bin, I noticed something sticking out of the sand. Crouching to retrieve it, I couldn't believe my luck. An antique spoon, black with tarnish, nestled in my hand. On the handle it bore the inscription 'MBL' with a silver hallmark, and the engraved letters 'Pat 1907'.

Dr No explained the highway was built over 100 years ago and, although he doubted it belonged to a worker, someone probably lost it seeking shade under the bridge. I remembered Stumbling Norwegian saying 'the trail will provide,' and I smiled. I spent a few minutes rubbing it in the sand, which removed the tarnish, and it came up like new. That spoon stayed with me for the rest of the PCT, and I still use it when I hike now. Weight penalties aside, we all have one item of luxury.

Five miles up the freeway, Cabazon beckoned with a hot meal, but my mileage wasn't meeting expectations and I felt compelled to push further. Only managing around 15 miles a day, I needed 20's. Besides, hitching on the Interstate is nigh on impossible; the vehicles travel too fast and it's illegal. This wouldn't have stopped me. 'Sorry, I'm English, I had no idea' and an innocent expression got me out of a few scrapes with the authorities.

I carried on through knee-high grass to the Mesa Wind Farm. Lizards darted about and startled me, especially after the snake earlier. Even my trekking poles kept catching the scrub and rustling, so I was a nervous wreck. I'd heard the wind farm maintenance crew welcomed hikers into their canteen and stocked their freezer full of goodies, asking only a donation to cover costs. It had closed when I arrived, and I hoped they'd be working in the morning. Burnie, Stumbling Norwegian, Pigpen, Your Mom, and Pony showed up afterwards with the same plan.

Excited by the rare opportunity to get a hot breakfast on trail, most of us were in the canteen by 7.30am, rummaging through the freezer and microwaving burritos, burgers, croissants, drinking coffee and washing it all down with ice cream.

The days were hotter, and we dripped sweat over unforgiving terrain. I couldn't believe how much water was available. It wasn't exactly abundant, but there were creeks every few miles. I sniggered thinking about England, which had drought warnings imposed after a few days of weak sunshine. The Californian desert rarely saw rain for weeks, even months, but still we found something to drink.

We descended through the Whitewater Canyon to the Whitewater River. At midday everyone was so hot that the chance to cool off was irresistible. For two hours we splashed and swam, did laundry, built dams to create pools and washed ourselves. Striped rock strata plunged diagonally into the ground like huge, angled slices of chocolate layer cake. It felt wonderful to be clean, and I took a siesta in the shade. Keen for solitude, I left before the others, progressing to the next valley, and picked up the trail weaving along Mission Creek. Soreness plagued my feet, and I blamed the sand and grit working through the mesh on my shoes.

Yelling as another blister burst, I hobbled to a painful

halt. Enough was enough for one day. Pitching tent among many scary-looking burrows, I hoped they didn't house a tarantula or something equally creepy. I checked my shelter for holes and made sure my zip was well sealed before sleeping. I slept fitfully to nightmares of huge rattlesnakes emerging from underground nests, devouring me whole.

I woke early, cooked porridge and just on the verge of leaving I noticed someone approaching from downstream, jumping nimbly over the creek like a mountain goat. Yvo had started at 6.30am, and I hiked with him for most of the day. He hailed from Switzerland and bore a striking resemblance to John Lennon, with scruffy hair meeting an unkempt beard, interrupted by wiry spectacles. I half expected him to whip out a guitar and play a rendition of Hey Jude. He walked quickly and effortlessly. Gliding along without sweating, he paused every 30 minutes, commented on the view and continued. I gasped behind, leaving a trail of sweat in the grit. It was like trying to follow a pacemaker. If you needed to be somewhere, and could keep up, Yvo was the man to stick with.

We fumbled aimlessly along Mission Creek, hemmed in by towering cliffs either side as they narrowed like a huge funnel. Feeling the sun's heat when we left the shade and a chill as we returned. With the constant gurgle of water for company, we must have crossed the creek 30 times. Balancing our feet on one side, ready to leap, the weak soil gave way beneath us, the icy water chilling our toes. Straining our eyes, we tried, sometimes in vain, to find the elusive trail. A rattlesnake glided casually across the path, startling me. Normally, they'd signal a warning, but it remained silent, seemingly without malice or intent to confront, and nightmares aside, my fear subsided. Forest fires had left trees stark and bare, twisted into bizarre shapes. We climbed, praying for the unrelenting hills to finish.

The end came ten hours later. Yvo, who had long since disappeared, had camped under the Ponderosas at 8,000 feet. I nodded a greeting and gestured I intended to carry on, and he signalled his understanding. 40 minutes later, after hiking 21 miles and climbing 4,500 feet, I pulled off the trail at 7.30pm. I laid down my pack, set up the tent and watched the sun sink over the Californian heights as a crescent moon rose, scarlet streaks merging to silver. Stars pierced the black as my saucepan lid rattled, the only sound in the mountains, letting me know dinner was ready.

I reached Onyx Summit in the morning and managed a quick ride into the town of Big Bear with a local fireman. I'd planned on staying at a hostel and after a bus ride, which I swore circled the same route twice, I finally arrived. Grayson, a very hospitable host, checked me in and told me to relax. A sombre Sugar Moma had arrived, explaining she'd got off at the top of Devil's Slide because of fatigue and dietary problems. She looked unhappy, but food and tiredness issues aside, I sensed something deeper simmered. I later learnt her relationship with the Stumbling Norwegian had ended.

Being spread out over a large distance, a situation I encountered often at towns, Big Bear didn't appeal. It sounds crazy that we hike from Mexico to Canada and then complain at having to walk everywhere once in town, but rest and recuperation was important. I concentrated on the usual tasks of showering, laundry, food shopping, and emails so I could relax, grab a beer and chill out. But it never happened that way. My plan to rest for one day a week wasn't working. I needed a day and a half, sometimes two, just to fit everything in.

The main time drain was sitting at the computer. My hike was gaining momentum, and my followers demanded updates. I kept receiving messages from people I didn't know, and the blog was proving popular. Most sent good wishes, which was heartening, but it took a while to answer, which I felt obliged to do. Internet facilities constantly frustrated me. The library usually had several computers, but they came with a ridiculous one-hour limits, nowhere near enough. I should point out that at the time of my hike, my cell phone was basic, and smartphones had only been around for three years. My phone wasn't even capable of emailing or internet access.

However, most errands were obscured by the importance of food. My appetite in town was off the scale. On the trail I was hungry, but no more than usual. Once rested, my body somehow sensed I'd arrived in town and it demanded I make inroads into my calorie deficit. I always had a huge breakfast, and the wait for lunch was so long I had to munch on something at 10am. After lunch, I'd already put away 4,000 calories and needed to snack mid-afternoon as well, only to feast come evening. Of course, I managed ice cream before bedtime too. Consuming 6,000 to 7,000 calories a day, I still constantly pondered when I'd eat next.

Grayson took me back to the trailhead after two days, and I set off alone. Weaving along classic single-track, I longed for my mountain bike. Pine needles dusted the trail, cushioning my feet and suppressing the dust. Huge

Ponderosa pines, famous for their rich, butterscotch scent sweetened the air. Elk had originally pointed out their sweet, rich aroma and we'd spent time a few days before pressing our nose into the bark like kids in a sweet shop. I kicked the occasional pine cone, pretending to take the winning penalty in the World Cup (and missing). Fallen trees blocked my passage and I approached, sizing them up, calculating whether best to climb over, squeeze under or walk around.

I daydreamed, and miles passed without realising. I missed turns in the path and reminded myself to concentrate on directions, to watch for rocks, snakes, and obstacles that could cause a twisted ankle. Annoyed at having to scan the ground in front of me, it denied me the chance to admire my surroundings, so I'd pause to gaze about. I tried to look behind as well; sometimes the best views stared me in the back. Days vanished in a blurred trance as the repetitive rhythm of footfall lured me into utopia. I saw no one or heard another sound except the crunch of my feet, the regular stab of my trekking poles, and my breathing.

Passing some hot springs, I was tempted to plunge in, but being Friday evening, everywhere teemed with townsfolk. Beer cans littered the banks, and hoarse shouts disturbed me as I walked past graffiti covered rocks. Innocuous slogans like 'I love Kate' or 'alcohol forever' mixed with lewd sexual suggestions. This behaviour and vandalism reminded me why I'd escaped to the PCT in the first place.

Town outskirts often shattered the wilderness experience, and I resented the human race, retreating further into myself and forgoing company for fear of being dragged from the solace I savoured. To protect my selfish tranquillity, I waited when seeing hikers ahead so I'd stay alone, and if people were behind, I might speed up. I camped well off trail to prevent being disturbed. For days I yearned for nothing more than to get lost in the desert, pretending to be a sole apocalyptic survivor, roaming at will. I begrudged roads, cars, and buildings their existence, even planes grated.

Addicted to a self-imposed solitude, I savoured the prospect of the remote Sierra Nevada, where I'd further indulge the isolation from my normal life. I tried to berate myself for allowing such feelings, convincing myself they were negative, but I couldn't. I was happy in my solitary meanderings and dreamt up ways to stay infinitely detached.

Then, suddenly, I'd snap out of it, eager to walk with others again. I liked company but relished the isolation equally. I flitted between the two according to my mood changes.

Snake count: 3
False alarms: 62

After only 350 miles I already needed new shoes. The rocky trail rasped at my footwear like sandpaper, but even taking that into account it surprised me. With that average I'd need eight pairs by the end of the hike. An English company called Inov-8 had sponsored me with Gore-Tex boots, which Uncle Tony was looking after. I only intended using them when and if the weather deteriorated. In the desert, as comfortable as they were, my feet would have fried. Philip Carcia, otherwise known as Lo, pointed me toward Montrails, which he swore by and I then purchased. My wide feet seemed better suited to this brand. After a day they blocked out more sand as the fabric was a tighter weave, but my blisters persisted regardless.

The town of Wrightwood impressed me immediately. It was compact and everything lay in walking distance around a central square. The Evergreen and Grizzly cafés dished up admirable breakfasts, the large supermarket made my re-supply easy and hikers gathered at the Evergreen bar in the evening.

Many had stopped for a few days, waiting for snow to clear on top of Baden-Powell. A similar backlog was due at the start of the Sierras, but I wasn't lingering over snow melt. An extra day wouldn't make any discernible difference, and I remained unhappy with my mileage. I'd pulled in a few 20 to 25-milers but, after taking rest days into account, the actual daily average totalled a dismal 15. I had to get moving; less time in town and more hours on the trail. I should have heeded this decision, for it came back to haunt me later.

My blisters were the problem, and they limited mileage. If I pushed too hard, then the existing ones worsened, or new ones appeared, so I had no choice than to stick below 20 miles a day. The days I exceeded that, I paid for it.

They took weeks to heal. The body is the best judge during a thru-hike and will generally fix itself. I'd always suffered from blisters, whether on the PCT or shorter adventures. They normally appeared after two days, which made a week's walking somewhat painful. Having learnt to accept them, I had to pay attention and watch for infections.

Every night I religiously washed my feet in a creek (ensuring I was downstream of anyone else!). Then I dried and inspected them. I didn't enjoy looking after them because it made inroads into my spare evening time, but I had little choice. The fresh ones required the most attention: sterilising my pen knife and needle in a lighter flame, I pierced them to squeeze out the liquid, then cut the loose skin away. The excruciating part was dabbing rubbing alcohol on the exposed, raw flesh underneath, which had me rocking back and forth like a baby, gritting my teeth and stifling a scream. I never dressed them, preferring instead to let the air do its work and, although this proved painful afterwards, they got the message and healed quicker.

Despite this care, one foot became infected near the town of Agua Dulce. The soft pad below my big toe was alarmingly red and tender. I tried to pierce it several times, but my feet had toughened (when thru-hiking the skin hardens). The needle wouldn't penetrate, so on the third evening I acted: the pain had worsened, and the area was changing colour to white and even shades of blue. I inserted the needle, broke through the skin and kept pushing, probing and testing each part. I watched, disgusted, as a thick, congealed mixture of pus and blood oozed out and a nasty smell hit me. Even Stumbling Norwegian held his nose, and he was 20 feet away.

I have tried nylon socks, wool, liners (a thin pair worn under the main ones), waterproof boots, non-waterproof boots, washing, and wearing blister patches, but nothing worked. However, I become immune to the pain and once moving, it faded after the five-minute hobble. I thought of Gabe every time it happened.

The heat made my feet sweat and wasn't helping, nor was the grit. I removed my shoes at breaks to air them, but they still looked wrinkled, like after a hot bath. I hadn't researched properly to start with either. I'd always walked in

Gore-Tex (or similar) lined footwear because I dislike wet feet, but in the desert, it invited breathability problems; so, just a week before leaving, I had switched to a low-cut trail runner with mesh inserts for ventilation. But I hadn't worn them in. That, I figured, was the main issue. Now that the first pair had worn out, I'd trusted Lo's advice and bought a brand I'd not tried before. He claimed his Hardrocks had covered 2,500 miles. By the look of them, I believed it!

Stumbling Norwegian hiked in water sport shoes. They were open to the air and highly breathable. Elk used full-blown leather boots, Burnie the same but fabric, others wore sandals and I even saw a few pairs of Crocs. Blisters settled at varying times for different people, some didn't suffer at all. After the first few weeks, the complaints died as our feet healed, or we just became immune to the pain. Like a headache that lasts for days, eventually you stop moaning and just deal with it.

I was on my second espresso in Mountain Grinds Coffee Shop the morning of my departure from Wrightwood. A sign on the wall made me chuckle: 'Unattended children will be given an espresso and a free kitten'. Filling up with breakfast afterwards at the Grizzly Café with a new face I'd met called Borders, we discussed plans for tackling Mount Baden-Powell. Hojo, Vicki, and Dennis had returned from a failed attempt, wet and blown around by the last of the poor weather. The forecast looked good, so I left with Borders, Grey Fox, Spiller, Jake and Upchuck. Reports filtering back revealed snow higher up, but the going was easier than Fuller Ridge. I remember thinking later that sometimes other people's advice sucks.

I walked with Jake at first, who proved great company. Descending to Vincent Gap, suddenly we met a never-ending stream of Japanese hikers coming up. Trail etiquette suggests giving way to those ascending, so we stepped to the side. Patiently, we waited as they filed up, one by one, ignoring us, making no eye contact and offering no thanks.

After about 40 had passed, displaying no manners, we threw politeness to the wind. Increasing our throttles, we stormed down the hill, as each of them yelped and jumped off the trail to get out of our way. We tempered our haste by thanking each one of them.

"Thanks! Nice one! Very kind of you! Cheers! Kon'nichiwa!"

We snacked with the rest of the group at the car park while several tourists came over, offering congratulations for our endeavours so far and wished us well for Baden-Powell. Perhaps it's me, but I'm wary when anyone offers me good luck before climbing a mountain. They'd returned from the summit and left us their surplus food, which we devoured gladly.

Switchbacks coiled up the north flank of Baden-Powell. Despite the chillier elevation, we sweated copiously and drank to stay hydrated. It was four miles uphill, and on each turn the snow deepened until we lost the trail altogether. We drifted apart, finding our own pace and direction. Before long I played a guessing game with my location. I didn't have a GPS, but my map showed a steepening gradient to the summit, with no tight contour lines suggesting dangerous drop-offs. I followed a compass bearing north and aimed for the high point. Snow came up to my thighs and, gasping for air, I lunged one step at a time, breathed deeply and ploughed on. The sun glared off a crisp, white surface, reducing my eyes to narrow slits behind my sunglasses.

I stumbled onto the path, saw the crest of a hill and then heard laughter. The group had made it to the summit, apart from Upchuck, who was nowhere to be seen. I assumed he was catching up with his beer hydration therapy.

Stunning views surrounded us. To the north mountains plummeted to plateaus stretching as far as I could see. To the east, south, and west more peaks soared, many capped with snow. We looked back to Fuller Ridge where we had been eight days earlier, its classic triangular silhouette still visible, commanding the surrounding hills. A glider soared past, so far below I barely saw it.

I left the others, suggesting we meet at camp, and followed a rollercoaster ridge, skipping around and over snow banks, trying to stay away from the edge and surveying the best line to take. I inadvertently veered right at Dawson's Saddle before realising my mistake when the trail filtered into nothing and steepened. I heard traffic far below and aimed there to have a better indication of my position as opposed to wasting energy returning to the top. The loose soil and steep slope made progress extremely difficult, and I spent two hours either sliding or falling on my arse. Finally, I reached the road and a welcome creek as dusk moved in. With water to hand, my fatigue and the chance to get a bearing in the morning from the road decided the spot for me.

As I looked back up towards Dawson's Saddle, I saw several figures at varying positions descending. I figured it was Jake, Spiller, Grey Fox, and Borders, who had either followed me or made the same mistake themselves. With daylight fading fast, I placed my head lamp on a tree stump pointing at them and turned it to the flashing strobe setting while I hurriedly built a fire to act as homing beacons. Either side of me, rock faces shot up, and I wanted no one falling over the edge.

One by one they emerged, having made the same navigational error, and glad to have heat and water. We commandeered the corner of an off-road parking area and busied ourselves making evening meals, rehydrating and relaxing. A car pulled up and an anxious-looking guy approached.

"Have you lost a hiker?" he asked.

Unsure, we replied in unison, "No?"

"Well, someone called Upchuck damn near fell in the road in front of us after tumbling down a slope, and we nearly ran him over!"

We'd forgotten about him, having last seen him on the ascent. He'd made the same mistake coming down Dawson's Saddle, although his final bearings must have gone astray and he found an unexpected drop-off. Minutes later he stumbled into camp a sweaty mess, with blood oozing from several lacerations to his legs.

"You OK, Upchuck?" I asked.

"Yeah, man, just lost the trail."

He unpacked his sleeping bag and then slid inside.

"You going to eat some food, dude?" asked Jake.

"Nah, too tired. I'll have a beer. I'm doing OK."

You couldn't reason with Upchuck; he did his own thing regardless. He could have arrived minus a leg, an eyeball hanging out, a branch through his chest and a case of diarrhoea but he'd still have drunk a can or two and turned in. We smiled and just shrugged our shoulders.

Chapter 5

Eat

I've never seen skinny people eat so much.
Unknown

Food is an obsession when long-distance hiking. As soon as I woke, I thought about breakfast; once moving the mid-morning snack beckoned; then I yearned for lunch. My afternoon break loomed and the evening meal couldn't come soon enough. It is the most hotly debated subject on trail bar none.

I usually resupplied once a week from a store or supermarket. After a month I'd honed my rationing to a fine art and judging quantities came easily. Amounts were important: too much meant a heavy pack; too little and I'd run out. If in doubt I took more, despite the weight penalty, as running out of food was sheer misery. If I had access to a weighing machine, I knew around 1.2 kilos of food per day was enough.

I have mentioned porridge, which became a staple, although sometimes I craved crunchiness so I had granola. Lunch consisted of tortillas with various fillings: often salami or cheese, both of which lasted well, tuna, peanut butter, mayonnaise, and fresh vegetables such as onions, avocados, and peppers. Firm vegetables kept for around three days before expiring. Evening meals provided the most calories, and I relied on pre-made rice and pasta meals with sauces such as cheese, spicy Mexican, and Spanish vegetable. I tried to keep my snacks healthy, using nuts and dried fruit, which provided valuable fat, protein, fibre and vitamins. Extras included a small bottle of olive oil, hot sauce, cookies, grated parmesan, spices, stock powder and my favourite dark chocolate almonds. To drink, I had coffee, tea, and a product called Emergen-C, which provided valuable electrolytes and minerals lost through perspiration. During the later stages I also carried protein powder. A few people used this, but I only became familiar with it later. If I'd known earlier, it would have been a staple: a little heavy but it packed small and proved a rich source of protein. The chocolate flavour filled me up and when mixed with water, it tasted like a milkshake. Occasionally, I added Emergen-C, powdered milk and green super-food powder. Before dinner it got to work repairing my body and tempered the immediate hunger. A revelation for breakfast, it was quick and fuelled me for three hours. Coupled with a coffee, no one could catch me, even Yvo.

When I tired of the packet meals, I experimented with other concoctions. Powdered French onion soup with rice, peanuts, and hot sauce became a favourite. It tasted like takeout Chinese.

I craved meat and ate my fill when in town, also carrying jerky, which developed into an addiction; I consumed mountains of the stuff, especially the peppered and teriyaki varieties. The camping stores carried a varied selection of freeze-dried meals and although expensive, I occasionally treated myself to bacon and eggs or beef stew. Chocolate cheesecake and even freeze-dried ice cream were available.

My weekly shopping totalled around $60. To cut costs, I sought the cheaper brands, made my own mixes or plundered the hiker boxes. I found hiker boxes in various places but usually in the camping stores, hostels or at trail angels' houses. They contained items that others no longer required, including old footwear, clothing, repair kits and a lot of food. The sell-by dates needed checking, but with the rubbish most of us consumed, our stomachs handled anything. I stuck to unopened packets to ensure better quality, and I found some excellent stuff.

Many hikers kept strict budgets to the point that they walked the entire PCT using only food from these boxes. I met Scorpion in Tehachapi and walked with her on occasion. She carried a lot of food, not knowing when she'd find the next box or how well stocked it would be. Others joked about getting to hiker boxes before Scorpion or there wouldn't be much left. This was somewhat harsh as she only took what she needed and also traded her surplus with others. I liked her, with less funds than some, she relied and thrived on being thrifty.

Camping one evening, I offered her coffee, and she reciprocated with a few sun-dried tomatoes. I accepted, but when I put one in my mouth, I regretted it. The dry, grainy, gritty morsel with a leather texture suggested the sell-by date had expired years earlier. I tried to look pleased and finished chewing it, but had to force it down, rinsing the aftertaste away with a generous swig of bourbon. In retrospect, perhaps I should have soaked it in the liquor first. Jack Daniels infused sun-dried tomatoes held much potential.

In the latter stages of my hike, I became acquainted with Nick Levy, one of only two other English guys on the trail that year and a source of many food stories. Nick had travelled on and off for most of his life, existing on meagre budgets, which drove him to drastic measures in his search for food. Over the years he had become skilled – if you can call it that – at judging a food's edibility.

He often sourced from trash bins in the street. Yes, that's what I said: trash bins. Many times in town, walking down the street, I'd wait for him to reply to a question, only to turn and find him 20 feet behind me with his nose and arms in a trash bin, smelling the offerings. He cherished half-eaten hamburgers, carefully unwrapping them (if indeed they were still wrapped), offering them tentatively to his nose to greet with either disgust or delight. After the initial shock, I accepted it as normal.

For Nick, rubbish skips, known in the States as dumpsters, were further horns of plenty. These scored highly because of greater quantities and improved quality. Supermarkets regularly threw out food even before the sell-by date. Bakeries threw unsold goods away daily, offering prime dumpster-diving opportunities. Nick disappeared inside dumpsters for alarmingly long periods to the sound of rustling plastic bags being torn open. He'd resurface, grinning, with a bag of bagels or clutching a cake.

He recalled one time when a friend had found an unlocked dumpster outside McDonald's. The fast food chain treats dumpster diving seriously, threatening arrest, and to stumble across an unlocked one was a treat. This trip scored well with his friend locating several fried eggs. Under the misguided impression that an expert chef merrily fried several of these to order, I now realise reality is somewhat different. The skip housed a large, plastic 'condom' (as Nick called it), with twenty-four compartments, four along the top and six down the side. With a perfectly cooked egg in each, presumably for microwaving or heating in hot water. His friend ate the lot and got a two-week protein fix in one hit, not to mention constipation.

Dietary issues such as coeliac disease, food intolerances and the usual difficulty sourcing vegetarian or vegan foods complicated plans. Most dealt with intolerances and allergies by preparing, dehydrating and mailing their supplies to various points along the trail. Many hikers used food boxes, not just those with specific dietary needs, but I never understood their appeal. My mind boggled at the sheer amount of effort needed to source, mix, pack and post up to seven months' worth of food. It forced the hiker to stop at certain points to collect packages where they often encountered delays because the post office was closed. I did have a 'bounce box' – a term used to describe a package we mailed ahead of ourselves. It contained items used occasionally but not worth carrying because of this infrequency; for example: shaving equipment, batteries, toothpicks, spare pens and recharging equipment. Any surplus food I didn't want to throw away or leave in a hiker box I'd leave in my bounce box, which was as near as I got to mailing food ahead.

Trooper, a vegetarian, whom I first met in the Sierras, mailed most of his food along the trail, a total of 26 boxes. A dehydrated vegan soup provided his main meal, which he supplemented with cheese from town to increase his fat intake. He never tired of his lunch staple; a tortilla with vegan jerky, cheese, and mayonnaise.

Sugar Moma was hypoglycaemic (low blood glucose levels), protein and iron deficient, and vegetarian. Hell, why make life easy?! She mixed and pre-packed most of her food and organised mail drops. Scrutinising ingredients and surviving mostly on protein shakes for breakfast, she also added powdered milk and TVP (textured vegetable protein) to most of her meals.

Others survived on simpler rations. Ryan 'Steve Climber' Bishop Ashby swore his success in Oregon was down to Snickers and the McDonald's Dollar Menu.

Fat intake – or rather, the lack of it – caused weight loss for many. Dehydrated food generally lacks fat, and because most fat sources were heavy, we neglected carrying them until we started getting skinny. Carbohydrates are the staple energy source; after these deplete, the body turns to its fat reserves. If fat isn't topped up, serious weight loss can occur. My main sources of fat came from peanut butter, which I'd eaten since childhood, along with nuts, olive oil, and cheese. I, too, neglected these at the start until noticing my weight loss after a few weeks.

An average week's re-supply was comprised of oats supplemented with raisins, sugar, dried milk and nuts for breakfast, plus coffee and tea. Snacks were a mix of crunchy oat bars of various flavours (chocolate, honey, maple syrup, etc.), nuts, a bag of tortilla chips, jerky, chocolate, M&Ms, Snickers and hard candy. Tortillas provided lunch, filled with either cheese, tuna, salami, peanut butter, or Spam, and a tube of mayonnaise to moisten it, providing extra fat.

Different flavours of packet rice and pasta meals provided my dinner. Despite the weight penalty I tried to leave town with a few items of fresh fruit and vegetables. Apples, peppers, and onions kept well for a few days, and even avocados, if treated carefully, could go for three days. I also took bananas.

I removed the packaging and decanted the contents into Ziploc bags. This prevented the build-up of unnecessary trash, saved weight and made access easier. The whole process could take an hour.

A hiker staple was macaroni and cheese. Kraft seemed the preferred brand, but it never appealed to me. Firstly, I try not to mix protein and carbohydrate because the body digests them differently, and secondly it looked and smelt disgusting. The cheese sauce, sealed inside a plastic bag, was added to the cooked pasta. It looked like liquid plastic in a disgusting, lurid yellow. The smell itself made me retch.

By far the most popular hiker staple, and most famous, is ramen noodles. These are thin, dried noodles shaped into a block, sealed in a packet with a foil sachet containing the flavoured powder. Choose from popular varieties such as pork, beef, shrimp, mushroom, and chili or venture into California vegetable, oriental, creamy chicken, and Cajun shrimp, to name a few. Ramen gets a bad press amongst hikers, but you'll find those complaining have a pack in their supplies. There's much going for it; it's light, small, incredibly cheap and reasonably filling. It's not healthy, but if you think eating on a thru-hike can be, you've been misled. It has a lot of salt but even that was a bonus in hotter conditions.

Most stores sold them for about 60 cents, even cheaper

if bought in bulk and mailed out, reducing the cost to an incredible 30 cents per meal. I bought them but found one didn't curb my hunger. I enjoyed the taste but drank a lot of water after, presumably because of the salt content.

Good old raisins and peanuts, known as GORP, was invented by a couple of surfers in the 60s. Since then it's been tweaked, added to, messed with but remains a staple amongst outdoor folk. Other ingredients have found their way in such as soya beans, cranberries, apricots, pretzels, banana chips, you name it. I like raisins and peanuts but not together.

I remember watching a video about one hiker preparing enough GORP to mail out for her entire thru-hike. She filled a large bucket with huge quantities of various dried fruits and nuts, mixed them together, and divided it into twenty-four portions for mail drops. After four weeks he hated the stuff. Enough said.

After the navigational mishap descending Dawson's Saddle, I followed the highway for a mile and reconnected with the PCT. There were washrooms near a parking area, which gave me the rare opportunity to sit down for my number twos. I emerged, a little lighter, and met Bigfoot, Wide Angle, and Stanimal. We hiked to Cooper Canyon campground, busy with people enjoying themselves. Wisely choosing to sit at a family's table laden with large amounts of food wantonly on display, we practised our hungry expressions, doing our best to look emaciated. Before long, after hearing of our hiking exploits, the family plied us with chilled sodas and fired up the barbecue. We stuffed ourselves with burgers, chicken and even a large rack of sticky ribs. Smiles all round, and licking of honey-glazed fingers rounded off a very successful lunch, and we thanked them profusely.

The temperature now climbed at night as well as by day. My sleeping bag research advised taking one rated to 20 degrees Fahrenheit. Cosy at the start, when the nights hovered around freezing point, but now it was too warm. During the night I kept opening my bag up more until eventually I climbed out and just slept underneath, using it like a quilt. Before long I'd need a cooler bag.

On the PCT each year, detours are inevitable. Usually because of forest fires or areas cordoned off to encourage regrowth after past fires. Nearing the end of a 47-mile road detour, my sore feet ached. Off road trail cushions feet somewhat but tarmac is harsh. The constant pounding meant several new blisters had flared up, and my leg muscles screamed. Motorists asked after me and I explained I was walking 47 miles to get back on trail. Met with bewildering looks, most couldn't comprehend walking this distance. So, when I explained further about hiking 2,640 miles to Canada, their brains couldn't compute; it was incomprehensible to them.

I lightened my road walking boredom by playing games. As cars approached, I glanced at the occupants; and during those split seconds, I tried to guess their lives.

Business people on their way to meetings drove smart executive models such as BMWs and Audis. Elderly couples in sun hats and sunglasses, most likely just out for day trips, drove cautiously, peering at the scenery. Larger cars with kids in the back and roof boxes suggested the holiday season was underway.

Unbearable heat recoiled off jet-black bitumen and assaulted me. The sun glared painfully. Sweat ran off my forehead, around my eyebrows and into my eyes, stinging. I wiped them instinctively with the back of my hand, only to make matters worse as the sunscreen hurt them further. Despite my frantic arm-waving, insects buzzed relentlessly, like someone constantly poking me in the side to gain a reaction.

I reached a KOA (Kampgrounds of America), where a few hikers had holed up for the day to take advantage of a shop, swimming pool, and showers. Elk, Brittany, Mojave, Cheeks, Stanimal, Bigfoot, Wide Angle, Vicky, Dennis and Hojo had cordoned off several picnic tables. Elk busied himself preparing a rattlesnake for dinner. He'd seen it being run over by a car and put it out of its misery. I'd not sampled it before, but I was impressed. It tasted like chicken, with a hint of fish. Elk prepared a few separate dishes, spiced up with various herbs and spices including curry powder. Rattlesnake curry, I thought, could catch on.

Elk also had a staple recipe for the trail I saw him make before a week's hike. He called it Raw Dawg, perhaps not a tempting sounding menu choice. It comprised a chopped onion, avocado, a can of pork and beans, a head of garlic, a can of Spam or corned beef, hot sauce and ketchup. Everything went in a Ziploc, then he left it in the sun for twenty-four hours (when hiking he'd place it on the outside of his pack). It kept for a few days on the trail because the garlic and hot sauce fended off any bacteria.

That night, while trying to doze off, I hoped my ears deceived me. Then I heard the sound again. I sat up, momentarily comforted that the flimsy piece of tent canvas would keep me safe. Perhaps from the odd snake or spider, unable to find its way in – but from a mountain lion? I hoped I'd been dreaming, but then it roared again and this time it sounded closer. My watch showed just after 3am. Mountain lions hunt at night, and this one seemed to be creeping closer. I drifted off but woke again at 6.30am, dressed and got out of the tent. Bigfoot snoozed in his sleeping bag.

"Mate, did you hear that roaring last night? Scared the crap out of me. Sounded like a mountain lion or something," I said.

"Oh, yeah," he replied casually. "There's a farm up the way that keeps lions and bears. They use them in the movies." He rolled over and snoozed again while I felt like a bloody idiot.

I left the KOA to pull in more miles. After taking a wrong turn crossing a railway line, I climbed. Nothing serious, but with the ever-increasing heat, I dripped with sweat. It rolled down my nose and caught the edge of my mouth where I tasted salt. My arms glistened as I gulped more water.

I passed Elk, Brittany (now known as Logic, in acknowledgement of her simplistic problem solving), Mojave and Cheeks. They'd made camp on a ridge, and I listened as Logic recounted how she'd woken in the night and watched two coyotes sniffing around camp before she shooed them off. I walked further, steering a course around a bees' nest in the middle of the trail. The PCT wound down a few switchbacks, levelled off and entered a tunnel around 200 feet long. It was dark and pleasantly damp as I avoided a stream of water in the middle. As the circle of light grew bigger, I made out the silhouette of someone sitting by the exit. The familiar features of Tomer came into focus as I reached the end. He looked up at me casually and said, "Welcome to the other side."

After the wide space of the trail in the morning, a canyon narrowed around me. Rocks, outcrops, and cliffs loomed up on either side, towering above a creek which I hopped over several times. Layers of different-coloured rock, millions of years old, streaked across the cliff face. I spilled onto the road, a mile from Agua Dulce. Being suddenly swept out of wilderness into civilisation always caught me off guard after days on the trail. I reached the intersection of Darling Road and turned left for the last mile, approaching what is fondly called 'Hiker Haven'. This house on the hill is home to the Saufley family, who every year offer their grounds to thru-hikers who wisely choose to stay there. John provided a guided tour, and my laundry disappeared, emerging later smelling of lemons. I collected the packages I'd mailed there and found a spare camp bed in one of the tents.

The Saufleys proved a great place to unwind. There must have been 50 hikers scattered about, relaxing, collecting mail, resupplying, eating or listening to music. There were too many for my comfort after days spent on my own, and I made plans to move on the next day, still keen to increase my mileage tally and seek further solitude. I picked up a new water filter and sent my old one back, wrapped in a complaint letter suggesting, politely, that they market it as a bicycle pump instead.

The town café cooked an excellent breakfast, and I concentrated on consuming as much fat as I could handle after the scales confirmed I had lost a few pounds. In the store, excitement got the better of me in the condiments aisle after stumbling across a hoard of hot sauces. It was red hot, devilish nirvana. With the local café devoid of any fiery sauces to top up my bottle, and not knowing which of the many brands to choose, I settled on the lightest choice: the ever-reliable Tabasco.

I enjoyed and immersed myself deeper into the PCT experience. I'd honed my camp routine, resupplies were well-judged and my body coped well. But the desert was starting to annoy me. The constant battle with heat and dust had me yearning for the High Sierra, another 250 miles away. Some had already made it to Kennedy Meadows, a small town at the foot of the mountains. Considered the start of the higher elevations, with cooler temperatures, abundant water, and stunning scenery. I craved it like a cold soda. Others felt it too: the sand continued to bug us, insects buzzed annoyingly, and the temperature soared. My focus of attention centred on Kennedy Meadows. Everything between Agua Dulce and there needed wrapping up so the next stage of my adventure could begin. I pined for the mountains, the grander the better.

Trying in vain to find a camp spot one evening, I became frustrated. In mountainous areas, the trail is often cut into the side of a hill with slopes above and drops below. Locating a flat area to pitch my tent was difficult. Many times, I walked for miles waiting for a patch of suitable ground to no avail. Thwarted by the terrain and, at the end of the day, tired and hungry, I often just slept on the trail itself. The chance of another hiker coming along that late was unlikely, and even if they did, there was enough space to either step round, or join for company. It's not advisable to pitch on trail because wild animals use it as well. They're not stupid and pick routes requiring the least effort; a trail saves them tramping through undergrowth.

Having set up camp, an airborne squadron of biting flies descended. Flapping and jumping around as if I had caught on fire was futile; even swearing had little effect. Eventually, as twilight set in, they quit. I relaxed for a few minutes, then the mosquitos arrived. Mozzies love me. Some people fare worse than others; maybe it's the smell of their blood. If there's a mozzie within a mile of me, it sends out a general invitation to its mates that there's good eating in the vicinity. My flapping routine started again and, stifled by the intense heat, my mood sank.

I surrendered, quickly cooked my meal and dived into the tent, zipping up frantically and settling down to eat in peace. The temperature inside was overwhelming, and damp blotches of sweat appeared on my t-shirt. I then realised I'd not cooked the ideal meal in the circumstances – curry with an extra helping of Tabasco.

News had filtered back from hikers at Kennedy Meadows that the snow levels had not receded as far as expected and much of the Sierra still lay under snow. My ice axe, crampons and cold weather gear waited for me at the post office there, and I hoped that by the time I reached them, the snow would have receded enough for the backlog of people to clear.

Before then, and only 17 miles away, came the Andersons. I'd met Terrie and Joe at Lake Morena and they opened their house for hikers each year. The Saufleys have a two-night maximum stay; the Andersons have a two-night *minimum*. Everyone slow-clapped as I walked up the drive, part of the arrival ritual. I took a Hawaiian shirt from the rack, conforming to the strict dress code, and had a guided tour by a bloke so drunk he didn't even know where he was, let alone anyone else. Familiar faces peered around beer cans, laughter filled the air, and the atmosphere was laid back and relaxed. I pitched my tent, grabbed a beer and chilled.

I spent two days at the Andersons in an alcoholic daze. Everyone helped with cooking, cleaning, and other chores. There was only one shower for everyone, which proved interesting: as soon as the bathroom door clicked open, a stampede of dusty hikers descended, eager to grab a wash. The slow-clapping routine continued every time a new face arrived, as did the guided tour and Hawaiian shirt ritual.

I left nursing a hangover at 5pm on the third day with Hojo, Swayze, and Dinosaur, who were also keen to get going. Walking late into the night was a new experience for me and an enjoyable one. Mesmerised by a setting sun, the temperature had thankfully cooled. The mosquitoes droned, and coyotes howled.

Hojo was 42. When he didn't hike, he worked as an emergency medical technician, preferring to spend his winters as a National Ski Patrol member. He'd completed the Appalachian Trail a few years before and had been in remission from cancer for eight years. When you have such a close brush with death, life seems more valuable. That, I believe, is why he walked the AT and now the PCT: you never know what's around the corner. His trail name came about after his second day on the AT when he arrived at a shelter for the night. As he removed his hat, another hiker noticed his ginger hair and commented that it looked the same colour as the roof of a US motel chain called Howard Johnson's. The name stuck.

I enjoyed his easy-going company; his plans were loose, and he never rushed. Fair-skinned, he took care in the sun and regardless of the temperatures he always covered up, head to foot, including wearing a modern-day hiking variant of the cowboy hat. He liked his equipment and was looking forward to cooking that evening.

"I sent my old stove back, Fozzie," he announced while preparing camp.

"Why?" I said. "No good?"

"No, it was OK, just too slow. I bought a Jetboil."

Jetboils were gas cylinder-based stoves renowned for a fierce heat and super-quick cooking times.

"I demand more immediate gratification," he explained.

He walked with a water bag strapped to one side of his pack exterior, which made refilling easier. Once full, one side of his pack became heavier and he'd counteract this by leaning to the opposite side. He joked he knew when water was short because he began tilting the other way.

We passed the 500-mile mark, which someone had marked with an artistic cluster of pine cones. Hojo and I shook hands, and he congratulated me.

"Well done, Canadian."

I never asked him why he called me the Canadian, but I assumed it was because I wasn't American. Despite my protestations and reminders that I was English, I eventually realised his weird sense of humour was to blame.

At mile 519 we arrived at the Hiker Hostel. I can only describe the place as bizarre. In the middle of nowhere; the nearest sign of life was a store a mile away. Bob, the owner, used to work in the film industry, and the grounds were littered with movie props. Complete with a mock-Western shop front with a post office and store, an old police car and even a Rolls Royce. Creepy mannequins peered at me through breaks in the sand storms.

Nursing more blisters and watching a toenail drop off, I went to check my email but, on the way, stubbed my foot sharply against a chair. After a minute of hopping around stifling a shriek, and enough swearing to make my mother cringe, I looked down. My hands and foot were covered in blood, which dripped on the floor. Leaving a series of red-splashes behind me like a murder scene, I hopped to the kitchen where Hojo inspected the injury, proclaiming it nonserious but a nasty cut nevertheless. I cleaned the mess up and surveyed a flap of skin, which lifted up and down like a submarine hatch. Not wanting my mileage to suffer any further, I left the following day with the Stumbling Norwegian and several layers of Band-Aid wound round my toe. Trying to keep up with him, my leg buckled in pain every time the wound rubbed.

We followed the Los Angeles Aqueduct for 17 miles. Funnelling millions of gallons of prime mountain meltwater to the big city, a covering of grey concrete made it look like a road. Norwegian had devised an ingenious method of reaching the water, although it was apparently inaccessible. Indulging my curiosity, he unclipped his pack, rummaged around for his filter, attached an extra length of plastic tubing and lowered this through a tiny hole in the concrete. Sure enough, as he pumped, a steady stream of water dribbled out. We celebrated by taking a break and seeking shade squeezed under a low bridge.

Snake count: 5
False alarms: 117

Magnificent cloud formations adorned the sky. One elongated specimen stretching up from the horizon looked like a giant lava lamp bubble. The wind intensified, blowing us about like litter in a storm. We reached Cottonwood Creek at dusk then continued a further six miles to Tylerhorse Canyon, which we hoped would shelter us from the wind.

Turning around to check Norwegian was still with me, I smirked as a furious gust caught him and carried him sideways. He executed a brisk jump over a bush and just managed to keep his footing. Occasionally, I thought, the Norwegian does indeed stumble.

We descended the canyon in darkness, our head lamps navigating a slim trail to the bottom where a creek tinkled. The wind roared, and after trying to pitch my tent, I gave up and followed Norwegian's lead, spending my first night cowboy camping. Lying back studying the skies, I listened to a howling gale rip through the canyon.

After reaching Tehachapi, I rested for a day and caught up on England's progress (or rather lack of it) in the Soccer

World Cup. Mocking and taunting Stumbling Norwegian and Jake, both avid USA supporters, that they'd lose against us, I ate my words after a 1-1 draw.

England's games dictated my distance targets and town stops over the coming weeks. I noted the date of the games and worked out a plan to hole up in a bar or motel to watch them. After their lacklustre beginning, and early exit, adjusting my routine to make town for the next disappointment proved a bad idea.

Three hours out of Tehachapi, I realised my calculations were a day out. To get to Ridgecrest, I needed two days of 28 miles, plus a 15 miler. Not impossible, but bearing in mind the Mojave Desert, with its searing temperatures, lay over the adjacent ridge and with water in short supply, the going proved difficult. I stopped at Bird Spring Pass water cache, where Burnie, Cheeks, and Elk were sheltering from a fierce midday sun. Elk had a mild case of Giardiasis and boasted about a 30 second fart. I advised that farting with Giardiasis was risky.

"Fozzie," he said, changing the subject, "did I tell you about my trout fantasy?"

"No, but I'm in the mood for a story, so go," I replied, looking expectant.

"Well, I'm on the trail and suddenly come across a bear pulling fish from a pristine mountain stream. It's caught a golden trout the size of my forearm. Now, what I'll do in this fantasy is scare the bear away, purely with my anger, and steal the trout from it." He laughed. "Then, I'll take a quart-size Ziploc, half-fill it with lemon juice, section the trout so it fits inside and hike with it for 20 minutes. Then I'll remove it, build a fire and sprinkle it with salt and pepper.

I'll then let out a huge roar of triumph and feast."

"Elk," I replied, "do you walk with your shrink or just make regular phone calls?"

I walked with Elk all afternoon, finding him interesting company as always. We sweated profusely climbing the 2,000 feet up Skinner's Pass. He slowed so I threw fruit candies as an incentive when I rounded each switchback. We crested to our first views of the Sierra Nevada: ridge after ridge stretching away to infinity, most still covered in snow.

Elk became excited about a hidden food stash. He'd buried many along the PCT the previous year, with staple contents that included canned meat, alcohol, and pipe tobacco. Checking his GPS and beaming, he left to home in on his prize, saying he'd meet me at camp.

It was busy that evening, and I had Burnie, Littlebit, Bigfoot, Stanimal, Wild Angle, Cheeks, and Mojave for company. The talk centred on black bears, and I cringed when I learned of three sightings in as many days.

Little did I know I'd soon be witnessing the next one.

Chapter 6

Bears

Not all who wander are lost.
But, to be perfectly honest, most of them are.
Shane 'Jester' O'Donnell

I left the others sleeping at 6am, eager to hit Highway 178 and get a ride to Ridgecrest. I couldn't find any trail signs and stumbled across McIvers Spring, which according to my map, lay 500 feet too far east of the trail. I returned to camp, still unable to find the route, then ended up back at the spring again, increasingly frustrated. I filtered water and brewed a coffee to calm down.

Twigs cracked from the forest behind me but, having become accustomed to sounds from the trees, I ignored them, losing myself in the morning stillness.

Suddenly, I tensed. The hairs on my arms rose, and I sensed something behind. I heard a loud animal noise, somewhere between a snort and an aggravated sigh. I feared a bear – it couldn't have been anything else. I turned around slowly.

A black bear, standing a good eight feet tall on its hind

legs, raised its nose, smelling the air and, presumably, me. It dropped to all fours and most of southern California shuddered as it landed. It looked at me; I returned the favour and then remembered the advice to avoid eye contact. Bears consider this aggressive, so I focused on the ground a few feet in front of it and quickly planned who I'd leave my limited estate to.

My first and natural reaction was sheer terror, but at the same time I felt lucky to witness such a commanding creature. Those feelings vanished quickly as it moved closer. I knew I shouldn't back off or run, but that's another story when a bulk of hungry muscle weighing several hundred kilos is approaching. I stood up, petrified. The others were just two minutes back at camp, still waking up and oblivious to my situation.

I'd never been so scared. I shook, confused and helpless. Then I remembered to make a noise. Lifting my arms to appear bigger, I screamed, "Get out of here bear! Hey! Go on! Sod off! GO!"

The bear bolted back into the forest, covering ground quickly. I crouched to get a better view through the trees as it sped away. Any hiker walking through the forest at that precise moment in the opposite direction would have jumped off the nearest cliff.

I stopped shaking, calmed down, and congratulated myself for remembering my bear research and reacting appropriately.

The black bear, Ursus americanus, is the smallest and commonest bear in the USA. The grizzly, Ursus arctos horribilis, is found in Canada and Washington, the northernmost state on the PCT. Snakes scared me, although

I'd accepted them, but bears terrified me. Their sheer size doesn't do much for one's confidence. They are, however, misunderstood. The media ignore the non-aggressive incidents, preferring biased coverage of the rare attacks.

Bears are docile creatures. They go about their business, focused on eating over the course of the warmer months to build up enough fat reserves for hibernation. Attacks are rare, and there haven't been any fatalities on the PCT, a fact I recalled in earnest during my encounter. Because of the media bias, bears are considered a dangerous menace. This is a shame and it's untrue.

I saw eight bears on my hike but heard many more. Usually they came sniffing around my tent after I'd turned in. It's not just food that attracts them, but toiletries too. I always cleaned my teeth a good 50 feet away from camp. Sometimes, nearly asleep, I'd hear scratching or snorting. A shout or whistle normally sent the bear thundering off into the night.

In areas where many people congregated outdoors, bears were common. They're not stupid; they know where food is, and trash bins (even if bear-proof) act as magnets. Yosemite is a classic example and one of a few places where hikers must, by law, use a bear canister.

It's like a bucket with a lid that bears cannot access. The plastic is tough and the screw lid is tamper-proof. It's left away from sleeping areas overnight with food and toiletries inside. Curious bears cannot open it and eventually give up. Pots and pans placed on top can help because of the sound made when disturbed, which scares bears and notifies campers. Many a hiker has woken in the morning to find their canister a fair distance from where they'd left it, dripping with bear saliva. The standing joke is that bears find one and then play hockey with it.

I hauled my canister through the designated zones, resenting that it took up half my pack. Outside the danger areas, most kept their food in or near their tent, or they hung it in a tree. Suspending food bags has long been the accepted method of protecting it, and I often used it. Pick a branch around 25 feet high. Tie a 50-foot length of cord to the bag and wrap the other end round a stone. Throw the stone over the branch as far away from the tree trunk as possible to prevent bears climbing up and along the branch. Once thrown successfully, hoist the bag above 15 feet, remove the stone and tie the end to a suitable anchor point.

Because our friends in the forest have learnt to climb and retrieve bags, bear cannisters were introduced. I hated them, as did most hikers. In fact, many stuck with their usual bags, taking their chances with ranger spot checks. I don't know if rangers had a legal right to search rucksacks. I met three on my trip, all of them respectful and polite, and only one asked to check my gear.

I heard of an incident at Lost Lakes, just south of Lake Tahoe, where Elk, Your Mom and others had camped. After they'd settled for the night, Your Mom called to Elk, as she thought something was lurking in the camp. Elk discounted this as he'd camped only a few feet away and would have heard any movement. However, he turned on his light and got out of his tent. He noticed his medical kit and backpack were both covered in drool. Your Mom remained uneasy, and they hung their bags, except for Elk, who had a bear canister. The others placed their bags by their tents and everyone settled once more.

Elk's bear canister fell over, the clatter of the pots resting on the top causing one hell of a commotion and scaring the life out of him. Everyone woke up but Elk saw the bear first.

He shouted and caused as much noise as he could to scare the intruder off, which worked, but the villain made three further visits that night. Your Mom found her food bag in the morning minus the contents except, unsurprisingly, a packet of chicken ramen! They named the bear Two Socks after the wolf in Dances with Wolves because he kept returning.

"He must have been 300 pounds," Elk told me afterwards. "The ground shook when he ran away."

I found the trail and hiked to Highway 178 with Bigfoot. His large feet dictated his trail name, and he found it difficult to find big enough shoes. He'd ordered several pairs of the same brand before starting. He towered above me but, to use a cliché, was a gentle giant, very amenable, and we chatted freely. One of the most identifiable characters on trail, his standard hiking apparel was a kilt and white cotton shirt which one might wear to a black-tie occasion.

We reached the road where some locals had set up trail magic. Hojo, Your Mom and Elk rested in the shade. I drank a Coke and went to catch a ride to Ridgecrest, as the soccer game between England and Algeria beckoned. In the other direction lay Lake Isabella, which I'd have opted for if I'd known what a disappointment Ridgecrest would be.

It took over two hours to get a ride; the highway was busy enough but long and straight, and the vehicles flew past with little chance of stopping. I almost got down on one knee, beseeching anything to stop. The heat in town was unbearable, especially after the mountain coolness. The main street stretched for miles. Jet-black bitumen disappeared to the horizon as a lazy heat haze hovered. I thanked Brian, who'd brought me in his truck, and walked through the endless monotony, looking for a cheap motel. The lurid red, yellow, blue and white logos of the fast-food chains stared from both sides, interrupted by hotels or supermarkets. The occupants of passing vehicles stared at me rudely as if I were a wild animal.

The Budget Motel looked cheap enough, and I checked in. Ridgecrest reminded me of a holiday destination that looked gorgeous in a catalogue but not in person. At the launderette, an annoying 30-minute walk away, trash spilled out of bins and a meagre choice of magazines draped an old wooden table. The detergent dispenser and washing machine both ate my money in return for nothing. I found a nearby barber and had my beard shaved off while my clothes dried.

I spent my time in the motel room, as it was the coolest place I could find. Coolest in temperature, that is, not reputation. I'd added my nose to the list of bodily functions that were failing. It itched, was incredibly dry and kept bleeding. The pharmacist at Walgreens told me the desert heat caused the same problem for many, and he gave me a tube of moisturising gel. A sore red rash had appeared on the soles of my feet; they were tender and it looked like prickly heat. Thankfully, my blisters had improved, but the rash took three days to disappear after several Epsom salt foot baths and good old fresh air. I occupied myself with the

World Cup, slept a lot, chastised myself for not going to Lake Isabella, and worked my way through several tubs of Ben & Jerry's Cherry Garcia.

The day after, I gladly fled Ridgecrest back to the trail, but I felt depressed. My body felt different; lethargic, tired, lacking in enthusiasm, and I cursed the constant heat. My nose worsened: I resorted to holding one nostril shut and blew out the contents of the other. A mix of blood, snot, dust and other dried debris shot out with a very unpleasant crackle. After a few minutes I had to repeat the process.

I approached Kennedy Meadows around the 700-mile mark on day 65. Everything seemed to take its toll and my mood sank deeper. I slept later in the morning and food breaks proved the only motivation. I longed for the next town stop where I could hide in a motel room and swim in self-pity. I'd spoken to my girlfriend back in England and we'd argued, which upset us both. I plummeted over a precipice of misery into a raging river of despair. I kept missing daily targets, and my finish date based on average mileage looked like December, a whole three months over schedule. I was late, but I didn't give a shit.

At lunch I sat by Fox Mill Spring, the sun beating relentlessly. I cried, holding my head in my hands, ashamed of my weakness. Trying to muster a morsel of energy, I convinced myself I was on the verge of throwing in a threadbare towel and quitting the PCT.

You'd miss Kennedy Meadows if you weren't paying attention. A few mobile homes scattered the roadside as I rounded a corner and the General Store appeared. Hikers sprawled everywhere and tents filled the back yard. A few familiar faces greeted me – Stumbling Norwegian, Cheeks and Mojave, Walker Texas Ranger, Flannel and Elk. This unassuming place in the middle of the desert proved the proverbial iced tonic.

My mood lifted, everyone was in good cheer, and the prospect of the Sierra Nevada boosted me. I relaxed and concentrated on reclaiming the hiking experience I'd originally wanted. I called my girlfriend and we lifted each other's spirits. Knowing she was fine always made everything OK. I ate good food, drank beer, caught up with everyone, made new friends and reminded myself to stop being a miserable little shit.

The morning after, I walked out of Kennedy Meadows a new man. I joined Chad and Justin, who'd just started, planning to get where they could before money and time ran out. Both in their early twenties, Chad was more dominant, making them more like father and son than friends.

At midday I emerged from a forest to one of the best views on the entire trail. Monache Meadow didn't just suggestively wink at me; more like it grabbed and kissed me passionately. It was stunning. Cumuli drifted lazily and the Kern River wiggled between sandy banks cradled by a wide, gently sloping valley, speckled with pine trees rising to the surrounding hills. I sat and rested, feeling very humbled.

Several times Chad, Justin and I stopped, speechless with wonder. We feared Monache Meadow could vanish from view and we'd never see it again. I regretted not camping by the river to enjoy the meadow's exquisite company.

Snake count: 9

False alarms: 347

The new equipment I'd picked up in Kennedy Meadows had increased my pack weight. I now carried an ice axe, Kahtoola spikes (a lighter version of crampons), a mosquito head net and the bulky bear canister. I balanced the weight by carrying less water; the mountain creeks and rivers flowed well, so I drank my fill, then carried a further bottle. Mosquitoes droned relentlessly in the evenings.

Mosquitoes love me. I don't know what attracts them but I have a load of it. In Europe I suffered the usual swollen, red, itchy bites. The bites from American mosquitoes bothered me less – I didn't need to scratch as often and my physical reaction was milder. Enough to weaken the strongest person's resolve, they attacked incessantly. They didn't party much during the day; come evening, however, all hell broke loose.

I'd camped in the forest with Chad and Justin, just off the trail in a comforting spot with water nearby, plenty of firewood and good, flat tent spots. We'd just arrived as the mosquitos descended. I wore my head net for the first time and immediately discovered a major design flaw; I couldn't see a bloody thing out of it. I moved my head in all directions to find a sweet spot in the mesh where I could see. Occasionally, the angle of my head, direction of light, and other random factors meant my sight returned. The three of us spent most of the evening slapping, shaking our heads, scratching and sitting in fire smoke to repel the critters.

My colleagues left before me in the morning. I ate more food at elevation, depleting my stocks, and I needed to re-supply. As I descended Trail Pass Trail onto Cotton Wood

Trail, I reached the parking lot. Chad and Justin sat by the road along with Farm Boy and Splints, who'd camped there hoping to get an early ride into Lone Pine. The road terminated at the car park with no through traffic and little chance of a ride. Two cars came and went in as many hours, so we reluctantly succumbed to walking.

As we plodded dejectedly, a minibus rolled by and we flagged it down. Bill, the driver, ran a taxi service up to the car park and couldn't take us for free, but we jumped at his offer of $10 each. He insisted on a guided tour, making the journey 30 minutes longer than I'd hoped.

We stumbled into the Alabama Hills Café like a pack of mad, hungry hounds. Regardless of being famished, I always tried to find a good, independent breakfast place. The restaurant was packed, which I took as a good sign.

We sat, long overdue a good feed. The waitress ambled over, eyeing us up: six soiled, aromatic and undesirable-looking hikers scratching insect bites. Chad licked his hand and flattened his hair in some vain attempt to look presentable, as I angled a nearby fan towards us to re-direct our body odour. We were health and safety's worst nightmare, but she took it in her stride. I never checked the menu; every breakfast place in America has what I need and they cook my food exactly how I like it.

"Two eggs, over easy. Hash browns, crisped on both sides please; bacon, also crispy. Toast, rye if you have it, wheat if not, butter on the side. Orange juice and coffee, black, strong and keep it coming," I requested, violently scratching my right forearm.

And they do it! Believe me, American breakfasts are the best in the world.

I enjoyed Lone Pine. With its rich history, it felt good to walk around, had everything a thru-hiker needed, and it commanded a spectacular view of the High Sierra, with Mt Whitney peering from above. As usual it was tempting to stay in town just that one extra day, to see if anyone else showed up, or just to visit the Alabama Hills Café one more time.

I pulled myself away and found Trooper hitching in the same direction. I'd met him a few days earlier, hiking with an Australian woman called Vader who made me laugh (unintentionally) because her face was muddy. I saw her in town afterwards, and the first thing she demanded to know was why Trooper or I hadn't told her. She'd only discovered upon looking in the motel mirror. We didn't carry mirrors, so after a week of sun and filth, the results were surprising.

Trooper was a true gentleman in his mid-forties and said, 'Ain't that the truth' a lot. He always apologised if he swore, as if his mum was nearby. He'd attempted the PCT before, getting agonisingly near Canada before a storm blew him off trail and ended his hike. Trooper didn't just go back to that point; he started again from Mexico. He loved it out there as much as anyone and boy, did he want to finish.

I walked with him for half a day and asked if he'd like to camp, but he wanted to push on another five miles. His tenacity impressed me. Somehow, I knew I'd be seeing more of Trooper.

The following day I met Flyboxer, Indie and Answerman sitting at the trail side and smiling in the sun. We exchanged a quick greeting, and I continued.

I couldn't believe the beauty of the Sierra Nevada. The wildness and remoteness reminded me that the nearest help could be hours away. This taste of danger and detachment added to our excitement, and we thrived on it like an addictive drug.

It was stunning, a pristine mountain wilderness embellished with shimmering lakes, thundering rivers and majestic forests. It proved tough going, the hardest section of the entire trail, but because it rewarded me with so many visual treats I couldn't blame it. I was in awe, humbled, and never wanted the Sierras to end.

I camped that night at Crabtree Meadow for two reasons. First, I just wanted to see it; and second, a side trail ran up to the summit of Mt Whitney at 14,505 feet, the highest mountain in the contiguous United States. When someone first told me this, I had to look up 'contiguous' in the dictionary. I just had to climb it.

Humming Bird and Flashback had left two hours before me in the morning, and Indie, Flyboxer and Answerman were behind. The trail climbed steadily at first, dipping in and out of pine trees as I glimpsed the night sky, a rising sun and the dark silhouettes of the mountains far above. As the sun intensified, more of my surroundings emerged. I'd never seen anything like it. As a bright light broke over the mountains, inky skies surrendered from black to deep blue. Sunshine crept down granite giants, bathing them yellow. Snow-capped peaks mellowed to green meadows dotted with wild flowers and shimmering lakes.

A long, wide valley eased up to Mt Whitney. Marmots peeked at me curiously. I giggled because they studied me intently but ran off when I got too close. Glance back, however, and they'd peek from their hiding place to have a last look.

After four hours, at 12.50pm, I summited. Being the highest person in the entire US on Independence Day, my Englishness seemed somehow more satisfying.

As if Whitney isn't enough to whet a hiker's appetite, the ascent of Forester Pass, the highest point of the PCT at 13,200 feet came next. The final section to the pass is the most feared part of the PCT because it involves crossing a snow chute, which can be slippery or mushy depending on the time of year. I'd seen it countless times on video; it's a long drop and it gave me the willies. None of us had ropes; they were considered unnecessary and bulky.

I struggled over Tyndall Creek, which a ranger warned me to treat with respect because of high water. I rose through the warmth of the lower elevations, crossing paths with Flyboxer, Indie and Answerman.

A call of nature forced me off trail to the only tree for miles that offered any privacy. As I assumed position, I noticed a squall rapidly approaching. Disregarding it at first, it arrived with shocking speed. The wind slammed into me first, then the rain stung. I watched in horror with flailing, outstretched arms as my toilet paper took flight. Even my soap catapulted skywards, and I fell flat on my arse. The squall passed as quickly as it had arrived and soaked through, I waddled off carefully to retrieve my toilet roll.

I found Indie and the others before the final hour-long push to Forester. Grinder joined us as we attempted to save time by taking a direct route up and avoiding the switchbacks. Gasping for air, we sank into the snow and hauled ourselves up, bent double, sweating, then resting to catch our breath. As we topped out on the last switchback, we lay on the trail, our chests rising and falling, eager for oxygen.

We stepped gingerly across the snow chute, aware that one mistake could prove fatal. Indie and I were nervous, but we made it across, hugging the nearest rock in gratitude. Northwards, the Sierras stretched away to infinity. The mountain passes were like turning pages in a book, each one a mere dent in the bigger picture, an unnoticeable gain on an immense adventure. It reminded me of the journey yet to be conquered, both on a personal level and on the PCT. These were pleasurable moments though. Instead of becoming disillusioned with my modest progress, I smiled. The PCT still had much to offer, and I wasn't in any hurry.

We'd summited the highest point of the PCT, but we still had to get down. Coming off Forester Pass was the hardest and longest alpine descent I've made. It wasn't technical, although in parts my pulse raced, but it was long. I post-holed several times, and, as usual, navigation was difficult because of the snow. The valley bottom mocked me. Grinder and I reached the end of a flat-topped ridge which ceased abruptly and fell away. We checked the map and, after deliberating, negotiated the steep face to get back on track. We stumbled, toppling and sliding. I gripped my ice axe firmly and concentrated on foot placement. Looking up, I saw Indie peering over, and he followed us. Grinder pulled away, diminishing to a tiny dot in the mountains. I approached Bubbs Creek, which had matured into a crazed, raging cascade of ice-cold water. My legs numbed and shook from the force and chill of the water as I cautiously placed each foot on the next rock, trying to ignore the 100-foot drop to my left that threatened to gobble me up with the slightest mistake.

As dusk fell and the ascent softened, I searched for a

suitable camp spot. Pulling off trail, I lit a fire before pitching the tent. Crouching to push through a small gap in the trees, another tent surprised me.

"Hey!" I called. "Anyone at home?"

There was silence, so I presumed the occupant was asleep. Ten minutes later the reply came.

"Fozzie?"

"Yeah! How the hell did you know it was me? Who is that? Trooper?"

"Yeah, it's me. Man, am I ill." His weak voice lay between sleep and sickness. The tent's zip glided open, two hands stretched the canvas back and a forlorn pale face appeared, offering a resigned smile.

"Trooper, you look bloody terrible. What's going on?"

"Giardia. Fozzie, I got the shits big time. See that clump of trees over there?"

"Yeah."

"Don't go looking for firewood there; that's my toilet."

Giardiasis is an infection of the small intestine, caused by the microscopic organism (protozoa) Giardia lamblia. Giardiasis outbreaks occur where water supplies become contaminated and, more importantly, are untreated. Beaver droppings are a common cause, especially on the PCT, and the infection can also spread between people through poor hygiene. While not fatal, the symptoms are nasty and include vomiting, diarrhoea, bloating, abnormal amounts of gas (as Elk would testify), headache, appetite loss, fever, nausea and a swollen abdomen. I met several people on the hike who had Giardia, which was enough to make me treat all my water.

I'd spoken to Stumbling Norwegian about it. He'd

caught it before and explained the worst symptom, known as sharting. Sharting is a mix of a shit and a fart. I feel I needn't explain this further.

The accepted course of treatment is a drug called Flagyl, which cures most cases. I'd tried to get this in the US at a pharmacy as a precaution, but it wasn't prescribed unless one actually had Giardia; it was also expensive. Several hikers carried it, and luckily, Trooper had a supply. It clears up in a week to ten days, sometimes longer, but can flare up again later in life.

Trooper spent that evening sleeping, interrupted by sprints to the 'toilet'. I offered to help him (I hasten to add not with the toilet trips), but he politely refused.

Indie, Answerman and Flyboxer appeared and, although lured by the fire, said they would hike more miles before pitching camp. I left Trooper in the morning. My conscience nibbled at me because of leaving someone sick in the mountains, but Trooper insisted, saying he'd be fine.

After the pain of coming down Forester Pass, the next challenge of Glen Pass and many other testing ascents beckoned. I was consuming food quickly, and despite my stop in Lone Pine, I needed to re-supply again.

However, in the High Sierra, access to the outside world was never easy.

Chapter 7

The Sierras, Water Crossings
and Battery Karma

As long as I live, I will hear the birds and the winds and the
waterfalls sing. I'll interpret the rocks and learn the language
of flood, of storm and avalanche. I'll make the acquaintance of
the wild gardens and the glaciers and get as near to the heart of
this world as I can.

John Muir

John Muir was born in 1838 in Dunbar, Scotland. His parents were deeply religious and considered anything that distracted from the Bible as frivolous. The family emigrated to the United States in 1849 and set up a farm near Portage in Wisconsin.

Aged 22, Muir enrolled at the University of Wisconsin-Madison. He achieved average grades, with geology and botany kindling his interest. In 1864 he went to Canada to avoid the military draft, returning two years later to Minneapolis, where he worked in a factory making wagon wheels. The turning point in his life came after a slipped tool struck him in the eye. Confined to a darkened room for six weeks, he feared he'd never regain his sight.

"This affliction has driven me to the sweet fields. God has to nearly kill us sometimes to teach us lessons," he said.

He promised afterwards to be true to himself and follow his dreams of exploration and the study of plants.

His legacy is the John Muir Trail, a route better described as a work of wilderness art. Starting near Mount Whitney, it continues 215 miles to Yosemite National Park and is one of the finest examples of our great outdoors. The PCT shares this route, and its designated trail status needs no explanation. The John Muir Trail is ludicrously difficult; the elevation loss and gain are the most punishing on the entire PCT.

It was, however, proving enjoyable punishment. A regular pattern emerged: For three weeks I ascended brutal climbs each day, often in snow, at altitudes of up to 13,200 feet as I summitted pass after pass. An insatiable craving for food never left me, down to increased exertion, higher altitude and cooler conditions. Some regard mountains as intimidating. If it goes wrong, you're in trouble. There's no quick medical help in the Sierras; not even phone reception to make the call. To many, this intimidation is precisely the attraction.

I took the Bullfrog Lake Trail to Kearsarge Pass, intending to hitch to the town of Independence and supplement my food for the coming section. Kearsarge Pass was off my map, so I had to work without directions, but the route was well-worn and obvious. I walked past lakes so deep blue they appeared black. The sun still hadn't completely managed to melt the ice, and I marvelled at the stark contrast between frozen white and turquoise. Brown trout darted in the creeks, jumping to catch flies. I dangled a line into the water, hoping for a fresh breakfast, but the fish scattered as they sensed me.

It was a day's hike to the Onion Valley parking area, where I sought a ride to Independence. As I crested Kearsarge Pass, a long series of switchbacks wound downwards. As much as I loved the PCT, I didn't love its miles of trail to towns. Others had followed suit, and I passed Cheeks, Mojave, Burnie, Brakelight, Splints, Farmboy, Uncle Gary and the two other English hikers Nick and Chris. They advised hitching back to Lone Pine, as re-supply options were poor in Independence.

I reached Onion Valley late-afternoon and stuck my thumb out at the first car. It stopped, and Damon and Renee Rockwell took me to Lone Pine, dropping me off on the main street.

I entered the Mount Whitney Hostel, where I'd stayed a few days before, and checked in with the same receptionist.

I forget people's names quickly. I listen, but my brain doesn't register, so I have to apologise and ask again. I thought a lack of confidence was to blame, so I decided to follow my instinct and be positive.

"Thanks, Teresa," I said.

"It's Jessica, actually," she replied, smiling and raising her eyebrows.

I didn't need two days in Lone Pine, but I filled the time with eating, drinking coffee, editing video and answering many emails. Feeling guilty about being off trail, I moved out the day after. I visited the Alabama Café for one last breakfast. The place was buzzing as usual, and I left fully fuelled.

I took a bus to Independence and managed a quick ride back to the Onion Valley parking area. Making short work of Kearsarge Pass, I was soon on the PCT with a full pack of food and a spring in my step. It was the longest section yet – seven days to the next town stop. I steeled myself and got going.

That part of the Sierra was brutal, with unforgiving climbs. Glen Pass (12,000ft), Pinchot Pass (12,150ft), Mather Pass (12,100ft), Muir Pass (11,950ft), Selden Pass (10,900ft) and Silver Pass (10,900ft) all loomed menacingly. The descents were more difficult than the ascents. Knees ached, and the valley bottoms teased from miles away. The ascents required more exertion, but I coped well. I had more grip in the snow and a smoother rhythm. Downhill was a series of leg-breaking jolts, and I post-holed alarmingly. I'd gained fitness since the start, and I needed it.

Coming off Glen Pass, I lost the trail, but I knew the approximate direction. At elevation I could see for miles, my route clearly visible in the terrain below. I simply had to pick the easiest and least dangerous line. I followed a fast-flowing creek to Rae Lake, identifiable because the trail hopped straight over a land bridge in the middle. I sank easily into unstable snow. Reaching the end of a snow bank, I rushed blithely to solid ground. My right leg post-holed as my shin smashed onto rock, and I screamed in agony. Wedged in, I couldn't push myself out; the pain was excruciating. Fearing a broken leg or fracture could spell the end, I pummelled the ground in frustration, angry at my mistake.

Eventually the pain subsided, I relaxed and took stock. Placing my pack on the snow to spread my weight, I hauled myself out as red streaked the stark white surface. With some trepidation, I peeled back a blood-soaked trouser leg to inspect the damage. A three-inch cut congealed and swelled. I cleaned the wound with snow, prising it open and squirting water to remove any debris. I applied antibiotic cream, dressed it and swallowed some ibuprofen, hoping nothing was broken. I brewed tea and tried to calm myself, concentrating on my breathing. After 30 minutes I hobbled away, figuring that unless I heard a nasty grating sound, I was OK.

Many rivers and creeks, swollen from snow melt, foamed and crashed impatiently. Some were only ankle-deep, others presented greater obstacles. Through summer, the upper Sierra Nevada warms and huge amounts of snow melt. Meltwater trickles into creeks and merges into rivers. The further into summer I ventured, the higher the water levels rose.

Each river fording needed careful judgement. I considered the depth, width and current. Narrow creeks had fierce currents; others were wider but flowed smoothly. Tyndall Creek on the climb to Forester Pass was the first crossing to catch me out. As I approached, I saw why the ranger had warned me. It was only twenty feet wide and three feet deep, but it crashed angrily. With 40 pounds strapped to my back, one slip and I'd be helpless.

Elk told me about a troublesome crossing. It rose to his waist, but moved slowly, lulling him into a false sense of security. Two steps in and the current took hold, whipping him down river for 50 feet before he clambered out.

I approached each crossing with the same mentality, never assuming where the trail met the river was the best place to cross. I walked upstream and downstream, looking for alternative spots, and I learnt this way. If the banks narrowed, the ford was shorter but the flow quicker. Wider crossings were usually preferable because of a kinder current. Sometimes, fallen trees formed natural bridges, getting me out of many a scrape.

Tyndall Creek didn't look threatening. It was narrow and seemed shallow, so I pulled off my boots, slipped on my Crocs and put my socks over the top. This was a trick I had picked up from countless internet videos – socks over footwear give a better grip on the wet rock. Three steps in, and the freezing water hit my legs, numbing them immediately. Panicking, I made the mistake of speeding up. As the current grabbed me, I strained to stay upright, leaning into the flow and using my trekking poles for balance.

I heard nothing except a deafening roar as water hit my waist. I glanced downstream; rocks poked from the crazed foam like preying sharks as Tyndall hurtled downwards. If I stumbled, there was no chance. I tried to ignore the pain and took slow, steady steps nearing the far side. Scanning the creek bed for good footholds was useless given the force of the current. By the time I reached the opposite bank, I was a wreck. My legs screamed with cold as I frantically sucked in air.

Nancy, in complete confusion, cried for updates from Reginald at Nerve Centre HQ. Gertrude, responsible for the left leg, studied her warning display, noting a severe temperature drop. Poor old Angela at foot level was hypothermic.

"What the hell's going on down there?" shouted Reginald. "I'm seeing cold shock, strong force to the legs, and apparently he's got socks over his Crocs. Is this correct?"

"I think we crossed a river!" Angela shouted. "He wore his socks over the Crocs. I'm not sure why, I mean, why the hell would he do that? We're out now. The temperature is stabilising."

The water crossings were never ending, as many as 15 a day. With practice, I honed my skills and grew confident. I started to leave my shoes and socks on, as much as I resented them wet, it was quicker than constantly changing to Crocs. Come evening, my footwear dried overnight by the fire. I'd mastered the rivers – until Evolution Creek spoiled an otherwise pleasant Sierra Nevada morning.

Evolution Creek takes the overspill from Wanda Lake. I woke from daydreaming as the trees cleared, revealing a stretch of water that seemed 100 feet wide. Because of the width, the current appeared docile, despite quickening in places. I made two mistakes: first, I'd become complacent. Second, I decided to capture the ford on video to post on the blog.

My camera mounted to the end of my trekking pole, so I only had one pole to steady myself. I scouted for an alternative crossing place but couldn't find one suitable, and returned to where the PCT intersected the river. The water rose to waist high except at one section where it deepened and the flow increased. I progressed carefully, then sank suddenly up to my armpits in freezing water, and the current hit me like a freight train. I couldn't lift my foot for the next step as the water threatened to send me flailing downstream. Helpless with fear yet somewhat taking leave of my senses, I carried on filming, not wishing to lose either the camera or such great footage.

I gritted my teeth and leaned into the current, with water rushing around my neck, I couldn't read the creek bed to find my next step. After a few seconds that lasted an eternity, I powered through to the far bank and collapsed, exhausted and shivering.

Peeling off my soaked clothes, I sat on a warm rock and grabbed my camera, eager to review what must have been great footage. I cried at the sombre message blinking on the screen: 'Sorry - memory card is full'.

The Sierra was certainly providing the solitude I craved. Now 800 miles and a third of the trail done, I saw fewer of my fellow hikers, assuming many had quit. My body was a powerhouse; despite the altitude, I'd never felt fitter as I stormed up passes and sped along the trail. I hiked harder than ever, amazed at my turbo charged leg muscles.

My daily routine meant tackling a pass, then descending to a lower, warmer, oxygen-rich elevation to prepare myself for more of the same the next day. My fear of bears was under control too – I relished the prospect of seeing more.

I loved the evenings. After the effort of 20 to 25 miles over another pass, having a few hours to wind down was bliss. I looked for a suitable rest spot once I'd reached my distance target.

I preferred the forest because firewood was available. This saved fuel for cooking, provided warmth and light, and fended off the mosquitos. My first goal was a flat patch of ground to sleep; my second a nearby creek for water but not close enough to attract mosquitoes. I stretched my legs and spine, then checked my feet. Next, I either pitched my tent, or simply laid out a groundsheet to spend the night cowboy-style, by now my preference. I inflated my sleeping mat and hung my sleeping bag from a tree to loft the down filling. I boiled enough water to provide a cup of tea or coffee and used the rest to rehydrate my dinner. I updated my journal and then, time allowing, read.

I loved listening to the wind rush through the forest. I focused intently, meditating, closing my eyes as one would with music. In the mountains, the wind and trees became orchestral. Sometimes the slightest of breezes glanced my face. Stronger gusts played with the forest as whirls and eddies wove through the trees. The pines parted like theatrical curtains, revealing a tantalising glimpse of the night sky before closing again. I heard it approaching hundreds of feet away, faintly, then intensifying as it neared, the anticipation exciting. Crashing through the forest behind me, leaving my little haven calm and undisturbed. Other times it slammed into me, a cool and exhilarating blast, the energy intoxicating. The forest lived when the wind played.

Mather Pass, however, took the wind out of me. Forester was the highest but not necessarily the hardest. Mather was a stiff climb and the descent long and difficult. I negotiated fallen trees and lost count of the water crossings.

At 6pm I reached the Middle Fork Kings River, where three mighty rivers converged violently. Indie and Flyboxer were cooking their evening meals before venturing off for a few more miles. They introduced me to Stacks, tending his mac 'n cheese over a fire. He'd walked the Camino de Santiago in Spain the same year I had, but we'd not met. He chopped a green plant which I enquired after, and he explained it was a wild onion, common in the Sierras. I knew it existed but didn't know how to identify it. He'd used his supply, and we tried in vain to find more. I left after him, and thoughtfully, two miles up the track, he'd left a neat bundle of wild onions on a boulder in the middle of the trail. I boiled them that evening with my usual rice dish, enjoying the fresh crunch and garlicy blast.

I walked with Indie past Grouse Meadow, which shone in the early evening sun as insects danced on its surface and spider webs glistened in the light. The river thundered, crashing and slamming downstream, at times deafening, then silent as it slid placidly through meadows. I pulled off trail as Indie carried on to catch up with Flyboxer. We agreed to meet in the morning for the assault on Muir Pass.

Muir boasted quite a reputation. From my elevation at camp, I had a 4,000-foot climb to the top and then more difficult miles down past the snow line to solid ground. I started early, at 7am, to make the most of a brutal day. I met with Indie again, along with Flyboxer and Answerman, teaming up for safety to tackle Muir together. Stax, Black Gum and Ursa Major were also breaking camp and soon passed us.

I crossed the Kings River and scrambled up a rocky outcrop where the river blocked my path again. Cautiously crossing using boulders, I reached the other side to discover a rock fall had blocked my way. I retraced my route back to join the others.

As we hit the snow and looked up, the terrain appeared

harder than we'd anticipated. The gradient was steep and slippery, and the river forced us into several crossings. We soon lost the trail. Other tracks provided clues but couldn't be trusted. I met a woman descending, who confirmed it was difficult, but a day should see us over the pass. She also warned of unstable snow, sure to soften further as the temperature warmed. She pointed out a dangerous snow bridge and advised taking a safer route. I thanked her and adjusted my course to take this into account while signalling to the others to veer up and follow me.

We tried to balance ourselves on the steepening camber. I wore shoe spikes and steadied myself with one trekking pole, my ice axe ready in the other hand. The snow alternated between soft and firm, broken up with damp, slippery rock sections that demanded using hands. We targeted a small saddle before Helen Lake and homed in on it. As we crested, floating islands of turquoise ice speckled the lake. We laboured on, our breathing heavy as we surveyed the top, still two miles ahead. Using firmer ground under well-trodden footprints, we descended to a narrow creek and crossed over a snow bridge that creaked beneath us. Flyboxer veered off, preferring a shorter and steeper approach, while Indie, Answerman and I took the longer but kinder gradient. At 3pm we reached a round stone shelter perched on the summit of Muir Pass. We ate a late lunch, took photos and mocked each other's appearance. After several days on trail, we were filthy.

We descended at our own pace, spacing out within sight of each other. Clouds billowed up and rain fell, the first I'd encountered in weeks. The snow gradually thinned. I removed my spikes and wove over rocks and meltwater until

Evolution Lake appeared. One last water crossing and I stopped for the day at the edge of the lake after 12 hours and 12 miles of gruelling hiking. The others limped in and set up camp. Watching the sun sink poetically between two mountains, we sat and observed in silence. Oranges and reds blazed, reflected in the waters as the clouds slowly dispersed. Although exhausted, we beamed, relaxing as steam rose from our stoves, and we ate like wolves.

This section of the Sierra was 110 miles between town stops and I'd misjudged my supplies again. I had a day's food at best, and my alcohol was a mere dribble. That's stove alcohol, not Jack Daniels. Shit, if I'd been running low on JD, things could have been really serious. A cut-off trail headed to the remote Muir Trail Ranch, and hoped I could re-supply there.

I descended past ferocious emerald rivers and foaming waterfalls. Immense granite rock-faces towered above as tumbling water streaked them like tears. I was miles from civilisation, hemmed in by wilderness. No buildings, no roads, no noise pollution.

I met Frank and his horse, Chief, out for an afternoon ride. He was the blacksmith at Muir Trail Ranch and as we chatted, he showed me an intricate key ring he had forged. He said I'd find food at the ranch, as there were several hiker boxes and the owner, Pat, kept stocks of stove fuel.

The ranch lay a mile off the PCT, and as I approached, it became clear that others had also stopped by to re-supply.

Pat, the owner, was an angel. She told me where everything was and confirmed they kept stove fuel. Five hiker boxes provided ample supplies to continue. Signs politely requested hikers take only what they required as food was in high demand. I needed two days' worth and scored a bag of dehydrated bacon and eggs, chocolate-coated sesame crackers, powdered milk, oats and two evening meals.

My next re-supply was the large town of Mammoth. After a 20-miler from the ranch, I'd left myself 20 miles the following day, then a short five to reach the trailhead and a ride to town. I calculated that the incentive of a cooked breakfast, albeit it 25 miles distant, increased my speed by an average of 0.2 miles per hour. I could therefore walk an extra two miles a day if somehow, I could reach a diner every morning. If only.

My second filter had broken in Lone Pine and I'd replaced it with a Steripen. This unit, consisting of an ultraviolet tube, destroyed any organism's reproductive ability. It was fragile, but its simplicity attracted me. Just wave in water for a minute and job done.

I passed a group of hikers at lunch and paused to chat. One of them asked what purification method I used, and when I told him, he said he also had a Steripen but his batteries had run out. I offered him my spares and refused payment, saying I'd reach Mammoth soon and could buy more. He thanked me profusely as I left. Two hours later I stopped by a creek to treat the water – and saw with frustration that my batteries were dead. So much for karma!

Chapter 8
Washed Away by the Tuolumne River

Shake your water, it makes the Giardia dizzy.
Cary 'Borders' Hart

I reached the trailhead at Reds Meadow late afternoon, making a beeline for the café to solve an insatiable craving for bacon and eggs. Once re-fuelled, I caught the bus heading to Mammoth and sat behind a guy near the front. As the bus left, he turned to me.

"Are you thru-hiking?" he enquired, clearly turning his nose up.

"Yes, I am," I replied, smiling.

"I thought so; you smell like shit." He then moved to the back of the bus.

I'd normally retort in such situations, but his outright rudeness left me tongue tied. He was right though; no denying it. After several days on trail, even I grimaced at the cheesy odour.

Mammoth earned its living from the winter ski season and during the summer, it becomes a mecca for mountain bikers and hikers. It had everything I needed, but I didn't like it. Again, the amenities were spread out, which meant time wasted finding the launderette, the supermarket, a restaurant and more importantly, somewhere to stay. Lodgings were in short supply because The Mammoth Jazz Festival was in full swing. I visited several motels but had no luck. Heading to the KOA, I called in at the Motel 6. Messages from hikers filled the reception register, some offering spare beds.

'Hey, Grey Fox in Room 6. Give us a call.'

I dialled the number.

"Hello?"

"Grey Fox, how you doing? Says here you have a spare bed," I said.

"Er, who is this?"

"It's Fozzie."

"Fozzie, hi. Yeah, er, a spare bed? No, sorry."

I got the distinct impression he didn't want me to take it.

"Well, you might want to change the message in the visitor book to reflect that," I replied.

I hadn't seen him for two weeks. He walked with Spiller, who I assumed was his girlfriend until I learnt they were just friends and he was engaged to someone else. The Grey Fox and Spiller saga proved bread-and-butter gossip for most thru-hikers. He'd driven back home from Kennedy Meadows because his fiancée apparently demanded they sort some issues out. I didn't know if Spiller had played any part, but they kept most people guessing for the length of the PCT.

I scanned the register further and saw a note from Pockets.

'Hey. Got chicken pox! Come say hello!'

I'd gone through my chicken pox phase aged seven, so I called him. I'd met Pockets at Kennedy Meadows but had not seen him since.

"Fozzie! Hey! What's up?"

"Pockets, how you doing? I'm looking for a spare bed for two nights. Any chance?"

"Man, I feel like shit, not good company. Tell you what though, come back tomorrow and I'll be through the worst of it. You're welcome to a bed then."

"Thanks, mate. I'll give you a shout in the morning."

I plodded to the KOA, confident I could at least get a tent spot and grab a shower. The warden said it was also full because of the festival.

"I only need a space seven feet long by three feet wide," I explained, outlining a rectangle with my hands, and motioning with my eyes to the abundance of possible spaces dotted everywhere.

"You have to stay at a designated spot and I don't have anywhere. Sorry."

After she'd driven off in her golf cart, I ducked up a track through the trees, and could have picked a spot among hundreds. The park was designed for vehicles, not individuals. Each plot was big enough to take an average American motor home, i.e. half an acre. I walked into the forest away from the prying eyes and camped.

Walking to the shower building, I heard the familiar cackle of Burnie's laugh and investigated. She'd camped with Cheeks and Mojave, and they too had experienced similar problems finding a spot until a kind couple let them pitch near their motor home. The showers were out of order, so I walked to the nearest eatery, a McDonald's, my lingering stench in hot pursuit.

I admit my aroma can't have been pleasant for anyone, and the insulting looks I received in McDonald's that evening amused me. People moved once they'd got a whiff. Dirt streaked my clothes, my hands were grimy, and my hair was so sticky it grew vertically. I took exception to the strange person peering back from the mirror.

What I and other hikers found peculiar were the townsfolk, who also stank. After being in the woods, you lose touch with how people smell. Perfume, deodorant, and hair products smell like offensive chemical cocktails. Even on trail, we could tell a casual day-hiker from a thru-hiker just by the smell.

I went to the Black Stove Café with Burnie in the morning for breakfast and began my usual 'zero' day tasks (a day with no hiking is called a zero). On my return to the Motel, Pockets said I could stay as long as needed.

I'd have trouble describing Pockets in under 50 pages, but I'll give it a shot. He earned his trail name after his AT thru-hike a few years before. He'd reached an outdoors store and agreed to a gear shakedown (where your pack is checked for unnecessary items). They scrutinised his pack, and he scored well. Then he emptied his pockets. All manner of items spilled out, and he earned his trail name.

Pockets was 27, hailing from a small town called Paw Paw in Michigan. He sported an impressive beard, the like of which I could only dream of growing. His eyes were a piercing blue that he claimed drove the women wild, and his passion was photography. Having only picked up a camera a few years before, he showed an uncanny knack for taking beautiful pictures. So much so he'd appeared in National Geographic, the holy grail of any photographer.

We went for a meal in the evening and Burnie joined us. She'd moved out of the campsite, so Pockets said she could sleep in the motel room. I offered her my bed, saying I could take the floor, but she declined and laid out her sleeping bag on the carpet.

"Yeah, so, I got this unusual problem when I sleep," Pockets said. "I figure I should warn you both in case something happens."

"Something happening? Like what?" asked Burnie, sitting up and raising her eyebrows.

"Well, I dream a lot and sometimes sleepwalk. It's nothing to worry about; I don't turn into a werewolf or anything. They hooked me up to a measuring machine a while back and apparently my brain is ten times more active at night than most people's during the day. If I make noises and talk, just ignore it. I've been doing it like forever. I was born in Germany but left when I was two. I can't speak German, but in my sleep I'm fluent. I also speak French and Spanish during the night. Most of the time I just ramble on incoherently. My parents had to watch me because I'd get up and move around the house."

Burnie and I looked at each other in silent astonishment. Pockets continued.

"When I hiked the AT, I was sleeping in the bottom bunk of a shelter. I dreamt of walking up a hill and suddenly all these logs started rolling down, so I tried to stop them. This woke most of the other hikers and, although still dreaming, I sensed a lot of head lamps shining on me. In the morning everyone said they'd woken as I screamed at them to get out. I leant hard against one of the wooden shelter supports, slipping back on the floor in my socks. 'Get out of the shelter!' I shouted. 'You could at least look appreciative, I'm trying to save you!'"

With that, Pockets turned over and went to sleep, as if he'd said nothing unusual. Burnie looked at me, shrugged her shoulders and we both nodded off, keeping an ear open for a German-speaking, crazed thru-hiker bracing himself against the motel wall.

Pockets was quiet that night, save a few mumbles. He'd skipped a section, so the following day returned south to Kearsarge Pass to complete the missing miles. I had a funny feeling we'd meet again.

I caught the bus back to Reds Meadow, and couldn't resist a slice of cherry pie with a chocolate milkshake to set me up for the afternoon. When the waitress handed me the bill for $12.02, I was shocked but paid at the counter.

"Could you fill my water bottle please?" I asked, holding up my grubby-looking bottle. She stepped back.

"There's a spigot round the back for hikers," she said.

"Would you have given me a glass of water with my pie had I asked?" I asked, surprised at her refusal.

"Yes, of course." Her look suggested she'd got my point before I'd made it.

"Good. Because I've just spent 12 bucks on a meagre piece of pie and an average milkshake. Now, please, could you walk the four paces to that sink and fill my water bottle?"

I put in a few miles that afternoon, stopping near the Vogelsang Trailhead. A pleasant breeze kept the mosquitoes at bay, and I camped near the river. It was a beautiful evening; the sun took longer saying goodbye, and the forest was silent except for the water sliding by. I sat on the bank and dangled my sore feet in the shallows, watching trout dart around. Lush, deep green grass banked up gently before disappearing into the trees, which in turn surrendered to towering granite outcrops, an orange brushed sky providing the finale. A doe and two fawns grazed, circling me cautiously, glancing my way. They came within a few feet, and it reminded me how lucky I was to be in the wilderness. Twigs snapped behind, and I looked round at a wolf skulking through the trees. It stopped and looked at me, chastising itself for making its presence known. We locked eyes for a few seconds, its nose testing the air for a scent, and it left.

The following day I made a beeline for the café at Tuolumne Meadows. This was a popular spot for tourists exploring the Ansel Adams Wilderness, the John Muir Trail and a huge rock-face known as Half Dome. I crested a hill and came face to face with Wyoming, whom I'd last seen in Idyllwild. Taken aback, I thought one of us must be going the wrong way. We hugged.

"Why are you walking the wrong way?" I stammered.

"I'm not, Fozzie! I skipped up to Ashland in Oregon because of snow in the Sierras. Now I'm walking back to where I skipped from, Kennedy Meadows."

"That's a big skip!" I exclaimed. "How was it from Ashland to here?"

"There's lingering snow in the Marble Mountains down to 6,000 feet; other than that, it's fine. Oregon is kinder, the trail is smooth and the elevation change is minimal. You can do good mileage there. How's the Sierras?"

"Difficult!" I said, smiling to lighten the news. "There's

a lot of hard passes and still plenty of snow. You can get through, but be careful. Take extra food: the altitude and temperature will increase your appetite. Oh, and watch out for Mather Pass; it's a bitch."

We hugged again, and I watched her trudge off south. It was strange meeting my first SoBo (south-bounder). I also felt a tinge of sadness. I'd first met Wyoming on the second day at a campsite off Fred Canyon Road when I walked with Gabe. Unassuming and gentle, she spoke quietly; I had to listen closely to what she said. Of slight build, she'd cut her hair short for the low-maintenance approach many hikers adopted. I dearly wished I'd spent more time with her.

SoBos thru-hike the PCT from Canada to Mexico. The norm is north-bound, NoBo-style. Because Canada and Washington State get more snowfall over the winter, which doesn't clear until later in the season, a south-bounder starts and finishes later. There are pros and cons for the SoBo. The main advantage is walking away from the bad weather towards California, which stays warm long after the northern states. NoBos play a game of chase-the-weather, trying to reach Canada before the snow hits. Wyoming wasn't a true SoBo as such, just south-bounding one section. I met more as I progressed further north. Generally, a SoBo starts in June and finishes around November.

The track levelled at 8,700 feet and bordered the Lyle River for eight miles. Overspill from the river softened the ground into a rich deep brown mud which clung to my shoes. I stopped several times to talk to other walkers, who congratulated me on attempting the PCT. The area is easily accessible from the road that runs through Tuolumne Meadows and attracts many visitors. That morning, it was easy to see why. As I walked through the meadows by the river, the flat terrain made for contemplative meandering. I felt at ease there.

I ate a good meal at the café and bought supplies from the well-stocked store. Tourists milled about, the air alive with the chatter of people expecting a day in the wild. I debated going to see Half Dome, but my distance had increased to 25 miles a day, and I was keen to maintain the pace. Although awe-inspiring, Half Dome wasn't any more spectacular than the sights I'd become used to everyday. Supposedly the inspiration for the North Face logo, it's the centrepiece of countless photos taken over the years, especially by Ansel Adams, whose work adorns many outdoor calendars. It would be teeming with tourists as well; I didn't see the point in hiking to the top with hundreds of others. I had plenty of mountains still to conquer in solitude.

I walked along the road, then followed the PCT as it turned up a side track scattered with parked vehicles and screaming kids. Holidaymakers stayed in air-conditioned cars, eating ice creams, and I wondered why. I found the place annoying and quickened my pace, disappearing into the forest again.

The woods were my home, my comfort zone. A meal in town boosted morale, but everyday distractions irritated me. I became frustrated at people asking questions, and I felt guilty for being unapproachable. "What are you doing?" they'd ask. "Why are you so dirty? Why is your pack so big? You're just wearing shoes; where are your hiking boots? Don't you miss the TV? Where do you wash your hair?"

Before long though, crowds became a distant memory, replaced by the tumbling rage of the Tuolumne River. I approached Dingley Creek cautiously.

Maybe I wasn't paying attention or my familiarity with river crossings had bred contempt. The creek seemed innocent enough; it flowed fast but shallow, and an assortment of boulders offered an easy crossing.

My trekking poles, Click and Clack, named after the striking sound on the ground, had been with me for 10 years since my walk on El Camino de Santiago. These constant companions offered security as they eased me up the ascents and stabilised me on the descents. They helped on river crossings; walking without Click and Clack would be unimaginable.

I jumped from one boulder to the next. I shivered as water found a way into my shoes. Mid-jump, I sensed hesitation with Clack, who'd become stuck in the creek bed. I let him go as my momentum carried me forward, thinking I'd retrieve him after. To my horror, as I looked behind me, the current tore at him. A boxer taking a last devastating punch, Clack slumped sideways, picking up speed as the creek took hold.

"No! Clack!" I screamed.

It was too late; as I jumped back and held out a flailing hand to rescue him, he succumbed to the flow and floated away. Dingley Creek travelled a mere 50 feet into the Tuolumne River. I ran along the bank, dropping my pack while trying to dodge fallen trees and other obstacles. I closed the gap, but as the river neared, Clack's speed increased as he looked at me pleadingly. The Tuolumne engulfed and tore him away in an instant. With his handle floating above the river, he swayed from side to side like a waving friend on a departing train. I waved back.

"Don't be sad, you still have Click! It'll be fine, I'll wash up downriver somewhere and a hiker will find me. I'll hike on. I will hike on!"

Click and I watched despondently as our companion bobbed into the distance. Our hearts sank. We turned north, paused for one last glimpse and left.

I got lost trying to navigate over vast sections of granite. Because of the hard surface, the trail was indistinguishable. Cairns marked the way, but they dwindled to nothing. A tent appeared.

Steve Climber, Borders, Jolly Green Giant, Dan, and Splizzard stretched across the trail, enjoying the afternoon sun. Borders sat in his tent, relishing a few minutes free of mosquitoes. I sat with my fellow hikers briefly before moving on.

Now the last week of July, in the higher elevations of the mountains, it was still spring. Elder shrubs dressed in white, meadow flowers splattered the grass with hundreds of colours, and squadrons of dragonflies hovered in formation over the lakes. A sandy trail carved its way through grass, and brown trout feasted.

I walked with Chrissie and Dodge for a morning as we donned our mosquito nets. Click did his best to keep me company, but I felt off-balance without Clack. The major passes were behind, and although the mountains were difficult, I'd conquered the hardest part of the Sierras.

My second pair of shoes had split. I'd tried to repair them by using rubber glue over the outside, but this had made matters worse. It had dried, leaving rough lumps on the insides which rubbed my toes, so I tried to pull the stuff off. This made the holes bigger. After 990 miles, my third pair of footwear beckoned.

Now at the tail end of the pack, I'd lost time resting my bad feet. I'd completed a third of the route, but it had taken 91 days, which put me on course to finish in January! This was four months after a typical end date in September. I needed to increase my mileage and keep town stops to one day a week at most.

On the plus side, the water crossings were less challenging. 700 miles ahead lay Oregon; a long way, but the terrain eased there. I felt strong, my feet were in good shape, but I knew unless my pace increased, I wasn't going to finish. After the hard work so far, the thought of failure gnawed at me. My daily mileage was great for the Sierras, but difficult to sustain.

I'd received good news from Chrissie and Dodge. The granite, typical of the Sierras, would soon merge to a more porous volcanic rock. This meant less standing water and therefore fewer mosquitos.

I reached the end of a hard day and looked for a camping spot, seeing smoke up ahead near a creek. As I hopped over the water, Mojave, and Cheeks waved. A new face, Mr Green, sat in the fire smoke, seeking refuge from the mosquitoes.

The surrounding rock-faces had turned from grey to a pinkish hue, which I took to be the transition Chrissie and Dodge had mentioned. Unfortunately, the mosquitoes hadn't noticed, and by sundown they engulfed us. Cheeks coped well, but Mojave had retreated to their tent, so I chatted with her through the canvas. By the time I'd sat down to cook, they attacked from every angle. I boiled my water, re-hydrated my meal and dived into my tent, quickly closing the zip. I stayed there for the rest of the evening, unwilling to get out to brush my teeth, and had to make a brisk dash to pee. I'd decided to go to Bridgeport, which meant an 11-mile morning walk to Sonora Pass and, with luck, a ride into town. Conscious of my need to increase mileage, I set the alarm for 4am.

I laboured up the 1,700-foot ascent of Sonora Pass in the early morning darkness. I slowly became familiar with my environment as the sun crept over the peaks and bathed my world in gentle orange. The PCT coiled up, heading for a pass just south of Leavitt Lake. I assumed I'd see Highway 108 as I crested, but I didn't. Not only did the elevation figures seem wrong, the distance did too. I walked along a wide ridge towards a notch which crossed over to the other side of the mountain, then down to the road.

I passed a figure huddled in a sleeping bag on Leavitt Peak and walked up to say hello.

"Morning," I said softly.

"Morning! Who's that? Is that Fozzie?" came the muffled reply.

I recognised the scruffy, early morning face of Swayze as he rubbed his eyes.

"Swayze!"

We exchanged a hearty handshake; it had been weeks since we'd last met. Back then he hiked with Dinosaur, and I assumed they were partners, and Scorpion had joined them at Tehachapi. But now Swayze camped alone.

"What happened to Scorpion?" I asked.

"She only wanted to do six-mile days, which obviously wasn't enough for us. I haven't seen you since that spring around the 600-mile mark," he replied.

"Yes, I remember," I replied. "There were a lot of people there. That's the last time I saw Stumbling Norwegian, Jake and the Israelis."

"You seemed in a hurry, Fozzie. You ate your lunch real quick and left."

I thought for a second. "Yes. I needed to get to Ridgecrest to see a World Cup game. Big mistake. I did 58 miles in two days and shredded my feet. Had to hole up for four days. That's probably where you got ahead of me. Where's Dinosaur?"

"She's camped up ahead maybe five miles; you'll see her."

We shook hands again. I liked Swayze. His name intrigued me but I never asked about it.

A mile further, I found Indie; he had also slept on the ground. I stopped and chatted to him as well. He was in good spirits.

I liked seeing familiar faces and indeed new ones. I assumed I'd stay within reach of the hikers I knew, so I had an indication of everyone's location. I couldn't rely on seeing anyone again though. For example, when I took the four days out in Ridgecrest, I imagined those who'd been near would then be four days ahead. It didn't work exactly like that; others took time out as well, so we constantly overlapped. Because our meetings were random and I might lose track of others, I made the most of them. Swayze and Indie were classic examples. Regrettably, it was the last time I saw either of them.

I followed the ridge towards the notch and descended to

the road, still a long way down. I spotted Sardine Creek, which teased my thirst, and I longed to drink from it. I crossed slushy snow banks and finally reached the highway. I'd done 11 miles, which felt more like 20.

Cars scattered along the road as Boy Scouts spilled out and grouped on the other side, where their leader drilled them about their hike. I tried to catch a ride just before a blind summit, figuring vehicles would slow down and I'd have a better chance. After an hour, my theory hadn't borne fruit, and I looked back at the Scout group preparing to move off. The parents returned to their cars, and I sensed an opportunity.

"Hi," I said, trying my best to look tired, hungry and expectant. "I'm walking the Pacific Crest Trail and need to get to Bridgeport to re-supply. Is anyone going that way? But I should warn you I stink." I hoped my humour would grease the wheels of kindness.

"Always happy to help someone who's walking the PCT," one woman said. "If you can bear with me for five minutes, then one of us can help you. How bad do you smell?" She smiled.

"Not good," I replied, shrugging my shoulders.

An hour later, I sat in the Sportsman Inn tucking into breakfast. I made my way to the Bridgeport Inn and passed a snack bar, where Nick and Chris, the other English guys, chatted between mouthfuls of fish and chips. Cheeks and Mojave were also there, grinning cheekily because they'd beaten me to town despite leaving later.

With all good intentions come a few surprises. I'd intended to spend the day, as usual, re-supplying, eating and checking emails before getting back on trail the following day. If someone had told me I'd be sitting on the patio at my Uncle Tony's in San Jose with a cold beer, I'd have shrugged off the suggestion as crazy.

Chapter 9
Light, Heat and Duff

Town? If I wanted to hang out in town, I could have stayed at home.
John 'Tradja' Drollette

My cell phone service provider in the US claimed their reception covered 97 per cent of Americans. Therefore, I put my constant lack of signal down to being English. I barely turned my phone on; I didn't need to. I used it occasionally to make a call or send a message. Most of the time it stayed off. The power off feature is underrated; when hiking I prefer silence.

Bridgeport had no reception either, but I expected that. I liked the place; walking from one end of town to the other took five minutes, and a smattering of history gave it a sense of purpose. There were good eateries, the supermarket was well-stocked, and they were within easy reach. The Bridgeport Inn needed refining though. There was no air conditioning, no TV and the bathroom was shared. All for the princely sum of $73 per night. The lodgings in town were expensive, and crazily enough, the Bridgeport Inn was the cheapest, so I checked in.

I bumped into Steve Climber, Splizzard, Mr Green and Borders eating breakfast at the Sportsman Inn. The chat centred on four days of thunderstorms. I peered out the window to blue skies.

"Are you sure?" I asked Splizzard, who twisted and curled the ends of his moustache like Hercule Poirot. The others followed suit.

"That's the forecast, coming in tomorrow. We're going up north to rest for a few days to ride it out."

Despite my eagerness to get more miles in, it made sense to avoid the coming storms. I'm used to walking in the rain; I live in England, after all. I'd planned to meet Uncle Tony at Lake Tahoe, 76 miles further on. We'd agreed I'd return to San Jose, rest for a few days, and sort out my gear. I reasoned I could do that while the weather deteriorated. I called Tony who, bless him, said he'd leave the next morning and collect me. This left a day to chill out and, for once, forget my usual chores.

I bumped into Burnie, who looked shaken after hiking to Sonora Pass in a thunderstorm, making me think Splizzard could indeed be right.

"I've never been so scared, Fozzie," she said, still looking ruffled from her experience. "Lightning was striking the ground everywhere. I thought I was finished."

She told me that Cheeks and Mojave had left to face the storms, come what may. I felt guilty for taking time out and continued to worry about the distance I still had to walk. Going to San Jose was a big gamble; I'd planned it from the outset, a short break to lighten my load, both physically and mentally. In retrospect, I blamed my lack of progress on frequent breaks. My downfall was approaching the PCT like a holiday, when I should have focused more on pushing miles, not days off. I'd only begun to realise my error, and it came back to haunt me later.

With the worst of the snow now behind, I had no need for my ice axe and crampons. Nearing the end of a mandatory bear cannister area, I ditched that as well, figuring I'd deal with questions from rangers if they arose. A cooler sleeping bag would save more weight. I needed new shoes again, and I leaned towards hiking boots, which I hoped might last to the end, and cope with any bad weather further north.

I returned to the Sportsman Bar that evening, taking a seat behind two feet of mahogany, with the sole intention of inebriation.

"Jack Daniels with ice, please," I said to Gordon, the owner.

"Can I see some ID, please?"

I looked at him, then at Brad and Steve, who sat next to me. They smiled, I sighed.

"I'm English," I replied. "The only ID I have is my passport, which is back at the hotel. I'd be more than happy to get it, but let me ask you a question first. I'm 43 years old, do I really look 21?"

"I have to card almost everyone in case there's an undercover cop in the bar," he replied, stony-faced.

This made me laugh, which didn't help my chances, but the idea of someone sinister lurking in the bar, checking on drinkers, was funny. Like the police didn't have enough to do already. I turned around, eyeing the patrons warily. No one looked like Mulder and Scully. I turned to Brad and Steve.

"Do I look under 21?"

They replied in unison to the negative. I turned back to Gordon.

"OK, if you want me to go back and get my passport, I can do that for you. I'm just here for food, to watch the TV and enjoy the atmosphere. I'll be drinking, probably too much but not enough to cause you any trouble. Do you want me to get my ID or can I please have a drink?"

"Gordon, give the English guy a drink; he's OK," Brad suggested.

Gordon sighed and poured me a drink.

Brad continued my education on Californian drinking law. It's illegal to have an open bottle of alcohol in a vehicle; but it's legal to have it in the boot. You can't take alcohol out of the bar, but it's OK to drink in the street on Independence Day or if the bottle is in a brown paper bag. I remembered this from the movies. The stupid part is if someone drinks from a container in a brown paper bag, then it's obviously alcohol! On the plus side, at least Californian law allows drinking until 2am. In England we still get chucked out at 11pm.

This got me thinking about other ridiculous laws. After researching, I found these American classics. Don't feel left out though, the English ones are coming.

In New Mexico, women are forbidden to appear unshaven in public. West Virginia states that children cannot attend school with their breath smelling of wild onions. In Oklahoma people can be fined, arrested or jailed for making ugly faces at a dog. In Florida, leaving an elephant tied to a parking meter is illegal unless the parking fee has been paid, just as it would for a vehicle. Citizens in

Indiana cannot attend a movie house or ride in a public streetcar within four hours of eating garlic. Finally, my personal favourite: in Louisiana it is illegal to rob a bank and then shoot the cashier with a water pistol. I never found out if the illegal part was robbing the bank, or using a water pistol!

As for us English, we've passed some equally bizarre laws. It is legal for a male to urinate in public, providing it's on the rear wheel of his vehicle, and his right hand is on that vehicle. Ladies can be arrested for eating chocolate on a public conveyance. Believe it or not, it's illegal to eat mince pies on Christmas day (this is true!). It's said that members of parliament may not enter the House of Commons wearing a full suit of armour. In Chester you can shoot a Welsh person with a bow and arrow inside the city walls if it's after midnight (isn't any time of day after midnight?). Lastly, in London, a Hackney Carriage (otherwise known as a taxi) must carry a bale of hay and a sack of oats (this dates back to the days when taxis were horse-drawn).

Apparently, in the UK at least, there's a government department dedicated to scrutinising laws going back centuries to revise or abolish them. Due to the sheer number of such laws, the task is huge; this is why some of these classics still exist, they just haven't got round to changing them.

Uncle Tony collected me the next day for the trip back to San Jose. It was weird being in a car again; we covered 600 miles that day. A distance that would take weeks to hike flashed by in a few hours. I watched the scenery change as we travelled further north, and with the sun in my eyes I fell asleep.

I'd discovered that Western Mountaineering, who made my sleeping bag, was based in San Jose. This was too good an opportunity to miss, so I called the owner, Gary Peterson. He agreed to loan me a summer sleeping bag until the weather cooled once more. I asked if I could to collect it, meet him and see the factory, and he agreed.

It took a while to find the place, tucked up a back street in the older part of town. Gary met me and took me through the manufacturing process. Skilfully operated sewing machines vibrated everywhere, and rolls of material teetered on benches. Western Mountaineering has an enviable reputation. Best known for their down-filled insulation products, they produce sleeping bags, jackets, down trousers and a few other accessories. As I strolled around, the air filled with escaping down fluffs, floating around like snow.

We discussed the options and settled on the Summerlite model, and he also presented me with a Flash Vest as a gift for the cooler evenings and mornings.

Three days whizzed past in San Jose, and before I knew it Uncle Tony was driving me back to Sonora Pass, with Rudy coming along for the ride. As I strode off waving at them, I shouted that I'd see them in October. How wrong I'd be!

My pack felt light; I'd lost four pounds changing or ditching equipment. I tried to fill just one water bottle where possible. I'd left Click behind for a new pair of hiking poles. I regretted my new leather boots, which were heavy and cumbersome. It was great to be back on the trail and I smiled, making short work of a 600-foot climb.

Now late July, I'd only covered 1020 miles. Sounds impressive (and it is), but I hadn't even reached halfway, and still had 1620 miles left. I ran the numbers and whichever way I looked, my situation was desperate. 98 days with 1020 miles covered, meant an average of 10.4 miles per day. Wait, it gets worse. With those figures, Canada was 154 days away. Or, in other words, five months, at the end of December.

I didn't know whether to laugh or cry, so I settled in-between and giggled nervously. The facts were inescapable; I couldn't ignore them or make them fit. Basically, I was in the shit. I needed to wake up and smash some miles, or my hike was over.

A pinkish-grey rock tumbled down to rolling green hills of lush grass. Meadow flowers splashed colour, and many lakes, rivers and creeks dotted the landscape.

I startled Walker Texas Ranger and Dozer, napping by the side of the trail as I rounded a corner. I had forgotten Dozer's name, which is no reflection on him; more on my failing memory. I didn't recognise Walker, as his beard had sprouted impressively since we last saw each other at Kennedy Meadows.

"Hey, Fozzie, it's Dozer," he said helpfully, as he stood up to shake my hand.

"Good to see you again," I said. "Sorry, not good with names."

"Fozzie, it's Walker!"

"Mate, I didn't recognise you," I said apologetically, offering my hand. He refused it, which puzzled me.

"Dude, I got Giardia," he said, with a resigned expression, suggesting it was bound to happen at some point. I drew my palm back faster than England's World Cup exit. Walker admitted he'd consumed untreated water from creeks in the Sierras. We walked together for 10 minutes before Walker stopped, and vomited most of his stomach contents. I hadn't seen as much sick since Margaret Holloway threw up in the school canteen when I was five years old.

"Dude, I purged a demon," he said, wiping sick from his beard.

Dozer and I couldn't stop sniggering. Unsympathetic, I know, but Walker smirked as well.

"No, I'm serious," he continued. "I just performed an exorcism." He smiled, trying to clear his nose.

"If you've got a sense of humour, Walker, you're halfway through it," I suggested.

We walked to the highway at Ebbetts Pass and cooked an evening meal by the road. Dozer fired up his Jetboil, boiling his water before I'd poured alcohol into my stove. He knew I was envious of his stove speed, and he smirked. By the time I'd emptied a dehydrated chicken stew into my saucepan, he was clearing up.

We tried to flag a car for Walker so he could see a doctor in Lake Tahoe, but the road was empty. Walker insisted on hiking the 24 miles to town so we carried on, but after two miles he stopped. We camped together and somehow, he slept. In the morning I left, telling the guys I'd see them in Lake Tahoe, where we'd agreed to share a motel room.

The morning was cold. I pulled the jacket zip up to my neck, shivered and walked quickly to warm up. The meagre 400-foot ascent over a ridge known as the Nipple soon had me sweating, so I stopped at the summit and lay my head down for five minutes.

I timed sections during the day so I could see my progress and keep tabs on my position. Here, though, I forgot about schedules. I knew getting to Highway 50 meant a long day, and I didn't want to be reminded of it.

I stopped for a break mid-morning and discovered I only had one snack left. I couldn't even cook rice as my fuel had run out. I passed a hiker who reassured me I would get water at the Carson Pass visitor centre.

"They don't have any food, though," he added with a resigned look and upturned palms.

I did my best to look hungry and thirsty as I reached the parking area, dreaming of a cold coke, but all was quiet. I slumped dejectedly on a chair outside the visitor centre and rummaged through my pack, hoping to find a long-forgotten morsel of peppered jerky cowering in the bottom. No such luck.

"PCT hiker?"

I looked up to see the kind face of a lady called Peggy Geelhaar, a volunteer at the centre.

"I am, yes," I said, smiling, still looking sorry for myself.

"You want a soda, maybe something to eat?"

Before I answered, she disappeared and came back with grapes and two apples. She told me to help myself to a soda from the cool box and gave me a slab of cheese. Her companion, Dan Quayle, sauntered to the car and returned with a bear-sized pack of crisps.

"Please sign the visitors' book," Peggy said.

I wolfed down the goodies and checked the visitors' book. Familiar names appeared, with dates and messages. Many of my friends were just a few days ahead, and I felt spurred to catch them. I scanned the entries: Burnie had passed through three days before, Answerman as well, Mojave and Cheeks were five days ahead, Bigfoot a week, Jake was still in the mix, and Stumbling Norwegian and HoJo were a good nine days in front.

'The trail will provide' rang in my ears as I carried on towards Lake Tahoe, thanking Peggy and Dan for their trail magic.

However, during the afternoon, my spirits slumped, as my new boots became painful. Lake Tahoe lay three hours ahead, so I pushed on through the pain. I thought of removing the offending boot to check my toe, but knew I'd have to endure the five-minute hobble, so I continued. It hurt like hell, and although a minor problem, I let it get to me and ended up crying. Why, I didn't know; I'd been through worse. Such a swing of emotions, positive at lunchtime to negative in two hours! My feet had been fine, only for blisters to plague me once more.

Leather hiking boots are notoriously difficult to break in and are best worn for many short walks, gradually building to longer distances. Of course, I didn't have that luxury, and despite deliberating my choice, I realised my decision was stupid. I decided to send the boots back when I reached Tahoe and return to Montrails, which suited my feet.

I reached the highway, hobbled to a halt and eased off my boot. A blister sat on my little toe, deep red with blood and ready to burst. Another swelled on the next toe as well. I switched to my Crocs and stuck out a hopeful thumb at passing vehicles. After 30 minutes without success, a taxi stopped and I got in.

The driver swept around bends as I listened to a voicemail from Dozer saying he and Walker had arrived at the motel. I found their room and checked on Walker, who lay on the bed looking pale; he'd seen a doctor who'd confirmed Giardiasis. He aimed to get back on trail after two days of medication.

I peeled off my boots and wincing, pushed a needle into the blister. A yellow and red liquid oozed out and dribbled onto the floor. I cut off the surrounding skin, leaving a tender wound, which would take time to dry out. I bathed my feet in a strong Epsom salt solution and hoped for a rapid recovery.

I relaxed with Dozer and Walker. Jack Straw knocked on the door, followed by Scorpion, Crow and Dundee, who made themselves at home. With the room getting crowded, I limped to town and the local outdoor store to check footwear options. The Montrails I'd used before weren't available, but a lighter, more cushioned and comfortable version looked promising. They felt wonderful, so I bought them and mailed the boots back.

Pockets had arrived when I returned. I was surprised he'd made up the time so fast, which reminded me of my slow progress. He was with a woman called Courtney, whom he'd met in Wrightwood, and she'd driven up to walk a section of the PCT. The five of us relaxed in the evening, watching movies and eating as much Ben and Jerry's as our stomachs allowed.

I spent a further three days in Lake Tahoe allowing my blister to heal. Walker had left, so I moved to a different motel. Dozer had given me the number of a guy who gave rides to the trailhead, and when I called he came straight over.

Back on trail I reached Echo Lake, stopped for a quick

drink and carried on skirting the shore. A ranger stopped me, appearing curt and impatient.

"You hiking the PCT?" he said, looking me up and down.

"Yes, I am."

"Where's your permit?"

All thru-hikers on the PCT have to carry a permit. As many of the areas and national parks require separate permits, the PCT Association offers one that covers them all. I'd applied for mine at the kick-off party in Lake Morena. I duly handed it to him. He asked if I carried a bear canister, which I wasn't. I'd left it in San Jose because I wouldn't be needing it for much longer.

"Yes," I lied, tapping the side of my rucksack where I knew a hard-plastic bottle lurked, hoping this would fool him.

"Be sure to use it, please," he ordered and walked away.

I hate being told what to do, almost as much as being told what I can't do. I have problems with authority. I don't know where it stems from, but I'm suspicious of anyone in a uniform. I don't get on with the police, and immigration officers are my worst nightmare. I'd met several rangers, all of them welcoming, pleasant to converse with and helpful. This guy was different, though. He seemed to revel in his position and look down on me, which riled me. In any case, I resented having to carry a permit. From what I gleaned from other hikers, the United States Forestry Service introduced permits to monitor the number of people in parks and recreation areas. I regarded the land as free. To register and pay to experience the wilderness annoyed me; it didn't seem fair.

Hikers also needed a fire permit. The online application included a questionnaire about campfires. Passing was easy; information containing the answers lurked in the text. But I learnt a few things. For one, all flammable material needed clearing around the fire to a distance of five feet (existing fire rings should be utilised if available). A shovel should be used for clearing and to extinguish campfires. A 'responsible' person (other multiple-choice answers included 'happy', 'reputable' and 'busy') should attend at all times. To extinguish the fire, separate any burning pieces of wood with the shovel, then drown the fire with water, stirring with the shovel to produce a sticky mess. This is known as the 'drown, stir and feel' method (other answers were 'shake, rattle and roll,' 'hit or miss or 'cut and run'!).

A substance known as duff caused many fires. This, I learned, is the decomposing layer of vegetation between the leaves and earth. It isn't highly flammable and its air supply is restricted, so it can smoulder for days from a stray ember. Once enough heat has built up, it can break free and start a blaze. I always tried to clear around the fire, removing the duff to get to dirt, and I always poured water over the finished fire and stirred with a stick. I never met anyone who had a shovel; they were too bulky, and besides, we used our feet to clear the ground and a stick to stir in the water.

At elevation, a fire provides warmth, light, mosquito protection, heat for cooking, a signal to others, and – maybe most of all – a morale boost. Watching a fire is a great way to relax. It dries out wet gear and indeed sometimes burns it! Often, I'd camp with others when we smelt burning plastic, followed by a stampede of hikers converging on the fire and pulling their shoes away.

I loved the warmth the most. Up in the Sierras and during the latter stages of my hike, the temperature dropped below freezing. In my sleeping bag I stayed warm, but in the evening, it got chilly. I'd write my journal in the light, and often just sit and stare into the flames. There is something mesmerising about looking into fires. Oranges, reds, yellows and greys fluctuating in a passing breeze, dancing as if alive.

Mosquitoes dislike fire smoke. The sure-fire method to escape them was sitting in the smoke, as eye-watering as that sounds. If you couldn't do that, the breeze would do it for you. Wind direction often wafted smoke over us. It was amusing watching others around a fire as they ducked, stooped and leant to one side, coughing and rubbing their eyes, trying to stay out of the smoke.

I began using fires for cooking. One disadvantage is the tendency of the cooking pot to get caked in a sticky mix of soot, small pieces of twig and pine resin. This put me off at first, and I used my alcohol stove; but the more fires I lit, the more often I cooked over them. It saved weight because I carried less fuel, and I could cook more adventurous meals with the limitless heat from a fire. For example, I could make several cups of tea instead of just one (an Englishman must have his tea) and still have plenty of hot water to clean up with afterwards. After a re-supply in town, I often treated myself to fresh meat or potatoes. Sausages suspended over the embers with a potato wrapped in tin foil (I always kept a small piece of foil somewhere), or some corn would round off the day splendidly.

Fire is a real danger on the trail. Fire damaged areas reminded us of its destructive capabilities. Some burnt sections dating back to the eighties were still regenerating;

the new trees hadn't reached full height and wide expanses of shorter vegetation remained. I passed through recent burns, a bleak landscape of black soil and white trees where the bark had burnt away. An apocalyptic aftermath, a stark reminder of the power of nature. One severe forest fire over just a few days can take years to recover. In 2018, PCT hikers endured one of the worst summers ever. Several, massive forest fires devastated large areas and many parts of the trail were either closed, or detoured.

Lightning strikes start many blazes, and nothing can be done to prevent those. Carelessness can cause fires; for example, at Apache Peak in southern California, a thru-hiker caused a serious blaze by accidentally spilling fuel.

I nearly did the same myself. I'd camped with HoJo and Ben in the desert. I cleared the grass away and set my equipment on the ground. As I held my lighter over the stove, I'd unknowingly spilt fuel on the ground, and it caught. It spread like, well, wildfire. I screamed at the others and they rushed over with water bottles, and we managed to dowse the flames.

Chapter 10

Ghosts on the Trail

This world is too cynical, greedy and self-serving for me.
I'd rather be poor and work from trip to trip than die rich.
We take none of our possessions to the grave, but hopefully
God grants us our memories.
David 'Walker Texas Ranger' Allen

I woke to a chilly morning, the tent damp from the overnight rain. As I peered through the hills, I saw Lake Tahoe flanked by mountains. She glinted as an upturned feather of mist floated above the water. Silence surrounded me, and vegetation glistened as it caught the rising sun. I'd managed an early start at 7am, eager to make up for lost time.

I concentrated on my breathing, which I'd learnt from yoga. Expanding the abdomen muscles as I inhaled and contracting them when exhaling forced more air into my lungs. I gingerly walked along tight ridges, marvelling at the land below. Even after 110 days, California still surprised me. I felt honoured to be in the mountains and forests.

It was the second week of August. The first thru-hikers

were a month away from finishing, and from Canada down through Washington, Oregon and northern California, hikers stretched out before me. I couldn't believe I was still in this southern state; at 1,700 miles long, it's twice the length of Great Britain! My current target was Oregon, another 530 miles distant. There, a wooden sign nailed to a solitary tree marked the state line. That alone would be an amazing achievement. After that, I had a mere 455 miles to my next goal, Washington State, and then a paltry 495 miles until the end of my journey. I hadn't even hit halfway yet; completing the PCT was daunting. Nevertheless, it's what I'd come to do, and I was excited. I'd only dreamt of being in the wilds for such a long time; now I was doing it.

I reached the Peter Grubb Hut, a haven for those caught out in the elements. Inside was vast, with a large kitchen, a smaller, cosier room to the side with an open fire, and further rooms upstairs. For the first time I tucked into a peanut butter and jam sandwich, which met with my full approval. Given my love for peanut butter, it was amazing I'd not sampled the mix before. I perused the trail register and saw Pockets had written a message.

"Foz! Catch up. I wrecked my tent. Got a great story for you!"

Intrigued, I wolfed down my lunch and left, hoping to catch him that day. Steve Climber had also stayed at the hut, along with a few others. What a sweet place to spend the night, but it was only midday, so I kept moving.

I saw no other hikers the rest of the day. I set up the tent on a flat spot by the trail just before a long ascent. A builder stopped on his quad bike and chatted. Unable to get a signal down in the valley, he regularly rode up to make phone calls.

I made a fire, cooked and turned in for the night. It didn't take long before I woke because of animal noises. I'd brushed my teeth away from the tent, but the smell had attracted a bear. I slammed the ground and called out, and the beast thundered off into the forest. From the reverberations, it must have been a fair size. 30 minutes later it returned, I shouted and again it charged off. It came back once more, and this time a hard blow on my emergency whistle did the trick. I lay silent, listening and looked at my watch. It was 4am. The forest was deathly quiet; no wind, no animals stirred, and I was miles from the nearest road.

"What are you doing here?!" a woman's voice screamed. Still awake in case of bears, I sat bolt upright, my heart pulling at my chest, panic-stricken. I shook with fear, focusing on the weak moonlight to get my bearings.

"What do you mean what am I doing here?" I shouted. "What are you doing here!?"

Silence. I peered out but there was no one there. I didn't sleep at all and come sunrise, I got up. The first thing I noticed was the number of twigs, sticks and dry leaves on the ground. Nobody could have approached the tent without making a noise. What the hell was someone doing at that time of morning, creeping up on hikers anyway? The builder rode up again and stopped. I told him what had happened, feeling rather stupid.

"Oh, I'm not surprised," he replied. "Depends on your beliefs, but this place is littered with old, derelict homesteads from the pioneers who tried to scrape a living here. It's not the first time someone's said they've heard voices in the forest at night."

"You mean a ghost?" I asked, astonished.

"Like I say, it depends on your beliefs." We shook hands, he wished me good luck and sped to the summit to make another phone call.

I walked for two hours and filled up with water at Haypress Creek. I knew Pockets was ahead of me because I recognised his footprints. He wore an unusual brand of shoe, and the prints were easy to spot. Crossing a logging track, I heard laughing behind, which startled me, not for the first time that day. I spun round to see Courtney standing there, smiling at me.

"Where the hell did you come from?" she asked, laughing.

"Where the hell did *you* come from?" I replied.

"I went for water back there. Pockets is up ahead; he said if he stopped he'd leave his trekking poles by the side of the trail."

"Let's go find him then," I said, eager to see my mate again.

Only a few hundred feet further, we spotted his poles.

"Pockets!" I cried.

"Fozzie! Up here!"

I ducked through the trees to an opening. He was taking time lapses of the passing clouds.

"Hey mate, how's it going?" he said, smiling.

"Good, didn't expect to catch you so quick. I was only at the Peter Grubb Hut yesterday."

"Yeah, I've been taking loads of photos; great skies, and Courtney walks slower, so I kept with her."

"What the hell did you do to your tent?" I asked, remembering the message he wrote in the hut.

"Dude, you will not believe the story I've got for you!" he cried, rubbing his hands in anticipation.

Courtney arrived, smiling as she'd already heard it.

"It's so far out that you have to believe it!" she cried.

I took out my Dictaphone to record the conversation.

"Pockets, go."

"Just as an intro," he began, "a few years back I'd camped in a slot canyon, a flash flood washed me and the tent away. I was OK but a bit shaken. Anyway, after I summited Barkers Pass, I hiked along that big ridgeline by the ski lifts – you know where I mean?"

"I do," I said, adjusting my position to get more comfortable. When Pockets told a story, it lasted forever but was always riveting.

"Well, this storm rolled in and it looked really bad. I ran down, hitting switchback after switchback. I reach the bottom and set up my tent just before it starts raining. I eat, chill out and go to sleep. At nine it's pouring, lightning and thundering, crazy weather. I dozed off somehow and started dreaming."

"No shit?" I said. "You, dreaming?" I looked over at Courtney, who giggled.

"I know! I put my hand on the groundsheet where a puddle had formed from a leak. This got me dreaming I was back at the slot canyon in the flash flood and I must have tried to get out of the tent. I knocked the pole over and the tent collapsed on me. The canvas flapped on my face so I started biting it to escape."

"You did what? Are you serious?" I asked.

"Yes! I can piece this shit together after the event. I keep biting until finally, I made a hole, grabbed it with both hands, tore it open and squeezed out. Remember, I'm still dreaming! I grab the ground because I'm scared I'll get washed away. Then the rain wakes me. It's pitch black and I'm in the woods. I'm like, 'What the fuck?' I see the damage to the tent. I'm sitting there with my torso sticking through the canvas with the rest of the tent lying around me."

Courtney shook with the giggles, and I laughed hard at the absurdity of it all. Pockets continued.

"I had to spend the night poking out with my umbrella up! I'd done a 34-mile day and was really tired, didn't sleep at all. I even called the guys at Tarptent and they believed me! They're sending out a new tent!"

His story was so unimaginable that I could do little else but believe it. He ran off to Highway 49 to get a ride into Sierra City, where he needed to find the post office before it closed, so I carried on with Courtney and we agreed to meet him there. We'd heard great things about the Red Moose Café, run by Bill and Margaret Price. They allowed camping in their yard, and the food was not to be missed.

Courtney was 28 and came from Troy, Michigan. She claimed she could trace her ancestry back to the First Nations, and her features indicated this: black hair braided in pigtails and olive skin. She'd taken the summer off before returning to Wrightwood to work for the ski patrol in September. She was attractive and easy to talk to, and I could see why Pockets had taken a shine to her.

However, it wasn't going smoothly. Pockets had also realised he needed to put in miles before the snow fell up north. He walked quickly, faster than my usual coasting speed, but I liked it because I clocked up more miles when we hiked together. But Courtney was frustrated, not to mention fatigued, trying to keep up. She'd only joined him for a short section, and we were now in great physical shape, which didn't help her. Not knowing where she stood with him was frustrating; I got the impression she didn't even know if there was a relationship.

We reached the highway. I did my usual chivalrous act, suggesting she stand by the side of the road as I loitered in the bushes. She signalled to cars going in the opposite direction to Sierra City.

"It's that way!" I cried, pointing in the opposite direction.

"I realise that!" she retorted. "But you never know, there's no harm in trying!"

I watched, amazed, as a car driving out of town pulled up, turned around and offered her a ride. I got in, thanking him and congratulating her on a job well done.

We peered into the Red Moose Café, and Bill came out.

"Come in!" he said. "Upstairs, everyone is upstairs."

We walked into the lounge on the first floor.

"Fozzie! Dude!" Dozer cried, and everyone hugged. Walker Texas Ranger had arrived, along with Jack Straw and Pockets, who'd made the post office in time.

Sierra City was a small village with a population of around 200. First settled in 1850, an avalanche destroyed it during the winter of 1852-53. It remained derelict for years before being rebuilt and earning a living from several gold mines established in the area. I look back on the place with fond memories. There wasn't much there: The Red Moose Café, the Buckhorn Restaurant, and the local store, providing a reasonable resupply and some substantial burgers. Pine forest surrounded the town, and the sheer, looming Sierra Buttes towered above. It was relaxed, quiet and a super town to hang out in.

We sat in the bar that evening. Bill and Margaret talked

about the Red Moose, how they ran things and the local gossip to boot.

First, we learnt that we couldn't camp in the garden. A few residents had complained about the tents and hikers, whom they called 'vagrants'. True, many thru-hikers had given up their homes, so could be considered homeless, unemployed wanderers. But we didn't wander idly; nor did we deserve to be called vagrants. Some people, especially town folk, don't understand the appeal of walking 2,640 miles. As for the notion that PCT thru-hikers are a bunch of soiled misfits who smell, drink too much and demand unreasonable discounts on food and accommodation, well, I agree wholeheartedly!

Trying to placate their neighbours, Bill and Margaret asked us not to camp, instead offering their lounge and balcony. They were a terrific couple; welcoming and helpful to a fault. Karma and Detective Bubbles, two thru-hikers who'd ended their hike in Sierra City, also helped to run it.

Margaret filled me in on who had passed through. Cheeks and Mojave had visited, departed, and then finished their hike. It saddened me to hear this as they were the first hikers I'd become acquainted with. Mojave had stepped on a nail which penetrated her instep. Veering on the side of caution they went to Reno where a doctor advised the wound would take three weeks to heal. They decided the wait was too long, would put them too far behind schedule and deplete their funds. They cut their losses and returned home.

An absolute feast greeted us at dinner. We lined the bar of the Red Moose in anticipation as plate after plate of ribs kept coming. Mashed potato and sweet corn appeared, followed by silence for 30 minutes as we demolished an obscene amount of food. They asked only a modest fee, which could have barely covered the ingredients cost. Afterwards, we went to the Buckhorn Restaurant for drinks.

We'd been warned about the Buckhorn. The proprietor disliked thru-hikers, and we weren't expecting a cordial welcome. We ventured over out of curiosity, and because we wanted a drink.

The owner, Joanne, said hello as we entered, and her opening line suggested the rumours were true.

"Perhaps you'd all like to sit outside?" she offered.

I took this as a hint rather than an invitation. We declined and lined the bar, ordering a good amount of alcohol. We drank sensibly and behaved ourselves. Joanne was pleasant enough for the rest of the evening, but a noticeable tension remained.

The following day, Courtney, Pockets and I returned to the Buckhorn for lunch. The garden was a great place to hang out. Joanne's daughter, Sierra, served us, and we ordered the hiker staple of burger and fries. Sierra was polite, the service prompt, and the food excellent. We wondered where the rumours had come from; until we asked to pay.

"Can we have separate bills, please?" Courtney said.

Sierra sighed and looked rudely skyward.

"Well, no. You should've told me at the start. I'm not rewriting the bill now, so you can't."

She stormed off to the kitchen. We looked at each other in astonishment. I left my share of the money and returned to the Red Moose as I had to check emails. The others arrived shortly afterwards and filled me in on what had happened.

"I couldn't believe it," Pockets said. "I went to the bar and asked her nicely if we could have separate bills. She did her huffy puffy routine again and said, 'I don't have time for this.' Joanne took over and sorted it for us."

Despite the PCT sign on the window welcoming hikers, perhaps 'Hikers not welcome' would've been more appropriate. We ate lunch at the store after that.

I slept on the balcony that night, but woke in the morning to a little sweet payback. Snoozing occasionally, I rolled over and peered through the wooden railings towards the Buckhorn. Joanne had just arrived for work and unlocked the door. Sierra plodded reluctantly behind and, thinking no-one could see her, picked her nose and scratched her arse in one beautiful, synced unison. Imminent revenge was a joy to behold.

"Morning Sierra!" I cried out, motioning to my nose. "Anything good up there?"

I received the evilest glare ever dished out in northern California. She gave me the finger and disappeared inside. It took me 10 minutes to stop giggling.

Pockets needed to wait for a trekking pole delivery to the post office, so he took a zero. I followed suit, making the most of the town's laid-back atmosphere. Brains, another thru-hiker, arrived; and Hawkeye, a section hiker, also turned up to sample the delights of the Red Moose.

Walker, Dozer and Jack Straw had left, so Courtney, Brains, Hawkeye, Pockets and I chilled out in the lounge that evening. Hawkeye regaled us with stories about Sasquatch. Also known as Bigfoot, this huge, hairy biped is the stuff of legends. Thought to be up to 10 feet high, ape-like and weighing two to three times the average person, sightings are common in the Pacific Northwest. The legend fascinated me. Pockets, also enthralled, listened intently, admitting he wanted to photograph the creature.

Scientists claim Bigfoot is a mixture of folklore, misidentification and hoax. The scientific world assumes something doesn't exist until proved otherwise. In my book, if something can't be proved, it's intriguing. Scientists argue that a species must exist in numbers sufficient to sustain a breeding population. Put simply, if Sasquatch is real, there should be more of them; and if so, there must be evidence. I understand the sceptical view, but I'm also a sucker for unexplainable legends, myths and stories.

Before the 1950s, Bigfoot was just a story. However, in 1951, the British mountaineer Eric Shipton photographed what he described as a Yeti footprint. With public interest aroused, the legend grew. In 1958, at a construction site at Bluff Creek, California, several large footprints were found. Gerald Crew, a bulldozer operator, decided the markings warranted further examination. A cast was made of the prints, and the subsequent photographs appeared in the Humboldt Times. This, in turn, fuelled speculation, and the Associated Press Agency picked up the story.

Film footage of the beast surfaced in 1967, when Roger Patterson and Robert Gimlin released what they claimed was decisive proof of Bigfoot, also taken near Bluff Creek. It proved a hoax, and the two men later admitted that Bob Heironimus, a friend of Patterson, had worn an ape costume.

In 2007, Rick Jacobs, a hunter, captured an image triggered by a motion camera he'd left in the Allegheny National Forest, Pennsylvania. He claimed it was Sasquatch, although experts thought it nothing more sinister than a bear with a severe case of mange.

Many cryptozoologists claim 80 to 90 per cent of sightings aren't real. This raises the obvious implication that 10 to 20 per cent are. Another possibility is that Bigfoot is a close relative of Gigantopithecus, whose fossils have been discovered in China. Migration across the Bering land bridge from China to America could have occurred, but no remains of a biped similar to Bigfoot have been found in the US.

After discussing the topic with Pockets and Brains, we decided that our next trip would be a Sasquatch adventure. Pockets would do photography, aerial footage was down to Brains, while I'd document and write about the expedition.

I'd received an email from a company called Back Packing Light in Denmark. The owner, Niels Overgaard Blok, had read my blog and noticed my alarming habit of damaging sunglasses: I dropped them, sat on them, and on one occasion just plain forgot them. He was the Danish distributor for Numa Sports Optics, based in Arizona. They claimed their shades were unbreakable. Niels said he'd be happy to send me a pair, and I readily agreed.

I also gained another sponsor. Brains hiked in a kilt made by Sportkilt, based in California. In fact, I'd seen several guys use them. Pockets had started from Mexico with one, but lost a waist size, so switched to shorts. Everyone spoke highly of kilts; the air circulation around one's undercarriage was reason enough to try one. Brains suggested contacting

Sportkilt, so I tried my luck, emailed them and a day later they agreed. I was excited; thru-hiking is the one situation in life where blokes can get away with wearing a skirt. When the temperature dropped, I could pair it with tights as well.

Courtney had decided to return to Wrightwood. She'd talked with Pockets and thought it best. I left Sierra City reluctantly, with Pockets and Brains, and we formed a loose group over the ensuing days. Sometimes we walked as a unit, occasionally one had a burst of speed and went ahead, but we usually ended up camping together. They both hiked faster than me, but their pace was comfortable, and it meant I could cover a couple more miles each day.

I peered at the Feather River below from the bridge. I liked camping near water; the mosquitoes weren't as prolific as in recent weeks, so we'd stay near rivers or creeks in the evening without fear. Hawkeye had left a note on the trail saying he'd discovered a nice camp spot by the bank, so I ducked and weaved through the undergrowth until I found him. I stripped off and lowered myself into calm waters, sheltered by a few boulders. I washed my clothes, taking time to appreciate being clean, and then sat on a rock drying off.

"Fozzie! Fozzie! Look what I got!"

I turned to see Pockets skipping over rocks like an excited child, with something wrapped around his forearm. I couldn't make it out.

"What you got, chap?"

"Look, mate, it's a rattler!"

In the split second it took my eyes to signal my brain, Reginald at Nerve Centre HQ hit panic alert. In a matter of milliseconds, he'd discarded a few initial responses, ranging from 'Back off quickly' to 'Keep a safe distance.' He eventually delivered a simple, but very effective 'Get the fuck out of there!'

At first, I didn't believe Pockets, but as the reptile merged into focus, Reginald's advice hit home.

"Pockets, get that thing away from me! Are you nuts?!" I cried, backing away.

"Fozzie! It's OK, I killed it! Look, no head!"

Sure enough, a bloody stump was all that remained. The body continued writhing and curling around his wrist. It made me cringe.

I found Pockets' behaviour curious. One minute he merrily hopped along like a kid, then he'd mischievously creep up behind me. At first, he seemed amused to have scared me, but he showed real concern when I appeared uncomfortable.

He explained later that the snake had struck the sole of his shoe as he stepped over a log. Taking exception to this, he turned around, waved to get its attention and then punched it on the head. Having stunned it, he cut off its head. I watched as he skinned, gutted and prepared the beast for cooking. Even when we placed the meat over the embers, it still moved. My second taste of rattlesnake was just as delicious as the first.

Pockets had a bottomless pit of energy. It was hilarious watching him chomp at the bit, then reign himself back. He got up last in the morning, but bloody hell, when he was up, he really was up.

His pace was faster than mine but appeared effortless. Backpacker magazine had given him a PCT image deal, so he stopped often to take photos, staying in one spot for an hour or more. He spotted artistic potential in trees, skies, water, snow; places that wouldn't occur to me as good photo opportunities. After burning off extra energy this way, he'd run off a few more calories by upping the pace to catch back up with us.

Then he played his games. I think Pockets just came up with these ideas that amused him to offload more enthusiasm. Sometimes, Brains and I would be walking through a forest when he'd jump out from nowhere, growling loudly. Most of the time I found it funny, but if I was tired, it annoyed me.

I couldn't figure out how he appeared in front, when I was convinced he was behind. And, adamant he was ahead, he'd pop out barking from a tree behind me. He did this several times a day; I started to think he was some sort of PCT ninja.

In town he went crazy. We didn't need a TV in the motels: Pockets laid on the entertainment. Often, he opened the back window and barked. Immediately, half the canine population within a mile went completely bananas. After a while they'd calm down, leaving just a few dogs still yapping. Then, trying different types of bark, Pockets tried to converse with them. Seriously.

Then he'd start with the cats. . .

At one motel Brains and I sat on the porch, smoking cigarettes and supping on Pale Ales, when the door flew open. Pockets stepped out completely naked, hands covering his genitals, and cried: "Boys! Come back inside! I haven't finished with you yet!"

We both held our heads in our hands and denied any association with him.

His other favourite prank was waiting until one of us fell

asleep. The other person then took a photo, while Pockets stood in the frame, facing backwards, flexing his muscles, with his shorts dropped. Not with his camera, but with whoever's was asleep. I can't tell you how many times I checked my shots at day's end to find a picture of me or Brains fast asleep with two buttocks in clear view.

Alluringly insane, Pockets was certainly the wild card of the group and perhaps the entire PCT.

Brains, on the other hand, was more laid-back, intelligent and had interesting points of view to share. He seemed well-informed, which kept me on my intellectual guard. We regularly sat outside smoking when staying at motels, and a 10-minute cigarette break often became a 30-minute chat.

He was originally from Long Island, New York. He grew up in a suburb of New York City and used to ride the train into Manhattan, Queens or Brooklyn whenever he could. Moving west when he turned 18, he'd travelled around ever since. Illinois, Utah, Nevada, California, Colorado and North Carolina all lured him. He found work, stayed for a while and then moved on. He seemed like a modern-day Jack Kerouac.

Sitting outside a motel one evening, I asked him why he was hiking the PCT. I didn't normally ask that; it was too common a question. Something told me he had a different story to tell though.

"Fozzie, there's two main reasons I'm on the trail," he began. "First, I'm not comfortable with where my life has taken me, and I'm utterly bored with it. Exactly the same thing day after day. Get up, work, come home, watch TV, sleep, wake up and do it all over again. I wanted a challenge, the bigger the better."

"And the second reason?" I pushed him.

"Well, that's somewhat controversial I guess. I'm expecting Western civilisation to crumble. The greed and corruption displayed by the ruling powers is astonishing. I've been paying attention for a while and noticed things were getting in a terrible state, so I started saving money. Sure enough, the financial sector melted and brought the world to the brink. I figure it's just a matter of time until someone, somewhere, makes an irreversible decision and the banks, corporations and governments will fall."

"I feel the same. Do you really think we're heading that way?" I asked.

"Yes, for sure. Anyway, this leads me to why I'm hiking the PCT. I thought if I hiked the trail, I'd learn skills for the future. Stuff like wood lore, hunting and trapping, orienteering, weather reading and so on. I've lived in cities my whole life, so I know nothing about camping; the last time I ventured into the woods was 20 years ago. I thought then, as I do now – be smart and get a jump start on the skills I'd need. I'd live a meagre existence, move quickly over long distances and be able to find water, food and shelter when needed."

"So," he continued, "I wanted to make a change in my life to test myself, and I sure have. I haven't learnt that much though. I can read a map better but I can't hunt, yet. I've grasped endurance though."

It was an unusual view but one I could relate to. I often wondered when, not if, Western civilisation will collapse. Being in the wilderness and not seeing a building for days, let alone another human being, only fed those thoughts. I agreed with Brains; we're becoming too greedy, we live in a democracy but our voices aren't heard. We elect leaders based on broken promises. What can we do? Not much – write a letter to our MP or post on social media. It's frustrating to feel so helpless. Democracy isn't democracy any more.

As for living in a so-called free society, do we? In America you can be arrested for standing on a street corner. In the UK, we're filmed everywhere, entering a shop or driving our car. Our retinas are scanned at airports. The extent of information-gathering is astonishing, but where is it going?

My opinion is that we're heading to a tipping point where everyone says 'enough'. I think we're tired of restrictions on the way we live, of rules and regulations and of being ignored. History shows that people revolt if they're not heard. At that point, when everything comes tumbling down and society collapses, I, too, will escape the riots, meltdown, disorder, disarray and disappear into the woods.

Hawkeye had left and Pockets still snoozed as Brains and I climbed from the river the following morning. The 3,500-foot ascent seemed easy; we both sped up like raging locomotives. Leaves from last autumn still carpeted the trail, cushioning our feet, and poison ivy reached out from the undergrowth.

Poison ivy shouldn't be taken lightly. Although not life-threatening, even the slightest brush against it can leave the oil on your skin. The plant alkaloid urushiol causes severe itching, inflammation, colourless bumps and blistering in four out of five people who come into contact with it. I learnt from other hikers how to recognise it, as it's not native to England.

It only grows a couple of feet high, but was commonplace along the trail. 'The poison oak dance', as I heard others call it, described the contortions one had to perform to avoid it, bending our bodies and swerving this way and that. I became complacent at times, but I remained unscathed. Could I be one of the lucky individuals with resistance? It could be precarious hiking at night; my head torch picked out the shiny leaves, and I'd exercise a tad more caution.

The air cooled as we rose, affording a welcome respite from the heat. Stunted oak trees allowed shafts of sunlight through, which patterned the ground. Brains surged ahead, and I let him go. An hour later I saw another hiker approaching. We both stopped and chatted; his name was Peacemaker.

"I'm a month behind where I should be at this stage," I said.

"No," he replied with a wry smile and a glint in his eye. "You're exactly where you should be."

Peacemaker looked like a lost hippie. I'd watched him climbing the hill as I descended. He strolled up calmly, taking his time. Stopping usually suggested someone was open to chat; if not, they'd step to one side and let you pass. If they removed their backpack, often it meant they'd decided to rest, and this was something of an open invitation to do the same. I sat and talked with him for 10 minutes, glad to be resting. He was section-hiking part of the PCT, said he found it enjoyable, and may continue further. I liked his relaxed approach. He appeared at ease, without a care. As I left him, his words reverberated in my mind.

You're exactly where you should be.

I felt happy and secure. Regardless of my limited progress, hearing those words validated my situation and reminded me the PCT wasn't a race.

I passed Brains as he took a break. We'd split off again into our different paces, and I tried to catch Hawkeye to camp with him but couldn't, but he clearly wanted to get more distance in. Approaching 27 miles, I left a note on the trail for Brains telling him I intended to stop soon. Sure enough, he joined me an hour later. I'd become grateful for the company at camp. During the day we each had our own routines; sometimes we spent the whole day together, other times we walked alone. Neither of us knew where Pockets was, but as night fell, I left my poles by the trail in case he passed.

The wind ripped through the forest as I listened, marvelling at the sheer energy of the night. I crawled into my tent and updated my journal, contemplating something Hawkeye had mentioned in passing earlier. I'd heard him but wasn't paying attention. However, if I knew then the repercussions of his words during the latter stages of my hike, I'd have taken more notice.

'Bad weather up north forecast later in the year, Fozzie. They say it could be one of the worst winters for years.'

Chapter 11
Setting the Limits

I found things in the woods that I didn't know I was looking for, and now I'll never be the same.
Jennifer Pharr Davis, 2011 record holder for the fastest ever thru-hike of the Appalachian Trail

I left Brains snoozing in the morning and progressed quickly to Belden, a small community established back when the nearby railroad was built. Hemmed in to one side of the surrounding hills by the familiar sight of the Feather River, it was a sleepy little place with a population of just 22. The iron bridge was a useful navigation point as I descended. The few people I'd spoken to about Belden were none too enamoured with it and advised not to stop. I was glad I did though, I liked it.

I'd also heard about a diner and store, albeit two miles along the highway, so I was pleased to find a restaurant, bar, and simple shop in Belden itself. Resting on a bench outside, Pockets suddenly appeared next to me.

"Where the hell did you come from?" I said. "You're a bloody trail Ninja, mate. You materialise from nowhere!"

"Got in last night, me ol' mucker. Walked most of the morning and slept in that old building over the road."

Pockets had taken my accent to heart and now had a string of English words and phrases to his bow. "Me ol' mucker" was his favourite (it's a general term meaning friend). He'd also come up with "You gonna 'ave a bacon buttie, mate? Wiv sum, yer know, brawn sauce and a cuppa tea?"

Brains arrived shortly after, and we went for breakfast, which merged into lunch. Before we knew it, it was afternoon. We swam in the river, and I thanked the Feather for giving me two good washes in as many days. Pockets showed us the old monument he'd slept in, which seemed a great spot to use again.

I often pondered the place of technology in the outdoors. Hikers carried various gizmos; head lamps, cell phones, maybe a tablet or GPS. All designed to make our lives more comfortable, and some, like the head lamp, were considered necessities. I wondered how outdoor science might advance, and what equipment we'll have in 20 years. Solar tent fabric? Heads-up displays? Body implants perhaps? Monitoring our temperature, water requirements, pulse, and other information. Kinetic trekking poles or shoes that produce electricity from movement? There's a line I couldn't cross though, a point where tech interferes with the experience. Even now it's going too far, I often saw hikers with earphones listening to music, something I did rarely. Instead, I liked to hear the sounds around me. There'll always be a balance.

Escaping computers, phones, and other annoyances was one motivation for me to do the PCT. Although I'd find life and work impossible without them, retreating to nature offered a tech vacation. I never missed the internet, and my phone was usually off. I spent time in motels watching the TV, but forgot it on the trail.

Experiencing the outdoors or – even better, the untamed wilderness – imparts a wisdom of what is truly needed for happiness. Though material pleasures provide a sense of achievement, the feeling is only temporary. Two weeks after buying a car, it is just a car. That bright, shiny new cell phone is exciting for a few days until the next model is released. It's a never-ending loop of buy and replace, a fake pleasure.

If you're after true fulfilment, I say take a walk in the wilderness.

We started the 5,000-foot climb out of Belden the following morning and bumped into Billy Goat on his way down. Perhaps the most famous face on the PCT in recent years, he's walked the route countless times, and each year ventures out in the summer to do more. He considered the trail his home, and spent weeks there. Wispy white hair and a long beard earned him his nickname. I'd met him twice before; first at the kick-off party and again on Fuller Ridge. We chatted for a few minutes and took photos, wishing each other well.

The chatter turned to distance. We now pulled in 25-mile days on average. This was comfortable and respectable progress. We discussed how far we could walk in one day. 30-milers presented no problem, mid-30s likewise. Silly mileage was anything over 40, 50-miles plus was classed as mad, and in the unlikely event that we ever managed a 60, that would be insane. I'd not reached the 30s before, at least not on the PCT, and neither had Brains nor Pockets, but it was a tempting prospect.

As with most sports, there are a few die-hards who set out to break records. Andrew Skurka is one of them. In 2006 he walked a 1,744-mile section of the PCT in 45 days and 16 hours, averaging 38.2 miles per day. To put this in perspective, it was three times quicker than my pace.

On the 3rd of November 2007, Skurka became the first person to complete the 6,875-mile Great Western Loop, averaging 33 miles per day for 208 consecutive days. On the 19th of July 2005, he hiked a 7,800-mile coast-to-coast walk from Cape Gaspe in Quebec to Cape Alava in Washington State, taking 373 days. He said of his section of the PCT:

"I succeeded in doing what I set out to do. I dropped 25 pounds and am currently a little leaner than I was at the end of my sea-to-sea hike. I now think of a 40-mile day as hardly unusual; hiking 45-50 miles a day successively presents a more notable but entirely doable challenge. And I have a much greater understanding of how I must manage my mind and my body while I'm pushing it to this level. Yeah, I only spent an afternoon at Kennedy Meadows; but I'm a more enlightened backpacker as a result. I'm now in a much better position to succeed in some of the challenging hikes I have planned over the next few years."

In 2004, Scott Williamson, on his fourth attempt, became the first person to 'yo-yo' the PCT. A yo-yo means completing a long-distance route, then hiking back to the beginning again, essentially hiking the trail twice. He took 205 days to complete the 5,280 miles, an average of 25.8 miles per day. In 2011, he set the record for hiking the PCT in an astonishing 64 days, 11 hours and 19 minutes, averaging 41.1 miles per day. His pack base weight (without food or water) was 8.6 pounds, under half of mine at 19.8 pounds. Scott has thru-hiked the PCT thirteen times!

He didn't use a stove, water treatment device or a bear canister. He slept under a tarpaulin and used a quilt (made famous by backpacking equipment designer Ray Jardine) instead of a sleeping bag. He removed the waist belt and sternum strap from his pack and didn't use trekking poles. Rising at 5.30am, he'd be hiking by 6am. His breakfast consisted of what he called a 'green shake', containing protein powder, a green supplement, spirulina, soy milk powder and water. Lunch was a swift 15-minute affair using his homemade 'Phat Doug' bars, and dinner consisted of a dehydrated refried bean powder, crumbled organic corn tortilla chips and a generous splash of olive oil.

"That may sound very unappealing to you," he once said during a presentation. "Actually, right now I'd agree, but it gets to be delicious and satisfying after several weeks on the trail."

If you're compelled to thru-hike long-distance and can't decide which trail to try, how about doing all three? Walk the Appalachian, Pacific Crest and Continental Divide trails and become a Triple Crowner. Many hikers have completed this feat and others, myself included, aspire to.

On the 31st of December 2000, Brian Robinson arrived at Springer Mountain, the southern terminus of the

Appalachian Trail. On New Year's Day 2001, he hiked north. Nine months and 27 days later he'd not only completed the Appalachian Trail, but also the Pacific Crest and Continental Divide Trails. He became the first person to hike all three American long-distance routes in one year, a total of 7,371 miles.

The Appalachian Trail also has its fair share of record breakers. In 2008, Jennifer Pharr Davis set the fastest women's time for a supported thru-hike in a remarkable 57 days, 8 hours and 35 minutes for the 2,175-miles.

In 2011 she vowed to do even better and subsequently beat the men's record of 47 days, 13 hours and 31 minutes set by Andrew Thompson in 2005. Having averaged 38 miles per day for her 2008 record, she had to pull off the same feat 10 days faster. 46 days, 11 hours and 20 minutes later she set the AT thru-hike record for both men and women. This equates to a leg-numbing 47.2 miles per day. My personal best for a day's hike on the PCT was 38.5 miles, 8.7-miles short of what Jennifer cracked out each day, every day.

"The first two weeks were a physical challenge," she said afterwards. "Adjusting to back-to-back 30 to 45-mile days is brutal, especially on New England terrain. The weather was bad, the trail was slick, and hiking in New England usually involves using your hands or butt to overcome significant grades. I'd finish each day looking like I'd come from a war zone: muddied, bloodied and bruised. After the first two weeks, the remaining hurdles were mental and emotional. Mentally, it was hard because I never had a break. It is really difficult to maintain mental focus for 57 days."

The unsupported PCT record was set on August 7th, 2013, when hiker Heather 'Anish' Anderson of Bellingham,

Washington smashed it. Having averaged around 44 miles each day, she beat the old record by almost four days, reaching Canada in 60 days, 17 hours, and 12 minutes.

It gets better. Heather's feat was trumped in 2014 by Joe McConaughy, who recorded 53 days, 6 hours, and 37 minutes. Wait, there's more. A 26-year-old dentist from Belgium by the name of Karel Sabbe romped home in 52 days, 8 hours, and 25 minutes in 2016.

His press release read:

The toughest day of the entire PCT was when, after a 2-hour sleep, I had to run 57 miles and do 3 major alpine passes: Pinchot, Mather and Muir Pass. Then I had to descend all the way to the Muir Trail Ranch where I'd booked a night. I arrived there at 11pm, but nearly everybody was asleep. There was one guy awake, but he didn't want to wake up the manager and told me to leave the property. I was desperate as I didn't have food nor sleeping equipment, and I was dead tired. In the end he woke her up, and she heated up my prepared meal, showed me my cabin and told me about the hot spring pool that they had in which I could soak. Oh, how a miserable day can end magically.

In August 2015, the AT unsupported record was beaten by Matt Kirk, who registered a time of 58 days, 9 hours, and 38 minutes. That is, until Heather Anderson completed her unsupported attempt a month later in 54 days, 7 hours, and 48 minutes.

The fastest AT hike at the time of writing was set in 2018 by a Belgium dentist, Karel Sabbe. He romped home in an incredible 47 days, 7 hours and 39 minutes, beating a record set in 2017 by Joe McConaughy of 45 days, 12 hours and 15 minutes.

I remember Jennifer Pharr Davis setting her record back in 2008, and being amazed. In just ten years that record has been shortened by an amazing ten days. By the time you've read this, I expect someone else will have knocked a chunk off again.

It's worth noting there are two types of hikers who take on these challenges: those who hike with all their gear and re-supply themselves, known as unsupported, and those who have assistance, such as a support vehicle, called supported. Pharr Davis was helped by her husband, Drew, on her attempts, and Matt, Heather and Joe deserve even more respect by setting their records unsupported.

And the guy that's trumping everyone? His name is Karl Bushby, and he's from England. Karl is making Scott, Brian, Jennifer, Andrew, and everyone else look like we're taking baby steps in kindergarten. Allow me to explain.

Karl is attempting to be the first person ever to walk around the world entirely on foot, with no transport. And before you question if that's actually possible in light of a small problem known as oceans, he's figured that out as well.

He started this mammoth undertaking from Punta Arenas, Chile, on November 1st, 1998, and he estimates the journey will take 14 years by the time he arrives back home in Hull. If the timespan doesn't grab your attention, then consider the distance: 36,000 miles! That's 14 Pacific Crest Trails!

He's walked the entire length of South America, through America itself, into Canada and Alaska – where he needed to get to Russia. Believe it or not, there's only 76-miles of ocean on his round the world walk. His first obstacle was the infamous Bering Strait, a stretch of sea separating the USA from Russia. During winter, the sea freezes either completely or partially. In 2006, Karl and a French explorer called Dimitri Kieffer walked (where possible), crawled and stumbled over ice and water to arrive in Russia 15 days later. When he reaches the French coast, he has permission from the authorities to walk through the channel tunnel.

Currently, Karl is battling Russian bureaucracy, as he's only allowed a 90-day visa. In 2008, as a result of these delays, he only managed three weeks of walking to reach Bilibino. This swampy area can only be traversed in the winter when the surface has frozen solid. He had to leave after his visa ran out.

From late 2008 to 2010, Karl spent most of his time in Mexico, for reasons to do with costs and funding. Because of the Russian delays, he lost valuable sponsors.

In 2011 he reached Srednekolymsk, again having to leave because of visa problems. He needs to complete another 560 miles to reach roads and not have to rely on the permafrost. As of 2017 he's not home yet.

People such as Andrew, Scott, Brian, and Jennifer fire the imagination. Physical boundaries are pushed and records smashed, setting extreme feats of endurance. I never set out to break any times; my goal was purely completion, but seeing what others have achieved makes me want to better myself. Distance is the obvious target; 2,640 miles is a long way on foot. As I hiked the PCT, the Continental Divide Trail seemed viable, as did the Appalachian Trail (which I subsequently completed in 2012). But I also started thinking about other, more original goals. Approaching mid-way on the PCT, I was already planning my next thru-hike.

Of course, let's not assume that America has all the best

hikes; it doesn't. There are numerous 'E' routes in Europe, and they're fantastic. The E8 starts in Ireland and finishes 2,920-miles later in Turkey. The E4 begins in south-west Spain and stretches east 6,250-miles to Greece. Or perhaps a round-the-coast walk of the UK? I could immerse myself in my home country over a year and increase my hiking total by a dizzying 6,500-miles. These challenges excite me.

Dozer told me after his thru-hike how he'd managed a 62-mile day. I didn't believe him until he told me about it.

"I'd not planned the day," he began. "But I was trying to catch Crow, Dundee, and Walker Texas Ranger. I'd been pushing hard doing a four mile-per-hour pace when darkness fell. I stumbled across the Pro from Dover, who was also hiking in the dark, and we startled each other. We pushed on to catch them but figured they must have camped off trail somewhere. Looking at the map, we realised we were only 25 miles from Mount Hood, and the Timberline Lodge, famous for their breakfast buffet. We carried on with that in mind, only stopping for water and ibuprofen. We hiked fast, but I began to hurt. My feet were blistered, I had chafing, and my knee was painful and swollen. The hardest part was the 2,000-foot steep climb to the lodge on sandy soil; we kept slipping. We took turns leading, which motivated us, and we made it as the sun rose. It was epic! 21 hours of hiking took its toll, but after breakfast and a hot tub I was happy that we'd done it."

I also contacted the Pro from Dover who gave me his version of events:

"I never set out to do a huge day. I planned to do about 50 miles which, although big, was something I'd done before. I've completed 40 miles at least a half-dozen times and one 50 to get across the Oregon border. I'm a strong hiker and relish big days. I liked to bust it out occasionally and prove my mettle.

The motivation centred on getting to Timberline Lodge on Mt Hood in time for breakfast. I figured I'd hike a 50 and then wake up early to crush another 15 in the morning to make the buffet. That would allow a couple hours of feasting.

The day didn't start well. I woke up before sunrise and it was chilly, but I just wasn't moving fast. I found water and took a long break. Dozer, Pyjamas, Uncle Gary, and JC found me. I hadn't seen these guys since Kennedy Meadows, so I was surprised and happy, especially Dozer, because I'd hiked with him; we started the same day way back in Campo. I still wanted to make the buffet, but they weren't keen. I was stubborn and wasn't backing down from my plan.

I hiked on, still firmly bent on doing 50. Dozer caught up as darkness fell, and we turned on our headlamps. He was hoping to camp with Crow, Dundee, and Walker Texas Ranger, but we couldn't find them. By this point, I had a 40 in place, and he'd done 35. He decided he'd keep going with me. Big days are better with someone to go through them with.

The thought of doing a big day enticed him, but his head was churning. I remember saying to him at one point, 'I'll hike as far as you want.' I wanted to get as close to Timberline as possible, and I needed his support. It became Dozer's golden carrot as well. The prospect of the morning breakfast buffet got him excited too. He'd never done a monster day of 40 or more miles, and now was his chance.

We kept going and neared the 50-mile mark for me, deciding we'd make it to the lodge no matter what. Once Dozer made that mental leap, we knew we'd push ourselves to the end.

The late night and early morning section took a while, and we slowed down. We used instant coffee every few miles to give us that recharge for the next leg. Rest for 20 minutes, make coffee, eat something and then get going again. The last stretch was the longest; it seemed never ending. Time moved slower, miles weren't clicking off as they'd been earlier. We were mentally tired from pushing our bodies. I would've loved a nap but knew I wouldn't wake up. We had to keep going all night; sleep wasn't on the agenda. The overnight part was methodical. I'd been hiking for three-quarters of a day, but my legs still kept moving. I was tired from the over-exertion, but the muscle memory remained and I carried on. On the final climb I just shut my eyes, and my legs carried me. I could keep my eyes closed for a minute and still hike. It was weird; I knew where I had to go.

The sun lightened the sky faintly, and we were basically there. Nothing could stop; we had just half a mile. The joy of accomplishment was awesome. We'd done this stupendous hike and pushed ourselves further than we ever had. I don't know how to describe that feeling. It was intense: we felt invincible but exhausted, both mentally and physically. I loved it.

But I never recovered from that superlative effort until my thru-hike ended. That run of miles beat up my legs and sapped the strength; I lost all my speed. I'd still hike big days, but they were mentally exhausting and from then on, I hated them, even 30s. I simply couldn't push myself as hard anymore. With my legs wiped out, all I had was endurance. I continued to enjoy the hike, but the physical aspect depressed me. As a result, my hiking style changed. Although I still did the miles, I switched to a new pace. I learnt about myself, and I'm much wiser for it."

Talk of a 40-mile day ebbed away, and after 26 miles we reached a clearing by the side of the trail before Humboldt Summit. It was a beautiful evening, and we left the tents in our packs, instead laying out our sleeping bags beneath an inky-black sky, which the trees framed perfectly. As our eyes became accustomed to the light, the Milky Way appeared, misting from one side of the horizon to the other. It was so vast I felt I could let go and fall into infinity.

I woke early, around 5am; got up and put some water on the boil. Brains still snoozed, and Pockets, who I thought was in his sleeping bag, appeared from behind a rock carrying his camera equipment.

"Mucker!" he cried, as though he'd been awake for several hours. "Got a sweet time lapse of the sun coming up, what a great morning!"

It was another perfect day. We left to complete the remaining 22 miles to Highway 36 and get a ride into Chester. A fine layer of powdery soil covered the trail, mixing with sweat on our legs and leaving a sticky mess. As we hiked into the night with our head lamps on, our view became obscured and glistened with billions of floating dust particles. Brains wore his bandana over his face to stop choking. Even our feet were brown with a congealed mix of muck at day's end. By now I'd stopped washing my feet, because I couldn't be bothered – and I felt a sense of achievement at coming to terms with my filth. Brains and Pockets had long since embraced the dirt, and after a week on trail we'd emerge from the woods looking as if we'd put in a shift down the local mine.

"I can't stop thinking about getting into town," said Pockets, breaking the silence mid-afternoon. "I'm gonna get some Ben and Jerry's, you know, buy four and get four free? Then, I'm gonna empty them all in the bath, lie in it and roll around till I'm completely covered. And, and, you two are going to watch me."

"Actually, I won't be there, Pockets," I said, stifling a laugh, and noticing Brains up ahead catching drift of the conversation and giggling uncontrollably.

Before the highway we stopped by a granite obelisk. I brought up the rear, and when I arrived, the guys had downed packs. Pockets grinned as though he'd just found a hidden 24-hour café serving free, all-you-can-eat food.

"What you smirking at?" I asked.

"Me ol' mucker! We're halfway!"

I did a double-take at the small monument with an engraved, gold inscription.

'PCT mid-point, Canada 1325 miles, Mexico 1325 miles.'

Suddenly, I focused and my situation became very lucid. I'd completed half the distance. It was August 20th, 119 days since I started back in Campo. This meant that at my current pace, I'd finish at Christmas. If I was to complete before winter, I needed to hike the same distance again in half the time. Immediately, Hawkeye's words returned.

"Bad weather up north forecast later in the year, Fozzie. They say it could be one of the worst winters for years."

I looked at Pockets and then Brains. They both beamed, as did I, but I sensed an underlying worry, and I'm sure they thought the same. We pushed our fears to one side, shook hands, jumped about, took some photos and set off to celebrate in Chester.

"Guys, do you know the name of the town that's famous for where most thru-hikers quit and end their hike?" asked Pockets, after we'd walked in silent contemplation for a few minutes. Neither Brains nor I responded.

"Chester," he added. "The town we're heading for now."

Chapter 12
Paw Fall would be Awful

You will never make it to Canada.
Billy Goat

I did make it to Canada.
Patrick 'Wideangle' Pöndl

P ockets was right. Many hikers crashed out after reaching
Chester. When the euphoria abates, the full extent of
the situation smashes into them. They now know what
hiking 1,325-miles feels like, and with shock, realise they have
to do the same distance again. After celebrating their
achievement in town, a few cannot comprehend what faces
them. It was a sobering thought we didn't entertain, but mind
games can creep up on you. Feel fine one minute but slowly it
sinks in; fears surface and doubts crumble one's resolve. We
walked in silence to the highway and caught a quick ride into
Chester with Rick, a passing builder.

"I always stop if I see you guys," he said. "I take my hat
off to you."

Reaching town after dark, we decided against a motel but

planned to get one early the following morning, making the most of a full day in comfort. We wolfed down a burger at the Kopper Kettle café, and after scouting for suitable sleeping spots we slept in the park, tucking ourselves away from prying eyes. A few kids kicked a ball around, smoke rose from a family barbecue and as dusk fell the park gradually emptied.

We stayed in a motel the following day and moved out after one night. Pockets' words rang in my ears, and I was keen not to quit my adventure there as many others had before. Trooper had turned up at the motel and, while Brains and I ate lunch, he got a ride with Pockets eight miles back to the trailhead.

Trooper had left by the time we caught Pockets, and we made our way to the Drakesbad Ranch. We were on a roll in terms of food availability. Our stomachs still groaned from Chester, Drakesbad loomed and a day's hike away lay Hat Creek resort, home to trail angels Georgi and Dennis Heitman. We entertained no thoughts of quitting. In fact, it was quite the reverse; leaving town quickly was a good move, and the prospect of eating always proved an incentive.

We set a good pace through intermittent forest dotted with open spaces and stopped at Boiling Spring Lake. A warning sign advised not to approach the small expanse of water that happily bubbled and steamed 50 feet from the trail.

I treat signs telling me not to do something the same as I treat someone in authority. Albeit with caution, I walked near the bank as Pockets took some photos and Brains rested and smoked. Being near volcanic activity gives me the willies, so I was glad when Pockets finished, and we continued to the ranch.

The forest melted into lush meadow stretching away either side. Despite breaks in the trees that afternoon, it was a relief to be in the open. We'd barely dropped our packs outside the Drakesbad Ranch when the front door opened and a waiter appeared.

"Guys! You thru-hiking? It's end of August; you late!" he said in broken English.

We laughed nervously, painfully aware of our situation.

"Come in! Sit!"

Drakesbad Ranch was nestled in the middle of nowhere. I couldn't even see a road leading to it. Guests feel welcome at this forest nirvana. There's a chance to relax in the hot springs, eat great food and forget the nine-to-five. They gave us water and our waiter came over.

"Guys, what you want eat? You're a little late, kitchen is closing but we have leftover quiche and plenty broccoli." Smiling often, his grasp of English was amusing as he left out the occasional, unimportant words. I tried to guess his nationality.

We looked at each other and paused.

"I'm not actually hungry," Brains offered first.

"Strangely, neither am I," I added before Pockets also agreed.

The waiter looked momentarily perplexed. During the season, a steady stream of hikers visit Drakesbad and demolish obscene quantities of food. Everyone seemed as confused as us. Whispers floated over from the waitresses, the kitchen door twitched, and eyes peered round from nooks and crannies. Silence fell in the dining room for a few seconds.

"Don't want any food?!" said Billie, the proprietor,

leaning against the kitchen door. "First time in 10 years a hiker said that. Is it a money thing?"

"No," Brains replied. "We have money, just not much of an appetite."

"Well," she continued, "You're all eating, and I don't want to hear another word about not being hungry!"

We fell silent as though the headmaster had rapped our knuckles. Billie was jesting, of course, but we weren't about to argue with her. The food arrived, followed by chocolate mousse, and we realised how hungry we actually were. Pockets tried to eat but became distracted by several lovely Slovenian waitresses.

"I'm moving to Slovenia after my hike," he said.

We thanked them profusely, and they didn't even want payment. We left a 30-dollar tip, which they reluctantly but gratefully accepted. They gave us towels, and we headed to the hot springs.

For an hour we floated, laughing and relaxing. The water soothed tired muscles as steam lifted skywards, catching the beams from a full moon. If it weren't for a staff member who had to close up, we'd have stayed another hour. Walking a mile along a track away from Drakesbad, I kept glancing back as the forest slowly engulfed the building until it finally disappeared.

Four miles into the following day, we emerged at a campground.

"Guys, this isn't right," I said sheepishly. I'd been leading and following an unwritten rule, responsible for navigation.

"It's not, no," Brains confirmed, checking his map.

We eventually pinpointed our location, and lethargy set in. Having put in four miles on the wrong track, and needing the same to get back, we decided the clear and obvious solution was to drink beer. Pockets managed to flag a ride, and we soon arrived at Old Station. Trail angels extraordinaire Georgi and Dennis Heitman showed us round their home, fed us and provided a bed each.

The guys camped in the grounds, and I grabbed a spare bed in the tree house, complete with TV, ageing video recorder and a wonderful selection of 80s movies.

Before embarking on my journey I'd contacted Matt Swaine, editor of Trail magazine, a popular hiking publication in England. I asked whether they'd be interested in a PCT feature. They liked it but the timing was off. I'd spoken to Pockets, and he was keen to have his photos published too, so I tried again.

We sent them six of the best shots. I made our adventure sound as enticing as possible, and two hours later I received an email.

"Hi, Keith. I'm heading out on holiday for a couple of weeks, but I am interested in this and I've passed it forward for discussion. I'll hopefully reply before I leave on Wednesday. All the best. Matt."

Two days later another email arrived.

"Hi, Keith. We will run with something but the current issue is looking very busy, so might have to wait until the next one. The editorial people will get back to you. Hope all's going well with you! Matt."

I went nuts when I read it.

"Pockets!" I cried. "POCKETS!"

"Mucker, wassup?"

"We got a magazine article!"

We jumped around excited and then realised we had to get to Burney. The internet connection at the Heitmans was slow, and Pockets stored his photos on a laptop, which was in his bounce box at the post office. Georgi kindly drove us to town, with Brains coming along, and before long we'd checked in at the Shasta Pines Motel. I had to write the piece for Trail in two days, while Pockets picked the best photos. They needed high resolution images, so each shot took an hour to send (the motel's internet wasn't any better than the Heitmans and the files were massive). Eventually, having sent the pictures, we celebrated by cracking open a case of Pale Ale.

I was keen to get going the following morning, but the guys wanted an extra day. I pondered doing the same, but guilt overcame me. I said I'd see them up trail and waited by McDonald's for a ride out of town. After succumbing to a chicken nugget temptation, I returned outside, then went back in for more.

It proved difficult getting to the trail. My first ride dropped me five miles up the road. I stuck my thumb out again, hoping someone else would hit the brakes. Steve, a plumber, offered to take me to the Lassen Volcanic National Park, which he duly did. Next, a local lady called Marjorie stopped and drove to the park entrance but no further, as she'd have to pay to get in.

"There's an entrance fee to the park," the woman at the gate told me.

"I'm hiking the PCT," I replied. "Just took a day out to resupply." I gave her my permit, and she waved me through, wishing me good luck.

I was still 10 miles from the car park where we'd strayed off the trail. I walked to the visitor centre and grabbed a cold soda from the machine. Then I looked for ride number four. A police SUV pulled up alongside, tyres crunching on the gravel. A smoky window lowered.

"You know you can't hitch a ride here, don't you?" she said.

"Really?" I asked.

"Yes. It's illegal to hitch in a national park."

I didn't know this but still flashed a mischievous grin and plumped for the innocent tourist routine.

"I'm English," I said. "Sorry, I didn't realise. Shit, how the hell am I gonna get back up to the park at Kings Creek?"

"I don't know, but you may be walking. What are you doing here anyway?"

"Hiking the PCT."

"Oh, really?" Her eyebrows raised. "You're late aren't you? You must be the last of the hikers, you're the last Englishman. You can't hitch though, I'm afraid."

"What are you up to now?" I hardened the accent and looked forlorn, but she sensed my attempt.

"No way!" she exclaimed. "I just clocked off. I'm going home to have a long, hot bath and to relax. Don't even think about asking me for a ride."

"Come on. You're gonna get back and feel guilty because you should've aided a helpless hiker instead of leaving me here in the wilderness. There's bears and lions out here, you know. Do you want that on your conscience? Please? It's just a few miles up the road."

She sighed, looked skyward and smiled again.

"Hang on," she said, reaching for the radio. "Guys, where

are you? Are you due at the entrance?"

The radio crackled, but I couldn't make out the reply.

"OK," she continued. "You're in luck, Mr Englishman. My buddies are starting their shift. If you wait 30 minutes, they'll grab some lunch and be here soon; you got a ride. I'm going home minus any guilt complex. And don't hitch in the national parks!"

With that she flashed me a cheeky smile, tossed her hair, slipped on her Ray-Bans and drove off.

Sitting in the back of my first American cop car, I quizzed her mates on why they needed seven guns between them. Two shotguns, two assault rifles, something resembling a sniper rifle all sat upright between them, plus their holstered pistols. For a moment I was Rambo, chaperoned back to the town outskirts. It made my day.

Finding the same track to Kings Creek easily, I soon came to the junction with the PCT where we'd taken the wrong turn before. It was late afternoon, and I needed to put in some miles to make up time. The section finished back at Burney, around 60 miles away. I'd rest overnight at the Heitmans' again and grab a bite to eat.

I hiked in fading light. The forest was dense, so I turned on my headlamp. I tried not to remind myself about walking in the woods after dark; it went against everything my parents told me. Bird shrieks startled me, and twigs snapped in the darkness amid an eerie, enveloping silence.

I looked up trail. A pair of yellow eyes reflected in my headlamp, pausing 50 feet ahead, and then disappeared. I thought of The Amityville Horror movie, where Margot Kidder's son tells her about his invisible friend who's just gone out of the window. As she looks out, a pair of menacing white eyes flash at her and disappear. My mind wasn't helping the situation. I was convinced a hungry wolf had crept through the undergrowth, flanked me and at any moment would jump on my back – and it wasn't after a tummy scratch.

Eventually, after 10 miles, I left the trees, entering a moonlit clearing. I walked for a further half-mile to the next forest and camped just in the trees with faint moonlight for company. It felt strange being separated from the guys, and I missed them at evening camp. For a while at least, I had to accept it.

I woke at 5am to light rain tickling my face and disturbing the dried leaves. Weak sunlight filtered through the pines, and I peered up at dark clouds racing overhead. It was September 1st, and my surroundings looked distinctly autumnal. Foliage withered and faded, and California had chilled. My watch showed 48F, and I shivered, wondering why the temperature had plummeted from the seventies yesterday. Skipping breakfast, I set off quickly to warm up.

I reached Hat Creek again and decided against calling the Heitmans because I knew, especially given the cold weather, that I'd struggle to move on if I stopped there. I went to the café and ordered the biggest breakfast they had. I chatted to two local hikers eager to hear about my hike, then headed off to make inroads into a brutal section of the PCT.

Hiking a long-distance trail is not about giving up a few months of your life. It's about having a few months to live. The harsh days, when everything goes wrong, when you doubt the whole idea of thru-hiking, when rain flies in your face and you've run out of stove fuel – these are only ever just days. Lying in my tent after a brutal few miles, when I thought the world was against me, I knew the next day would be kinder. And the bad times came rarely; a thru-hike is a heart-warming experience that made me glad to be alive.

I pondered the hard days as I approached Hat Creek Rim, a notoriously hot and dry 26-mile stretch out of Hat Creek, so hot it's more typical of southern California. The Heitmans maintained a water cache at the start. After a short climb to the top, I drank some fluids. The clouds dispersed, and the temperature rose alarmingly. The next water cache lay eight hours away, plus breaks, with no water sources in-between, so I filled my bottles and a further bag, which I usually used for camp. It sprung a leak and a jet of water shot from the side.

"Shit," I mumbled.

I pulled out a waterproof compression bag and emptied the contents back into my pack. Filling it, I strapped it securely and strode off. Two hours later, it had also leaked, leaving most of the water on the trail. I had just one bottle, but rather than return to the cache, I pressed on: perhaps not the wisest of decisions. But any thru-hiker will tell you that making miles is far more important than safety!

The heat was stifling, and Hat Creek was earning its reputation. Walking in that temperature, I should have been carrying at least 64oz, ideally 128oz; I had just 32oz. The rim dropped away to flatter lands. Scorched blonde grass waved weakly; the horizon blurred to a hazy apparition. Stunted trees appeared ill and withered. It felt more like the African bush.

Three hours and nine miles in, I stopped to eat. My throat felt rough as I coaxed the last few trickles from my bottle. I sucked on candy, hoping to elicit some moisture response, then picked up my pack and continued. I had no choice but to walk the entire rim; there was no water until the next cache, 17 miles away.

A reflection caught my eye. Cattle had gathered round a shallow pond; they dispersed as I approached. It wasn't water, more a black sludge with green organisms floating on the surface. Flies buzzed round my head. I pulled out my filter and sat by the edge. It stank, cattle dung littered the area, and a cow eyed me curiously, trying to convince me otherwise. I relented, put my filter away, and walked off. Even at this stage, I still contemplated returning to the first cache; now 10 miles behind, instead of 16 miles, or five hours to the next one. I had visions of diners in the café a week later, tutting and shaking their heads as they read the Hat Creek Herald, headlining with "English hiker found dead with no water."

Reginald at Nerve Centre HQ had also overheated. While trying to cope with borderline dehydration, heatstroke and sunburn, he sent out orders faster than a thru-hiker's mouth at an all-you-can-eat breakfast. His attention centred on Nancy, responsible for the main organs. Normally faultlessly efficient, she, too, was struggling to stabilise.

"I'm running way above normal temperature down here, Reginald. He must know he needs water; I need two bottles just to maintain all systems. Anything above that is a bonus."

"Do what you can," Reginald replied. "We're in a dry zone. I see parched, dusty soil. I don't think there's any water coming, so you'll have to shore up the defences and wait."

Five hot hours later, I saw a white sign by the side of the trail:

'Cache down here!'

Sheltered in the trees sat a solitary chair.

"Don't rely on the cache 26 miles in," Georgi Heitman had said a few days earlier. "It is maintained but not often; there's a good chance it'll be empty."

10 large water bottles were tied to a tree. As I gingerly lifted each one, my hopes fell further and further.

"There's a good chance it'll be empty..."

It was. I was coherent but in poor shape. I had a pounding headache, felt tired and lethargic. My throat was so dry I couldn't even muster a swallow. Then, I noticed a cool box under a bush. I lifted it and it felt heavy; my hopes rose. I pried the lid open and peered in. One lonely jug of water sat in the corner, and two sodas slid down and rested next to it. Speckled with thousands of condensation bubbles; they were still cold! I drank one quickly without coming up for air and subsequently spent several minutes burping. I swallowed more water and left one soda and some water in case someone was behind.

From the searing heat of the rim, I descended and camped near Lake Britton amid the gentle hum of a nearby waterworks. The countryside in the morning was transformed and reminded me of home. Lush green grass, lakes idling between hills, familiar trees such as oak and elm. A low mist hovered over the water, and a heron fished.

After the dry weather, rain caught me off guard. Feeling restricted in my waterproofs, I removed them and carried on regardless, dodging a few light showers. The undergrowth was damp as I brushed against wet bushes, chilling me further. I wondered whether Pockets and Brains had overtaken me. I checked for footprints, being familiar with their tread patterns, but there wasn't any.

The temperature had dropped, and this, together with the moisture in the air, attracted tiny insects. They drove me insane, constantly buzzing in my face and chasing me for miles. I'd long since ditched my mosquito net because I couldn't see out of it, so I waved my trekking pole across my face instead.

I passed a SoBo who'd seen Brains the evening before. I continued through dense forest, feeling constrained and hemmed in. I had mail in Castella, a few miles from Shasta, which I figured would make a good place to rest and resupply; the town had a great reputation with thru-hikers. I reached a road near Castella and ducked into some woods, too tired to take any notice of a 'no camping' sign. I settled for the night. Writing my journal that evening and tallying up my mileage, I'd completed 150 miles in only 5 days – an average of 30 per day, including a 33, the furthest I'd hiked in one day.

I walked to Castella in the morning, which consisted of just a post office and garage. No Pain sat on a bench outside, cramming a breakfast burrito into his mouth. He got up and shook my hand when I arrived. It had been a while since I'd seen him, and we chatted for an hour while I also ate.

"You won't reach Canada now, Fozzie," he said matter-of-factly.

"What makes you say that?" I replied, feeling somewhat offended.

"You're way too late. The snow will hit Washington. You won't get through."

There wasn't a doubt in his mind.

"Are you going to carry on from here?" I asked.

"Yes, but I know I won't make it. When it gets too cold I'll go home."

"You're wrong, No Pain," I said. "I'm late, yes, but I'm not backing off now. I've come too far and put in too much work. I haven't time for presumption. Good luck with the rest of your hike."

I shook his hand again and walked back to the highway. No Pain could be right, I knew that; but I didn't want to entertain it. A little into September and I'd completed 1,509-miles; with 1,131 left. Assuming I hiked six, even seven-day weeks with 25-mile days, I still had two months. This meant finishing early November, a good month over target. I respected his opinion; he'd been hiking the PCT and AT for several years and he knew the seasons. Emphatic as he seemed though, when someone tells me I can't do something, that's all the incentive I need to do it.

I checked my phone coming out of Castella, and Pockets had left a voicemail.

"Mucker, I'm in Shasta, call when you get here."

We agreed to meet at the local supermarket, and I got a quick ride. People talked to me as I sat outside; spotting my pack and soiled appearance, they assumed I was on the PCT. They were pleasant enough, but they kept reminding me of the obvious.

"You're late, aren't you?" or "Most thru-hikers passed through a few weeks ago."

With Pockets, whom I now called 'Rockets' on account of his fast walking speed, we went to find a motel. How he'd overtaken me, I didn't know. It transpired that he'd camped at Ash Camp, just a quarter-mile from where I'd spent the night in a clearing. I'd even walked into Ash Camp to get water from the river in the morning but somehow missed him. Brains had holed up in Dunsmuir seven miles away with the flu or something similar.

Shasta was one of the best thru-hiker towns ever, with a great choice of resupply shops and plenty of restaurants. Rockets had found an Italian place, so we went for lunch. It was all-you-can-eat, so we settled down to feast and placate the hunger gods. I watched him take a glass jar of grated parmesan. He unscrewed the top, poured the entire contents over his dish and then called the waitress. He showed her the empty jar, and she duly returned with another. He emptied as well. He ended with not so much pasta and parmesan, but more parmesan and pasta. Then he picked up the olive oil. . .

We left the following day, eager to move on and conquer a 5,000-foot, 18-mile climb. Halfway up, early evening, we were both tired and camped early. Rockets darted around the forest taking photos.

The morning was chilly, and I kept thinking of winter. Keen to make up for lost miles, we only managed 12 by lunch. We ate a quick snack, and Rockets set a four-miles-per-hour pace through the afternoon.

"I hate puds," he said.

"What, as in puddings?" I asked.

"No, puds. You never heard of a pud before? A pud is a pointless up and down, p, u and d."

"Oh," I replied, thinking. "Does that make this section of trail a paular then?"

"What the hell is a paular?"

"A pointless and useless left and right."

Once in the groove, we steamed up the hills, pulling up

at 6pm, having clocked 33 miles for the day and 21 for the afternoon alone. The camp site was stunning: a small, plateau offered amazing views for miles until Mt Shasta shot skywards. As the sun set, streaking the white flanks with orange, it rose supreme over California.

Four days out of Shasta and we'd both run out of food. Having re-supplied with a smaller amount to keep the weight down, we'd figured on getting more supplies at Etna, but hadn't considered the distance. There were two locations from which to catch a ride, the first was Carter Meadows Summit and Highway 93. We had two choices; either try there or camp and push out a 21-miler in the morning to the next road with nothing to eat. It was a no-brainer; we set down our packs and stuck out a thumb.

Three forestry trucks passed within 10 minutes, none of them stopped, then it went quiet. An hour went by, and we saw no-one. Finally, we heard the groan of an engine approaching. Both standing in the middle of the road, we waved and practically forced the car to stop.

The window lowered, and a woman stuck her head out. A cigarette dangled from her mouth while one foot contorted into a yoga position on the dashboard. The radio played Elvis.

"You two trying to get killed?! PCT Hikers?"

"Yep," we replied simultaneously. "Any chance of a ride into Etna?"

"No way!" she said. "I've just come from there. It's 20 miles, I ain't going back again!"

We hung our arms limply, explained we'd run out of food, hoping it might swing things in our favour.

"Listen," she continued, "I live six miles down the valley.

If you want to come with me, I can feed you and give you somewhere to sleep tonight. There's not many houses there, it's in the middle of nowhere, but maybe someone can give you a ride to Etna to resupply in the morning."

It was a good offer and certainly the best we'd get.

Her name was Laurissa, and her house, tucked away from the world, was wonderful. She grew many fruits, vegetables and seemed self-sufficient; she'd even stopped off en route to fill up several bottles from a local spring. The house was off grid, generated its own electricity and must have been a great place to live. It oozed character. Different types of wood clad the exterior, their different colours enlivening the walls. A hotchpotch of mismatched tiles clung to the roof. We sat outside under a porch while a gentle rain fell.

The interior was just as sweet as the outside. A wood stove provided the heat, and shelves groaned under books and rugs decorated a wooden floor.

Laurissa disappeared into the garden and returned with tomatoes, onions and herbs. She boiled rice, pan-fried some tempeh and mixed it together in a bowl with a generous dash of olive oil. It was one of the best meals I'd eaten on the entire trail, and even Rockets, who didn't like health-food, raved about it for days afterwards.

Laurissa's neighbour drove us to Etna in the morning, and we ate breakfast at Bob's Ranch House. The only motel was full, forcing us to get a bus to Yreka, where we stayed for the day. Rockets had been suffering with unbearable toothache and kept holding his jaw. He phoned around trying to find a dentist and eventually a family friend pointed him towards Portland, Oregon. Naturally, I couldn't wait for him, so we parted company, and he said he'd try to catch me. After a long series of rides back to the trailhead, I started walking in the hope of putting in a few miles before sunset.

As dusk fell, I tried in vain to find somewhere level to camp. The terrain was hilly, so the only place to sleep was on the trail.

It was a clear night, but in the forest my environment was dark. Not a breeze stirred, and I heard everything, even mice scurrying around in the leaves. I usually cowboy camped now; it put me in touch with the woods, and I looked forward to falling asleep waiting for a shooting star or two. Also, it saved time not pitching the tent or packing it in the morning. After laying out my ground mat, sleeping pad and bag on the trail, I settled down to cook and write my journal.

Sticks snapped and cracked in the forest above me. I ignored them and continued writing, but I paused to listen again as bushes swished and sprang back to make way for something. It sounded big, no mistake. It crept closer. Suddenly, I felt hunted and pleaded the footfall wasn't paws; paw fall would be awful. The intruder seemed to be making a beeline for me – certainly heading too close for comfort.

Please let that be a deer, I thought. Please, don't make it a bear or a mountain lion.

It crept closer. I felt the reverberations as it approached. I stood, heart thumping, waiting for this fearsome beast to emerge.

Thankfully, it adjusted its course, and veered off, thudding onto the trail 20 feet away. I could hear it, but only barely see it, so I turned on my head torch. The beam immediately picked out two big, menacing eyes which bored a hole right through me. It was a bear.

Chapter 13
Into Oregon

*If everyone in the world treated each other as we treat each
other on the trail, the world would be a far better place.*
Unknown

S
ize, apparently, is not important. This advice doesn't
apply to bears. The size of a bear is directly proportional
to the fear factor. It had been weeks since my last
encounter, and I'd been lulled into a false sense of security.

I didn't know what to do. The mere thought of facing a
bear, let alone being in the middle of nowhere with such a
creature, was the one situation that had haunted me before
my hike. They scared me so much that I'd nearly decided
against going to America because of the possibility.

I'd seen several since my last encounter at McIvers Spring
three months earlier. I'd become comfortable in their
presence, purely because they'd been some distance away or
were happily munching on berries and preoccupied. If they
were aware of me, they usually ran off anyway. This one was
different; it scared me.

Unpredictability and bears are not a good match.

Not wanting to shine my light in its eyes, I lowered the beam from my headlamp. It was dark, but I still avoided eye contact. Fear kept me frozen to the spot, unable to act, make a move or even process the simplest of thoughts. I waited for it to react, like a cowboy facing his arch-rival across a dusty street, guns at the ready. It was waiting for me, and I for it. A standoff with a bear; great.

It stood still, eyes glinting. I glimpsed my dinner-smeared pot lying nearby, and other culinary items dotted the camp. If this bear was hunting for food, it must have thought it had stumbled across the local Walmart. I half expected it to jot down a grocery list, disappear amongst the trees and emerge with a shopping cart.

It then moved towards me, slowly, deliberately and confidently. The animal's sheer bulk cleared aside the overhanging branches which had kept it in the shadows, and it emerged on to the trail as the moon bathed it in a weak, silvery light. I could make out the hairs on its back, shimmering as its nose moved up and down, smelling the area.

I started shaking and then kicked into self-preservation mode. If it was testing me, to see if I'd retreat and run or stand my ground, then now was my time to react.

"Hey, bear! Get outta here! Go! Go on!" I screamed.

It didn't wince and merely carried on staring at me. Now I really was in trouble. Bears are supposedly more scared of us than we are of them, but this one wasn't conforming to the rules.

"Go! Get out! GO!"

Nothing. I was a comedian; I'd delivered my lines, but no one laughed. Even more convinced that dinner was on the agenda and I was the main course, I wondered if it sensed my fear. Perhaps it could see my anxiety or detect my unease.

So far, I'd reacted as I should have done, standing my ground and making some noise. When the beast crept a few paces closer, my instinct was to retreat, but I knew that would've been a big mistake. Retreating is a sign of weakness and all the excuse a bear needs. It's like sizing up to the bloke in a pub when you've just knocked over his beer. You don't run – you try to resolve the situation rationally, and if things turn grim, you stand your ground and square up.

Bears communicate by establishing a pecking order. They fight only as a last resort, wary of sustaining injuries. That hierarchy is about dominance and submission; territorial disputes are usually solved by the alpha male. All this bear was looking for was a weakness. I was slap bang in the middle of a very serious game of chicken.

All or nothing, I thought. I raised my arms over my head, puffed my chest, and screamed.

"Hey! Bear! Get the hell out of here! MOVE!"

Slowly, it turned its head to one side, looked down the hill and sniffed the bushes. It took one last look at me, appeared bored, and sloped off. I felt exhausted, as though I'd just run five miles. I didn't sleep at all that night; every time a twig snapped, I shot bolt upright like a jack-in-the-box, headlamp at the ready. Like I said, I don't like the woods after dark.

Preparing breakfast in the morning, I had more bad luck – my Steripen wasn't working. I'd been using it since Mammoth because my second water filter had broken. When it worked it was brilliant, but it was temperamental. The batteries weren't standard, so I had to carry several spares just in case. A green LED illuminated when the purifying had worked, but there was also a red LED that blinked if there was a problem. Every time I used it, I dreaded that red light. It was like turning the key in your car's ignition and hoping the fault light didn't show. I looked in dismay as, sure enough, the red LED blinked mockingly and furthermore, I couldn't fix it.

I'd only been back on trail for an afternoon and night and my next re-supply was six days away. A few purification tablets were my sole backup, which would at best see me through one, maybe two days. I had to walk back to the highway, get another ride into Etna, and locate the nearest decent hiking shop to buy another water treatment device. Dejected, I plodded back to the road and stuck my thumb out.

Etna is a beautiful little town with much to recommend, but it lacks a dedicated outdoor shop. I tried the pharmacy, desperately hoping to find purification tablets, but it wasn't to be. The owner of the hardware store shrugged his shoulders when I asked him, and said my only choice was Yreka, again to catch a connecting bus all the way back to Shasta. I wandered off to the motel but then remembered a cheaper alternative at Alderbrook Manor.

The Manor had converted a large garage to one side for PCT hikers. The owner, Dave, showed me around and made me welcome. I dumped my gear and hurried to the bus stop for the 10.30am ride to Yreka.

As the bus trundled into the Walmart car park, I took a gamble, missed the connecting service, and entered the store. The camping section was limited, but a saviour appeared; iodine tablets. This purple chemical kills any nasty organisms, but I didn't like using it. It has a bad reputation; in fact, research suggests it should only be used as a backup and never for long periods. However, this particular brand came with another bottle of tablets that neutralised the iodine after it had worked its magic. Besides, I only had six days until my next stop in Ashland. So, I bought them and caught the bus back to Etna. I made a quick phone call to a camping store in Ashland, who confirmed they had the filter I was looking for and kindly agreed to put it aside for me. I got a quick ride up the hill, and I was back on trail five hours after I'd left.

I calculated that 25-mile days, with one zero a week, should get me to Canada by the 31st of October. I remained behind schedule, but if the winter held off, it was certainly achievable. Oregon was close, which meant two positives. First, I'd finally be out of California, a huge morale boost and tangible proof of progress. Second, Oregon is more hiker-friendly. Elevation loss and gain are less severe than California and Washington, and generally the terrain is easier. On the negative side, the temperatures were dropping at night, and dusk was now falling not in the evening, but late afternoon. I put my head down, increased my pace a touch and became stricter about leaving camp early, taking fewer and shorter breaks and meeting my target each day. I tried to stick to this plan; it was easy, surely? All I had to do was make sure I walked at least 15 miles by lunch and put in a brisk three hours in the afternoon to make up the distance. Anything on top of that would be a bonus.

Journal entry:
The weather is changing. It's getting cold, clouds appear

often and become darker by the day. Crawling out of my cosy sleeping bag each morning is something of a chore. Tentatively, I pull down the zip, groping for my clothes. I cringe as I slide into my cold trousers and top. Out of my warm little haven, squinting into a rising sun, I must decide whether to light the stove or jump-start my body. My brain splutters grains of a battle plan for the day. Come the evenings, I'm stopping earlier because of the diminishing sunlight. Fire is the first priority; food and erecting the tent can wait; first I must warm my tired and aching limbs. A cup of hot chocolate brings a glow to my face, and the pain begins to melt. I know that sustenance is imminent; the portions increasing as the temperatures drop. I sit by the orange glow of the fire, warming my front as my back chills. Twigs cracking and snapping in the surrounding forest bring thoughts of bears and Sasquatch.

They say the PCT starts taking its physical toll after halfway, and they're right. I am tired, the aches take longer to fade and new ones appear. It hurts a little more each day, and the ibuprofen supply finishes earlier each week. However, none of this matters. The trail continues to astound, surprise and welcome me. New views greet me; different panoramas bring more smiles. The relentless California stretch that I have been eating away at for the past 138 days is coming to an end. Oregon is in sight, five days distant, and in three days I will have 1,000 miles left. These things are huge confidence-boosters. My morale needs lifting occasionally, and targets help keep me focused and positive.

My mileage has increased from 15 each day at the start to 25 now. I need to keep moving at that tempo, because a finish in late October means walking nearly twice as far each day as I did during the first half. I continue to walk with Rockets, a fine companion. Brains left us, but we spoke on the phone. We expect to catch him because he rested owing to illness. Rockets is the crazy wild card. A veteran of the Appalachian Trail in 2006, he continues to make me smile with his larking around and mischievous antics. A true outdoorsman, he is at one with his surroundings and regales me with his adventures in hiking, climbing and mountaineering. He stops often and pulls out his camera when he sees something worthy of his photographic eye. He is one of a handful of people who I can see myself walking to the end with. 1,000 miles is still a long way, but I know it's the home stretch. Mexico, all those weeks behind me, is an eternity ago. Time has little meaning out here; I get up when it feels right and stop when I'm tired. One day melts into another, and I don't even know what day it is; but a small part of me knows that I am within striking distance of Canada.

The elements grow restless, winter draws its sword and I find myself at the tail end of the pack, but I walk with delight in my eyes and success in my heart.

I wandered off trail into a meadow to find Buckhorn Spring and fill up with water. A small clear pool tinkled as the spring trickled in, and I scooped up a litre, added an iodine tablet and waited for it to take effect. Despite being at 6,500 feet, it still felt like the middle of summer. A heat haze shimmered in the valley below, insects hovered and butterflies flew past.

Cicadas hummed a gentle, reassuring melody, the grass waved as a breeze wandered through and flowers splashed colour everywhere. Long grass tickled my bare skin as I rested.

Downing the first litre in one go, I filled up again and dropped in another tablet, setting me up for the next couple of hours.

I checked my route on the map and made a general plan. There were 20 miles to Seiad Valley and a 5,000-foot descent in the process. I planned to ingest some fat at the famous café there. Leaving Seiad, the elevation graph showed a 4,500-foot climb, which normally wasn't a problem, but it stretched out over only eight miles. That would make for a steep and tiring end to the day.

I met Colin, a SoBo, as I descended into Seiad. He agreed that I should be able to crack out good mileage in Oregon. He also advised that the ascent out of Seiad up to the summit at Devils Peak was long and steep. I was glad I was going down and he was going up, but that would change soon enough.

I reached Highway 96 and made quick work of the two miles to the café, store and post office. Seiad Valley Café is renowned among hikers for its pancake challenge: eat five inch-thick, dinner-plate-sized pancakes in less than two hours. A complimentary drizzle of syrup and a trickle of butter finishes off the dish. This innocuous-sounding test has laid out most of those who have attempted it. In fact, only a handful have succeeded since its inception. The only reward for success is there's no bill.

This was, however, the last thing on my mind. I'm not fond of American pancakes, and with the climb out of the valley imminent, I settled for a lighter bacon and eggs as I chatted to the locals.

"You're late," said Brian, a local decorator having lunch. "Most hikers have come through by now." I didn't need reminding again.

"There's a hiker holed up in the campground next door, by the way. He had Giardia but he's recovered. I think his name is Cash."

I'd bumped into Cash before and wasn't too fond of him; there was just something I couldn't put my finger on. I didn't want to see him again, so I cautiously peered out of the window. The coast appeared clear; I grabbed my pack and left.

"Fozzie!"

Shit! I thought. He's seen me.

He came over, looking tired and pale.

"Are you with anyone?" he asked.

"On my own, making tracks and still aiming for Canada," I replied.

"Wait for me? I'm just getting over Giardia, but I'm OK to hike. Let me pack up camp, get some food and I'll come with you."

I made my excuses and said I couldn't hang about. It seemed harsh but something about Cash didn't ring true.

Another SoBo called Two Dog stopped me. To my surprise, she'd bumped into Rockets two days earlier.

What the hell? I thought. Where does that guy get his energy? I leave him in Yreka to sort his tooth out and now, he's passed me?

I called his cell phone.

"How the hell did you get ahead of me, Rockets?"

"I don't know, mucker," he replied, chuckling. "I got the tooth sorted and didn't have to go to Portland, so I put my head down and ground out the miles. I walked late a couple of evenings, so guess I must have passed you while you were sleeping."

He was with Brains in Ashland and said he'd wait for me there although Brains was moving on.

I continued on the road for a mile and returned to the forest to tackle Devils Peak. It was hot and humid. The hill was steeper than expected, but it maintained a steady gradient, so at least I knew what to expect and I adjusted my pace accordingly. Stopping briefly at Lookout Spring, I gritted my teeth and let fly, reaching the top in one go. As I eased on to flatter terrain, my legs gently relaxed after their efforts. I battled on, trying to put distance between Cash and me.

Everyone I meet is walking south, I thought as I glimpsed another hiker descending towards me. As he came into view, I realised we'd met before.

"Patch!" I exclaimed. "I haven't seen you for weeks!"

I'd camped in a trail angel's yard with Patch in Wrightwood. He'd had a bad time there; on the approach to town, he'd left his pack and taken a side trail to a spring, and returning found that someone had stolen it. Apparently, this had happened to several hikers; the rumour was someone was lying in wait at the trail junction. The culprit presumably knew that the spring was downhill and a fair distance, so most hikers slipped off their packs to lessen the burden on the climb back up.

This was a major blow; equipment for a thru-hike is expensive. My main essentials – namely pack, camping mat, sleeping bag and tent – cost a small fortune on their own. If you're on a tight budget, having your gear stolen can end a hike.

I'd watched Patch at his computer ordering replacements, and then play the waiting game with the mail man, but he managed it.

He'd skipped up to Canada from the Heitmans' and now hiked back, on course to complete the PCT in two more weeks. He'd hiked 800 miles more than me in the same amount of time. I feared it was more my slow pace that was to blame.

"In anticipation of becoming a thru-hiker," I offered, "let me be the first to congratulate you," and I shook his hand.

"Go, Fozzie!" he shouted after me as we went separate ways. "You can do it!"

Fuelled by good progress since Etna, I rose early. I downed a litre of water, threw my only remaining snack, a handful of parmesan shavings, into my mouth and sped off.

Two hours into my 15-mile morning shift, I approached a couple of signs nailed to a tree. I assumed it was a 'distance to Canada' reminder, so I took no notice. I dropped my pack and rested for a few minutes. Curiosity got the better of me, though, as I got up, and a broad smile rippled across my chops as I checked the sign:

Welcome to Oregon
Interstate 5 – 28
Hyatt Lake – 51
Washington Border – 498
Canadian Border – 962

I felt a fire in my belly, a mixture of achievement, pride and determination. At last I was out of California and into Oregon! It was well under 1,000 miles now until the finish, and I could in theory get through Oregon in a month. Finally, after 146 days, I was on the home stretch.

"YES!" I screamed, running off. "Get in there!"

I spent the next hour kicking pine cones into a goal past a helpless German goalkeeper in an imaginary World Cup final. We won 16-0, I got six goals and became a football legend.

I walked well into the night and rested before vowing to walk a few more miles. Ashland's lights twinkled below me, and a full moon cast soft shadows. I called Rockets and said I'd get there by lunch the following day.

Searching for a camping spot, I reached a four-way intersection with a sign.

Grouse Gap Shelter – 0.25 miles

There's just a handful of shelters on the PCT. The Appalachian Trail, by contrast, is strewn with three-sided buildings where hikers spend the night in the dry; most will pass one or more each day. I turned right, anticipating the simple prospect of a picnic table where I could sit comfortably, and a roof.

I reached my goal at 10pm after a long day. Interior lights from a couple of RVs penetrated the darkness and Steve, the owner, came out to meet me as he saw my head torch sweeping around.

"You walking the PCT?" he enquired.

"Yes, I am; glad to find the shelter."

"You're a bit late, aren't you?"

This remark was becoming somewhat regular, but I

didn't mind. The look of surprise on most people's faces was all I needed to prove them wrong.

I smiled cheekily. "Yes, I'll make it."

I settled down, cooked the last remaining meal and tallied up the mileage. I arrived at the figure of 38.6 for the day. I was happy, but I also chastised myself for not keeping closer tabs on my progress and pushing on for another 30 minutes to achieve my first 40-miler. To my delight, I discovered I'd walked 95.4 miles in three days, an average of 31.8 miles per day. Finally, the need to crush the miles was starting to sink in.

I woke early, peering through the slit in my sleeping bag. The sun skulked under the horizon of a distant hill but cast enough light to see by. A low mist hovered over a field by the shelter, in no hurry to disperse. I was about to light my stove when Steve appeared, smiling, and handed me a coffee. We sat and took in our calm environment for a few minutes before he left, bidding me good luck.

I set off, eager to get to the highway 10 miles away. There was the prospect of breakfast at Callahan's Restaurant and maybe a ride to Ashland. I startled a huge bear in the forest and watched in awe as it thundered up the hill like a runaway goods train. Passing under Interstate 5, I arrived at Callahan's. It holds a great reputation among hikers; seeming a little upmarket for us, but we receive a warm welcome there.

Callahan's burnt down in September 2006, but the owners Donna and Ron Bergquist bounced back, re-opening bigger and better in August 2008. To keep attracting business from PCT hikers, they've kept their mid-week prices flexible. The place now has showers and laundry, and allows camping on the back lawn as well as offering one of the best breakfasts I'd eaten.

Being smelly and filthy as usual, I felt self-conscious, but the receptionist didn't bat an eyelid. I explained I was heading to Ashland and, despite my appearance, didn't need to shower or to do laundry; I purely craved sustenance. She led me into the dining room, introduced me to my waitress and wished me well on my hike. Angela the waitress floated over, poured me freshly squeezed orange juice, asked how I liked my coffee and gently placed a menu in my hands.

"You're running late for a thru-hike, aren't you?" she asked, looking me directly in the eye and smiling.

"Not enough decent breakfasts," I replied. "I need optimal fuel to perform."

Making quick work of the meal, I got a ride into Ashland from James, a staff member. I knocked on the door of Room 5 at the Ashland Motel, and Courtney answered.

"What are you doing here?!" I smiled as she hugged me.

"Came up to see Pockets and chill out for a few days," she replied.

"Mucker!" came a voice from inside the bedroom, as Rockets strode out and gave me another hug.

"You seen anyone in town?" I asked.

"Nope, I think we're the last of the pack. Brains left two days ago with Lone Ginger. You?"

"Saw Patch south-bound and due to finish soon, Two Dog, and also Cash."

His face dropped.

"Cash is here?"

"Well, I don't think he's in Ashland," I continued, "I left him at Seiad, and I've put in good miles since then but he's not far behind."

Rockets was not fond of Cash after they'd nearly come to

blows in Mammoth. Cash was drunk and tried to pick a fight. Rockets, a former nightclub bouncer, said he'd backed off with a little gentle persuasion.

We were in good spirits. I was still on a high from my mileage, Courtney was just happy to be with Rockets, and he bounced around full of his usual energy. We went to the post office to collect mail, and as we parked Cash strolled over, surprising me how he'd caught up so quickly.

When he asked if we'd found somewhere to stay, we confirmed we had but there was no space. We drove him to the hostel, also full, and eventually two miles out of town to a motel where he got a spare bed.

We spent two days in Ashland. As usual, I tried but didn't get everything done in a day. I had to update my blog, answer emails, download photos, re-supply, clean myself up, do laundry and eat a lot of food. It rained on and off and turned colder. I had a raging hunger, and the café next door was a godsend come breakfast. I worked my way through piles of hash browns, eggs, bacon, toast and sausage every morning. I drifted around in a caffeine-induced high after discovering an abundance of good coffee houses and finished off pizzas so big that I'd normally have struggled to eat three slices.

The camping shop had indeed put a Katadyn Hiker filter to one side. I hoped that this, my fourth water treatment device of the trip, would see me through to Canada. My waterproof pack liner had also reached the end of its life, so I replaced it. All my other gear was faring well except my tent, which would need replacing soon. What with the impending wetter weather and possibly snow, I knew I'd need the Gore-Tex boots that Inov-8 had provided. I called

Aunty Jillian, and she arranged to post them up trail.

Rockets and I zoomed off late morning, constantly aware now that the weather could close in. Winter was almost upon us, and snow was inevitable. Hikers up the trail reported that Washington hadn't had snow but was wet. The forecast bad winter was, so far at least, delayed.

Before long we spotted a hiker snoozing by the side of the trail, his gear strung out on branches to dry. It was Cash.

"Hey, guys! Wassup?" he said.

We stopped briefly to exchange pleasantries and continued. Cash appeared in no hurry. As we looked back, we expected to see him packing up and coming after us, but he just went back to sleep. However, two hours later when we'd stopped for lunch, he rounded the corner and sat with us, opening his food bag. He shared his supplies, which I thought was a nice gesture, and I started to think that maybe he wasn't so bad after all. Rockets raised his eyebrows at me, suggesting he thought the same.

Cash appeared to be taking the trail lightly and again stayed behind when we strode off. Reaching Hyatt Lake road, we spotted Keene Creek reservoir down the hill and camped on the bank to have access to water. It was a still evening; I watched the sun slide away and the moon rise, reflecting in the Keene's waters. Car headlights flashed on a nearby road and illuminated the forest as the driver negotiated the hairpin turns.

I went to pee before hiker midnight. There's something immensely satisfying about peeing outside. Sprinkling in a toilet doesn't come close. I often pondered this as I stood, legs astride, in the woods. I think it stems back to our wild days when we lived outdoors and it was the norm. It's territorial too, the marking of one's territory. Dogs and cats still do it, as do many animals. I'm sure that before humans lost their evolved, heightened sense of smell, they knew when they encroached on someone else's area. Even in motels, I had the urge to go outside to pee. At home, I nearly always go in the garden. I need to mark my dominion, and will tinkle in various spots to spread the scent around. It's an enlightening experience to relieve yourself outside. Try it; you'll be pleasantly surprised.

We woke to damp gear and ice crusting the tents. It had rained again during the night, and we knew it wouldn't be long before plunging temperatures turned rain to snow. Clouds streamed overhead and didn't disperse all day. We discussed tactics. Rockets had a friend in a town called Corvallis, accessible by a road 85 miles up trail. We debated getting a ride from there, resupplying and then finding transport to Cascade Locks and the Bridge of the Gods.

This impressively engineered bridge spans the Columbia River and separates Oregon from Washington. Our plan was to skip up to the border before the snow hit, knock off Washington northbound, get transport back to the bridge and then south-bound back into Oregon. It made sense; we were aware of the game of dice we played with the elements.

Oregon was living up to its reputation. Instead of a hilly rollercoaster, now the altitude graph had settled into a kinder, flatter line. We did 27 miles the next day, nearing Brown Mountain shelter, hoping for nearby water and a stock of firewood. Taking the short side track to the cabin, we were lucky on both counts. A hand pump provided access to clean well water, and inside the hut we found not only wood but a huge cast-iron stove in the middle of the single room. By the time we'd fired it up, it was so hot that we walked around casually in shirts and shorts. We cooked on the stove and relaxed to read and write journals. As I began dozing off, Rockets spoke.

"Hey, Fozzie."

I turned over to see him pressing his nose to the window, looking outside.

"Hmm. Wassup?" I replied, half asleep.

"I think there's someone coming."

Chapter 14
Jekyll and Hyde

The long trail can change us if we listen and let it. The longer we are on the journey, the deeper the truth penetrates and the deceptions of modern life vanish.
Ned Tibbits (Director of Mountain Education, who educate hikers on winter mountaineering skills)

Rockets peered out of the window, spotting a head torch bouncing along towards us.

"I think it may be Cash."

Sure enough, Cash poked his head through the door. I sat upright and acknowledged him as he entered.

"Sorry, mate," I said, "our stuff is everywhere, we weren't expecting anyone. Hang on, and I'll make some space for you."

"No, it's fine," he replied. "I can sleep on the trail."

Before I could answer, he left. I watched through the window as he sat at the table outside and started to read. 30 minutes later he stormed back in, a changed man.

"This is disgusting!" he screamed.

Surprised at such an outburst, I looked at Rockets, who

raised his eyebrows in equal amazement.

"Your stuff is everywhere, there's no room! What's this trash doing on the floor?"

"It's our trash, which we'll take with us in the morning, Cash," Rockets said. "We can make room for you. We weren't expecting anyone, which is why our stuff is spread out. Where do you want to sleep?"

"This is fucking disgusting!" he screamed.

To say he looked angry was an understatement. Rockets sensed something amiss, as did I, as Cash continued, having changed from Jekyll to Hyde.

"What's this?!" he cried and began throwing our gear about. He approached Rockets, zipped up in his sleeping bag, and shouted at him. Rockets glanced at me and narrowed his eyes. It was a warning that the situation could turn dangerous, a fact I was already well aware of. He gently unzipped his bag as Cash threw a torrent of abuse at both of us and encroached threateningly on Rockets's space.

"Cash! We can make room for you!" Rockets cried.

"You're both scum! Look at this shit!"

I broke in. "Cash, you're being a prick. Shut the fuck up and piss off."

"Fuck you!"

I got out of my bag as Rockets stood up and confronted him. Holding his ground, he pleaded with him to calm down, but he also told him in no uncertain terms to stop or else get thrown out. Cash motioned to throw another piece of equipment, but Rockets stepped in, holding him with a firm gaze.

"Cash, I'm going to say this once. Leave our stuff alone and get the fuck out of here or I'll throw you out."

Cash paused, glared at me and then at Rockets. The atmosphere tensed. Rockets stood tall, ready for anything, his body rigid and primed. I got up and returned Cash's stare. His fists clenched; his stance suggested violence. In the ensuing pause, I assumed all hell would unleash, but then he appeared to relax and retreated a few steps. Picking up his bag, he thundered off into the night.

"What the hell was that about?" I exclaimed.

"I don't know," Rockets replied, "but I never want to see that guy again."

We slept fitfully, half expecting Cash to storm back. Although he didn't, we knew at some point we'd bump into him again. Sure enough, the following day, Cash's familiar frame appeared ahead of us, seated by the trail side.

"What you wanna do?" I asked Rockets.

"I don't know." I replied.

I made eye contact a good 10 seconds before we passed Cash and locked his gaze. He showed no remorse, didn't move and said nothing. We left him and sped up to put more distance between us.

"I got a message from him," Rockets said, checking his phone as we finished lunch. "He's apologised, said he was out of order."

"It's a nice gesture, but it doesn't excuse his behaviour," I said.

Rockets nodded.

"Too little, too late. Good of him to apologise, but I still never want to see him again."

We hurried up, agreeing that mileage was the priority, and with luck we'd leave Cash behind. For once I led. I stopped near a spring, which over the summer had reduced to a small trickle. Rockets arrived a few minutes later, sweat staining both his top and the trail behind him.

"Where's water?" he gasped.

"Down there," I replied, motioning. "Ignore the first creek bed; it's empty. There's another further on that's flowing."

Rockets sweated more than a terrorist at airport immigration with a fake passport and a poorly concealed AK47. He literally dripped his way along. We discussed our intake when he returned. I drank two to three litres a day, regardless of the temperature, while he chugged between six and seven litres. We timed our rest breaks around water sources. If I arrived before him, his first words were always, "Where's water?"

The Oregon trails were indeed kinder, and we found ourselves finishing our daily 25-mile target earlier. The trail itself, a dark, sandy soil with a smattering of pine cones, felt softer and cushioned each foot strike. Temperatures warmed during the day but chilled rapidly in the evening, and mist often enclosed around us.

We reached Highway 62 and got a ride with John, who was heading for Mazama Village. This small cluster of buildings included a store, restaurant and post office. As we pulled up, I noticed a familiar figure leaning against a wall.

"Cash is here," I said, pointing towards the restaurant.

"Great," Rockets replied.

I walked over and completely ignored Cash but as I looked back, I saw Rockets talking to him and waited, catching wind of the conversation.

"I'm sorry, Pockets," Cash began.

"We appreciate you sending the messages apologising," Rockets said, "but what you did was out of order. You don't go crazy at people in the middle of nowhere. You threatened both of us."

"Where's Fozzie gone?"

"He's inside, and he doesn't want to speak to you. In fact, he never wants to see you again and neither do I. Good luck with your hike, Cash."

After downing a few hot dogs, John asked if we could use a lift somewhere. We checked the map and realised we were right on top of Crater Lake. At 7,700 years old, it's one of the finest sights on the PCT. It's also the deepest lake in the United States at 1,943 feet and the seventh deepest in the world, originally formed when Mount Mazama collapsed.

"Why don't we try to get a ride to Corvallis from here?" I asked Rockets. "Imagine walking back and finishing at Crater Lake: it would make one hell of a finale."

He agreed, and we jumped in the car with John, who drove to Benton. Dancing on the slip road to the highway to attract attention, we got another quick ride, which dropped us at Grants Pass. Now dark, we looked for somewhere to sleep and passed the Greyhound station. The Corvallis bus departed at 3am. After grabbing a bite to eat, we slept fitfully round the back of a factory.

"Your feet smell like a dead rat in a rotting, musky basement," he said.

"Thanks," I replied, laughing.

"And what is it with your Neoair?" (A Neoair is an inflatable sleeping mattress which has a habit of squeaking when the user shifts position).

"What do you mean?"

"It's noisy! Every night you sound like you're wrestling a dolphin."

"Have you not met my mate Flipper yet?"

We arrived in Corvallis early morning and found Rockets's friend Brett in his kitchen.

"Guys, if you're hungry, we can go down the local café and try the Beaver Buster!"

Tommy's 4th Street Bar & Grill served up the Beaver Buster. It's a breakfast named after the local Football team, the Beavers, and to call it monumental is something of an understatement. When I first read the menu, I decided that just good old eggs, hash browns and bacon would do. But Rockets, who can put away abnormally large amounts of food, appeared tempted by the challenge.

Said challenge meant eating the calorie-loaded mound of gluten, fat and cholesterol in under an hour. The diner must sit alone – I believe this rule stems from an incident when someone discreetly passed food to a friend on the same table – and a timer is set. You can only start when the waitress gives the nod, and the reward for success is a free meal. Otherwise, it's a $24 bill. In the four years since Tommy's had offered the challenge, only four people had succeeded.

Rockets looked at the menu, then at Brett, checked the menu again, looked at me and scratched his chin.

"I'll give it a go, me old mucker!"

A waitress appeared 15 minutes later, struggling to keep hold of a plate groaning with an obscene amount of food. She placed it carefully in front of Rockets, who sat at an empty table. He raised his eyebrows, picked up his fork, looked at me, then at Brett and finally at the waitress.

"Good luck. Go!" she said, starting the timer.

We'd discussed tactics. I advised making the most of the seven-minute rule – the time it takes the brain to register that the stomach is full. Therefore, Rockets needed to put away as much food as possible before his brain had a chance to realise. I also told him to eat the wheat products such as bread and pancakes first because these are the most filling; the sooner he got those out of the way, the easier it would be to finish the rest.

This, I thought, seemed good advice. The problem centred on the amount of food. When I first saw it, I couldn't believe my eyes. Two six-egg omelettes (that's an astonishing twelve eggs), a mound of hash browns, piles of home fries (sautéed potatoes), five pancakes, two biscuits (this is like a savoury scone in England), strips of bacon, sausages, ham, gravy, and eight pieces of toast! Eight!

As Brett and I tucked in to our modest servings, Rockets dived in, piling in the food as fast as he could. However, a mere 10 minutes in, he puffed out his cheeks and raised his eyebrows once more. The poor chap had barely made it through half the plate before giving up and holding his stomach, groaning.

We stayed in Corvallis for two days and then caught the Greyhound to Cascade Locks. Arriving late, we found a cheap motel. We were both eager to get back on the trail and tackle Washington.

We bumped into Uncle Gary the next morning. I hadn't seen him since Independence, where he'd hiked with the two Brits, Nick and Chris. I asked him about my fellow countrymen. He thought they were about 70 miles up the way.

We started late but walked until Panther Creek, only managing nine miles. Gary told us in the morning that Flannel, Walker Texas Ranger, Crow and Dundee were close behind. It was Rockets's birthday, so we got a swift ride back to town, secured beer and snacks, and sat by the creek, slowly getting inebriated. Sure enough, at midday the others arrived. They were surprised to see us as they'd heard through the hiker grapevine how far behind we lagged. We explained we'd skipped up to Cascade Locks to hike Washington, then we'd return to finish the Oregon section. We set off, and I felt good being among familiar faces.

Uncle Gary came from Petaluma, California and was studying outdoor education. He sported an impressive beard and mound of hair and, despite weeks of sunshine, he'd managed to stay impressively pale. We walked together for most of the day, until Rockets, Uncle Gary and I descended a series of switchbacks to camp by a creek.

Journal entry:
The bears know when it's time. So do the mountain lions, the squirrels and the snakes. They sense the snows coming, and they prepare for the winter. I can see the obvious signs, like leaves painted in reds, oranges and yellows. When the wind catches the trees, we walk through thousands of leaves cascading down, floating from side to side like a mother cradling her baby. The mornings are colder, and frost clings to our tents. We watch clouds of warm mist rise as we exhale. Gaggles of geese fly overhead, calling out and warning us.

The vibe of autumn approaching is hard to explain. It's not just the visual signals, as mesmerising as they are. This is my favourite time of the year: the temperature is perfect for hiking, the sunsets are magical and sitting in camp with a blazing fire is comforting. Something in my body makes me aware that summer has ended. It's more than the smell of musty leaves and it goes deeper than the mist banks swirling around me.

Rockets and I have been joined by Uncle Gary. At 26 years old, he is an interesting guy. A powerful hiker with thighs like tree trunks, he walks a good-but-not-quick pace and reels off a series of jokes. Many times, he stops to study fungi poking through the soil, and we feast on the forest's bountiful supply. His impressive knowledge in this area adds to my modest memory bank of edible shrooms. Our food stocks are well supplemented by the likes of cauliflower fungus, boletes, chanterelles and white matsutake. Throw in some leftover bacon, fresh garlic and a little parsley, and the finest restaurants would be hard pressed to come up with anything this tasty.

Washington State is great walking. We meander between pine trees towering so high that we strain to see the tops. The trail is dampened with occasional rain, which stops the clouds of dust we normally kick up. Occasionally, we glimpse valleys below us. Lakes peek through gaps, and peaks such as Mt Adams and Mt Hood tower imposingly above us, capped with fresh snow. Tough going after our brief Oregon excursion, Washington has the dips and crests we'd become used to in California. Climbs of 3,000 feet or more, and four-hour ascents, make our thighs and calves scream.

We progressed well, but I became concerned about Rockets; his behaviour wasn't normal, and he lacked his usual mischievousness. I'd noticed this over the course of a week and had broached the subject of whether anything was wrong a couple of times. He answered despondently, saying he was tired of walking, unhappy with his photos and lacked motivation. He seemed too blasé about taking zeros, and the snowfall threat didn't bother him. It was a strange departure from the carefree, positive and crazy friend I had come to know, and it threatened to demotivate me, too. I never needed an excuse to take a zero, and I enjoyed a more sedate pace than others, covering fewer miles than I should. But I was painfully aware of the changing season, and, unlike my mate, desperately wanted to keep moving.

I rose early with Uncle Gary, and we tried to rouse Rockets. He grunted and said he'd catch us.

Reaching a dirt track, we decided to clean up and re-supply in the small village of Trout Lake. We tried for 30 minutes to get a ride, but no one passed so we started walking the 13 miles. After two hours, a Ranger truck passed, and I saw Rockets sitting in the back, grinning and waving. It pulled over and took us to Trout Lake.

Rockets admitted he hadn't risen until 2pm. He complained of feeling constantly tired. That night he threw up on several occasions. He was getting worse and failed to get up in the morning again. I told him he should see a doctor, but he shrugged it off and said it would pass.

Walker, Flannel, Crow and Dundee showed up, re-supplied and left. They were late like me, but I could see in their eyes their determination to finish. They kept their rest breaks as short as possible, and I envied their dedication – I was still struggling to leave Trout Lake. The usual diversions of the café and hot food had lengthened my stay, and my concern for Rockets intensified.

I constantly battled to move, to find motivation,

especially when surrounded by town comforts. The woods were wet and cold, although I stayed warm when moving; stopping for camp meant fighting the chill. I also had a sense of duty towards Rockets – you don't abandon your hiking partner unless by agreement or illness. He was clearly ill, and I felt obliged to be there for him. He stayed in bed for most of the day.

Uncle Gary had found matsutake fungi in the woods. He'd picked them before so appeared confident in his identification. They can be elusive, but around Trout Lake we spotted them a few times. We discussed lunching on this expensive treat. I went into the Store Grocery where we'd rented the room above, and asked Greg, the owner, if he had a frying pan we could borrow.

His ears pricked up when I told him of our culinary plans.

"Really?" he said. "I haven't had matsutake for a while. How many you got?"

"Enough to barter if you like! I'd gladly trade for some bacon and garlic."

"I like!" His eyes lit up. I soon discovered how highly prized our fungi were when he also threw in some chanterelles and two slabs of steak. Shroom hunting held much potential!

Firing up Uncle Gary's stove, we let it heat up, dropped in the butter and watched a layer of liquid fat coat the bottom of the pan. We carefully added the seasoned steak, seared it for a couple of minutes each side and removed it to rest. The funghi hissed as it hit the skillet. Then, in went the bacon, and we cooked both to a golden brown, finally throwing in the chopped garlic. The resulting dish proved one of the best I had eaten on the entire trip.

Dundee appeared.

"What are you cooking? It smells amazing!" she exclaimed.

We let her try it. Her face contorted into ecstasy as she looked gratefully skyward, making approving noises. Even Mike and Murray, the two local cats, came to investigate.

Uncle Gary left in the morning, and I was keen to move on as well. Rockets, still unwell, seemed grumpy; annoyed at a couple of things I'd done, and he moved out of the room because I apparently made too much noise. He'd always let stuff like that slide; when you hike with someone day in and day out, you let the little things go because it's just not worth the tension. If thru-hikers don't get along, they go their separate ways. I didn't blame him; I knew the illness was causing his moods. Asking if he wanted me to do anything for him, he said no.

"I have to hit the trail and finish, Rockets. I can help you, but you have to make a decision: stay and find out what's wrong with you or come with me."

"Go, Fozzie; I'll catch you."

Greg dropped me at the trailhead. It was cold, a low mist lingered and moisture dripped everywhere. I looked at the track and watched water trickling around tree roots, searching for the path of least resistance. It fed the creeks and streams, which in turn found the rivers all the way to the Pacific Ocean. Water never took a zero, didn't fall ill and didn't quit until reaching the goal. It's funny, the comparison we make between nature and walking, I thought, as I skipped along, trying to keep my feet dry.

I camped in a small clearing circled by trees as meadows

stretched out towards distant peaks. A melancholic mist lowered and thickened, and my head torch struggled to penetrate a random mix of eddies, fluctuations and billions of twinkling water droplets. I managed to start a fire in the dampness, to warm up and dry out my shoes. The flames glowed, reaching out before the mist forced them back. An orange dome of heat and light formed around me, gently tickling the trees and illuminating the patterns on the bark. Beyond that, the forest engulfed any light that dared stray further. It felt oppressive, as if giant hands smothered me.

The murkiness subsided a little in the morning, just clearing the treetops. Sunlight occasionally lit solitary trees like a spotlight in a crowd of people. The occasional creak and groan from the forest broke the silence, and huckleberry bushes hemmed me in on a trail so worn that it was more of a shallow trench. Barely anything stirred or made a sound all day. My only company as I walked was the gentle crunch of my boots on crispy volcanic soil.

At 8pm, before the ascent to Goat Rocks Wilderness, I stopped for the day. It was late, and from the map I saw that the contour lines were about to have a party. I was approaching a climb and a knife-edge ridge walk. There was no way I'd attempt that in the dark, especially with ominous clouds rolling in. I tucked my tent into a tiny gap at the forest's edge for extra protection, lit a fire and cooked over the flames. A log offered a seat and, as I sat, I reached out for warmth. A faint glimmer from the moon bounced around the camp, but not enough to see by, so I switched on my head torch and sipped hot chocolate.

The beam picked out something falling, reflecting thousands of tiny particles winking at me. I assumed it was light rain, but then noticed the particles floating. It was the first snowfall, and though only a dusting, I knew the Washington winter was beginning. It threw me into a mild panic, which subsided but left a deep fear of failure in the pit of my stomach. All those zeros, all those days I could have walked a few more miles. Why didn't I get up earlier or walk further? Now, my nonchalance had caught up, tapped me on the back and chuckled. My PCT hike was in very real danger of faltering on the home stretch. I had 336 miles left in Washington, and then I had to return to Cascade Locks and south-bound the section I had missed to Crater Lake, a further distance of 322 miles. This 658-mile effort equated to 26 days, or a month, to be safe. I was looking at completion around the second week of November, a good two months over schedule.

The mornings and nights were cold, the days chilly. I woke again to ice on the tent and on the trail. My boots crunched on the frozen dirt as they broke through the crust into small puddles. Icicles protruded horizontally from bushes where the wind had forced them sideways. I drank from my bottle, and a mix of slushy water slid down my throat.

Entering the Goat Rocks Wilderness, I climbed for an eternity towards the ridge at 7,150 feet. I crested, dumbstruck, confronted with the best view in the world. The trail followed the ridge as it descended, and I walked carefully as my boots sought grip on shiny, slick, icy rock as smooth as glass. I was in the middle of a gigantic arena; the ridge fell away to green lowlands and then rose again, dipping and diving around me as it disappeared to infinity. White peaks merged into grey rock and plummeted into valleys where the silver ribbons of a river wove their way along the bottom. Mt Rainier stood majestic, a king perched on a throne, as low cloud whipped past and occasionally obscured my own personal panorama.

I negotiated the rollercoaster like a feather caught in the breeze, straining up hills and relaxing on the downs. Early afternoon I spilled out on to Highway 12 and turned left towards White Pass, with a roadside store. Walker Texas Ranger, Crow, Dundee, Flannel and Uncle Gary sat outside, opening mail boxes and cramming supplies into their packs. I grabbed a coffee, and the assistant told me that my mail hadn't arrived but had probably ended up in the town of Packwood, 19 miles away. I wished the others luck and caught a ride into town. The Packwood Inn had a reasonable room, and the owner took my laundry away. Reaching the post office just before it closed, I picked up a package from Dicentra, a food box in exchange for my last book I'd sent her. I tore it open eagerly and smiled as I found several dehydrated meals from her own recipes, proper coffee, almond and peanut butter sachets and a host of other goodies. My other packages contained a new tent, my winter sleeping bag, down jacket, thicker socks and a neck buff. My mood brightened at the thought of being warmer and better fed over the coming days. I sent my old tent to HQ in San Jose, and my summer bag back to Western Mountaineering.

The soles of my feet were in bad shape. Although blisters were a thing of the distant past, I had painful and tender areas of red skin. I'd no idea what caused them, but they had slowed my progress over recent days and I pondered resting for a day more. I secured comfort food along with Epsom salts from the store and sat with my feet in a strong solution while working my way through a tub of ice cream and occasionally pausing to drink Pale Ale.

Later, as I wandered aimlessly around town, I caught the tantalising aroma of coffee from a side street. Following my nose, I found the Butter Butte Coffee Shop. Not content with making wonderful espressos, they also roasted and ground their own beans. I returned several times, sitting in the corner reading and contemplating my hike so far and the challenges ahead. I can reliably inform you that the Butter Butte Coffee Shop served me the best cup of joe on the entire trail.

Rockets called me the day after and asked me to wait as he was due in town. Although he'd seen a doctor, who'd diagnosed possible E. coli poisoning, he sounded upbeat and eager to continue. We moved over to a twin room at the Hotel Packwood. The place was empty save the owner and her dog.

The doctor had told him to stop hiking. Most thru-hikers don't consult doctors, regardless of the ailment. The advice, 9 times out of 10, is to 'get off trail', and nine times out of ten hikers don't need to. Rockets simply said, "You can't keep Pockets down."

But he wasn't well. Apart from the physical problems associated with E. coli, it was his psychological state that troubled me. He was despondent, still sleeping a lot, and reluctant to move. He was constantly tired and struggling, but he wouldn't admit it. I looked up to him in some ways and was thankful for his lead when we walked together. But maybe because of my admiration for him, I let his disinclination rub off on me, and I became too comfortable doing nothing. Rain had covered Packwood for two days, only adding to the gloom, and I found myself repeating a mantra several times a day for motivation.

"I will finish the PCT and I will enjoy it. Foz, you have to move. YOU HAVE TO MOVE."

On the third day, despite the rain, I left Rockets again and caught a quick ride back to White Pass. He wanted to wait for clearer weather, but I couldn't. Recoiling from the spray of passing trucks, I found the trailhead and disappeared back into the damp forest. My shoes, now worn out, slipped on the mud, but they had to last until Snoqualmie Pass, 99 miles away, where HQ had mailed my Gore-Tex boots. Water seeped through the mesh as I squelched unceremoniously along. When dusk crept in, I pulled off trail near the shore of Snow Lake. I dropped my pack as drizzle started falling, and was two minutes into erecting my tent when I heard what sounded like the call of an eagle. I swung round to see Rockets peering out from behind a tree, giggling.

We spent the rainy evening under canvas, eating and reading. We discussed plans, our conversation somewhat drowned in the pitter-patter of water falling and trickling off our tents.

"I have to get going, mate," I said. "You're ill but it's your head that worries me: it's holding you back and, in turn, me as well. I need to finish this, there's way too much resting on it to consider failing. I'm late as it is; I must move. Come and hike with me, but you do have to start trying."

"I know, me old mucker, I know," he replied, his vague tone engulfed by the forest.

The inevitable happened: rain turned to snow at higher elevations early afternoon the following day. Venturing upwards, we hit dark, damp, sticky soil covered with snow. The cone-shaped hills around us were topped with a sprinkling of the white magic like huge iced buns. Rockets was ahead of me as I stopped for water at a creek which crossed the trail. A voice from behind startled me.

"How's it going?"

I spun round to see a very damp Trooper grinning at me.

"Trooper! Where the hell did you come from?"

Pleased though I was to see him, it again reminded me of slow progress. He'd hiked from Chester where we'd last seen each other. He'd made it through Oregon and the section from Crater Lake, which I hadn't. I couldn't help feeling a little envious of how far he'd walked. He knew how it felt to falter at the last hurdle after his previous PCT attempt ended a few years earlier. Determined to succeed this time, he was 313 miles away from doing so. He was smashing the distance to reach Stehekin, 251 miles away. That was the final town to re-supply before the end and lay 11 miles off trail. A bus service runs through the summer, taking hikers to this small settlement on the banks of Lake Chelan. There, they can rest and stock up for the final 65-mile section to the Canadian border. However, the buses had usually stopped by the middle of October, so time was running out. Anyway, Trooper was in good spirits and seemed glad to have company, as were we.

We camped that night and dried our gear by the fire. Through the day, we stayed reasonably dry in our waterproofs; only our socks and shoes were wet. We tried to build a fire every evening, but the damp conditions were making life difficult. Usually finding shelter in the forest gave us drier wood, but we constantly had to check and feed it before it spluttered to a moist and untimely death.

Trooper had left when I started in the morning, leaving Rockets taking photos of the appropriately named Dewey Lake, shrouded in a low mist. The target for the day lay 26 miles away: a cabin called the Urich Shelter, where we could dry out in comfort and, for once, warm up. I descended towards Highway 410 and Chinook Pass where the sun had emerged. A curling vapour rose from Trooper's gear, spread out over a wall drying by the roadside. Rockets arrived shortly afterwards, and I left ahead of both of them, eager to conquer a series of small passes between me and the shelter. I crested Sourdough Pass, Bluebell Pass and Scout Pass, the thought of a warm night spurring me ever onward. Rockets caught me quickly, and we finished the day with two fast paced two-hour stints. He pulled away from me as the sun set, saying he'd get a fire going.

Daylight was fading as I emerged from the forest, crossing a wooden bridge over Meadow Creek. I homed in on the cabin, seeing the windows glowing a faint orange in the murk.

"How is it in there?" I called out as I approached the large, impressive-looking shelter.

"Awesome!" came the muffled reply. "There's a stack of firewood, a good stove and seating. Come on in!"

You know your life is back to basics when seating becomes exciting. Rockets's head torch struggled to illuminate the interior. I turned on my torch too and found a few tea lights. The fire caught, and before long the gloomy cold warmed in appreciation, as the flames cast a flickering light which played a game of shadows and silhouettes on the walls. Trooper strolled in after dark, and we spent the evening drying out and eating in comfort. I updated my journal and saw a mouse sitting next to me, patiently waiting for a crumb or two.

Trooper had set off again by the time I left at 9am. Rockets said he wanted to zero at the cabin and take more photos. I left, crunching my way along an icy trail, guided by Trooper's footprints seeking out the dry landing spots. A solitary jet plane screamed over me, 20 minutes from Canada at that speed. Reaching Tacoma Pass, I was sitting and munching on snacks when two motorbikes pulled up and the riders approached. They congratulated me on my story, and gave me apples, pears and a pack of my favourite dark chocolate-covered almonds before zipping off home. The kindness of strangers still proved amazing.

My body was in reasonable shape after 173 days. I had an aching elbow and tight calf muscle which always made itself known wherever I walked. Otherwise, though, my only slight concern was a sore throat. I could handle a cold, but I sincerely hoped it wasn't the onset of flu. The weather had turned somewhat and, for the time being at least, I enjoyed a return to sunshine and rising temperatures. Fungi poked through the ground, topped with clods of earth, and announced themselves in vivid reds, browns, greens and whites. Sunset foliage painted the bushes, and leaves clung on with their last hope.

A hum of traffic intruded on my solitude as I reached the brow of a hill looking down on Snoqualmie Pass and Interstate 90. Ski lifts crawled up from the small cluster of buildings, and beyond I grimaced as a series of peaks and passes fluctuated to the edge of the Earth. I followed a collection of tracks downwards, crossed the road and walked, shivering, between a lost time of summer's end and the start of winter. The Howard Johnson Motel beckoned me over and Trooper was in reception, washed and laundered.

"Pockets is here," he said.

"What? What the hell!" I spluttered. "I left him at the cabin! He said he was resting for a day. How does that guy do it?"

"Well, he didn't say much," Trooper continued, "but he didn't walk in. I think he got picked up by a couple of hunters slightly the worse for wear."

"Do you know what room he's in?"

"No, but Reception may tell you, providing the receptionist has cheered up and finished with his arsehole routine."

I approached the desk and checked the PCT book, left open on the counter. It included comments about the establishment as well as messages for other hikers. Confusingly, most of the notes were obliterated by a black marker.

"Hi," I said to Dominic, seeing the name etched on to his shiny brass badge. "What's with the deletions in the PCT book?"

"I block out the negative ones," he replied curtly. "I don't want other customers reading them."

"Aren't you missing the point?" I asked. "That's what they're there for, to provide feedback."

"Is there something I can help you with?" he asked, ignoring my remark.

I looked at Trooper, who, in turn, raised his gaze skyward.

"I'd like to check in but will be sharing with Josh Myers."

"I'll need to speak to him about that." He checked the records, picked up the phone and called the room.

"There's a gentleman in Reception who says he will be sharing with you. I need you to come here and verify this is OK." He replaced the receiver and continued to ignore me while idly shuffling his paperwork. Trooper retreated to his room.

Rockets appeared, looking somewhat dishevelled and annoyed at being disturbed.

"I'll fill you in shortly," he said to me and then turned to Dominic.

"Wassup?" he asked.

"The room's on your credit card, so I need your permission to book this guy in."

Rockets glared at him. "Can you make my stay here anymore unpleasant than it already is?"

After checking in, I collapsed on the bed, and he filled me in on what had happened.

"I'm feeling terrible," he said. "I stayed at the shelter until midday and then started to walk but had no energy, I was struggling. I was stopping every few minutes to take a shit and then I virtually fell on to a forest road and had resigned myself to putting up the tent when a couple of hunters stopped in their truck. They drove me here; I got a bus to Seattle where a doctor took a stool sample. He thinks it's E.coli, but I have to wait for him to call."

"What are you going to do?"

"I'm not stopping now, Fozzie. I have to make the hike."

"And what's the deal with Reception?"

"That guy is an arsehole. He wouldn't let me check in till three-thirty despite the place being empty. All I wanted to do was sleep; he wouldn't give me the Wi-Fi passcode or my package he was holding, wouldn't let me change the channel on TV in Reception, wouldn't let me lie on the couch even though I made sure my feet were hanging off the end and wouldn't let me use the PC. He wouldn't let me do anything!"

The situation cooled in the evening as Dominic finished his shift and a more accommodating lady arrived. We ventured out into the rain to a local bar which had laid on a midweek all-you-can-eat Mexican feast. We ate heartily, including Rockets, whose hunger was alternating between non-existent and insatiable, despite his condition.

To my dismay, my boots hadn't arrived in the morning, so I left a note to return them to HQ and went online to order a pair for delivery up the trail. My existing footwear was splitting alarmingly, and the sole flapped around as I walked. Rockets also had to wait for new shoes and for the doctor to call, so as usual, he said he'd catch us up.

I puffed up the steep 3,000-foot climb from the pass into the Alpine Lakes Wilderness with Trooper, and camped in a depression, which offered shelter from the bitter wind whipping through the mountains. Trooper's pace was identical to mine. After slipping over a couple of times on icy ground, he was fast earning himself the new nickname of 'Tripper'.

There were 255 miles to the Canadian border and the end of the PCT, for Trooper, at least. Before the finish line were two re-supply points: 75 miles away lay trail angels the Dinsmores, near Skykomish, and 99 miles further lay Stehekin, the last chance to re-supply for the final 81 miles to the border. A further eight miles into Canada was Manning Park, where a solitary hotel stood by a main road, from where Trooper could get transport home, and I could travel back to the Bridge of the Gods to make inroads south through Oregon.

At our lunch stop, a succession of hikers heading back to Snoqualmie Pass came by. Instead of the familiar "You won't make it" comments, they were full of praise and fed us snacks from their packs. I felt like a duck waiting for bits of bread.

The forecast looked promising, but I knew that mountain weather patterns were notoriously temperamental. The ice was also becoming a nuisance. Rounding a corner cut into a steep incline, I gingerly placed each foot on a solid sheet of ice glued to the rock. Knowing Trooper was behind, I waited for him to round the bend and called out a warning: "Trooper, watch the ice, it's. . ."

It was too late. His legs slipped out from under him, and he went crashing down. I grimaced as he fell, hoping he'd grab the nearest lump of something solid to stop him careering over the edge. This was the third time I had seen him fall. He always laughed it off, dusted himself down, checked nothing had fallen off him or his equipment, and continued. He surveyed his trekking pole, which had snapped, and performed a spot of emergency repair with the aid of that good old hiker staple, duct tape.

We all carried duct tape. The wide, silver material is easy to tear off yet extremely strong. To save space in our packs, we wound it around trekking poles. We used it for pack repairs, broken sunglasses, ripped clothing and even taped it to our ankles. The strength and slippery surface were ideal for blister prevention. I considered it one of a few truly necessary items.

Our hunger was raging. The mix of mountainous terrain and cold weather was playing havoc with our systems. In extreme conditions, the body prioritises and conserves fuel to look after the main organs and to increase bodily warmth. This is its basic survival instinct. Remaining calories are used for energy expenditure. Fat reserves take a hammering when the temperature drops, and consequently I craved sugary sweets, oils, nuts, and cheese.

During the summer crunchy oat bars satisfied my sweet tooth, and I could get by on two a day. Now when re-supplying, I'd allow for no fewer than seven sweet candies per day. On a typical day, I'd polish off four bags of M&M's, a couple of munchy bars and a Snickers or two. I ate double portions of oats in the morning, laced with sultanas, nuts, powdered milk and sugar. My evening meal, usually a packet of pre-mixed rice with various flavours, got doused with pools of olive oil, chunks of cheese and bacon bits. My jerky consumption was alarming and expensive. 500 grams used to see me through the week: now I consumed three times as much.

My hands never fared well in cold weather. They'd started to crack, bleed and were very dry, despite taking care and using my gloves. My feet were permanently wet, and painful when I stopped, although once moving it subsided. The rest of my body was coping. I walked in a long-sleeved wool top and leggings, covered with my waterproof jacket and trousers. My wool hat stayed in place all day, and once at evening camp I put another wool T-shirt on and replaced my jacket with my down alternative. Despite advice from equipment manufacturers to wear nothing inside sleeping bags, as the body heat warms them quicker, I still wore most of my clothes. I knew it was getting colder because I was waking to ice on the inside of the tent as well as the outside.

The Glacier Peak Wilderness was stunning, a mix of all terrains. In places it was flat, but often it dipped, dived and wiggled its way through Washington. We clung to ridges, walked along a trail cut into the hillside, relaxed on soft soil and slipped on the rock. Enjoying the sun in the exposed sections, we shivered when we returned to the forest. Once the sun was up it was pleasantly warm, and even Trooper commented on how lucky we were for the time of year. The landscape was taking its toll at times, though, and 25-mile days meant 12 hours' walking.

Knee-jarring descents levelled out and rose into formidable ascents. It was a repeating pattern of bottoming out and then getting stuck into the uphill stretches. After five minutes, lungs were heaving, legs were screaming and calf muscles were ready to burst. Thereafter, however, the physical conditioning we'd acquired over the past few months came into its own, the adrenaline surged, and we settled into a good rhythm.

We left the Waptus River intending to cover 29 miles, leave nine miles to reach Highway 2, and catch a ride to the Dinsmores'. Fallen trees littered our path, the remnants of a major storm a few years earlier. We regularly had to clamber over slippery, moss-covered tree limbs or duck underneath them. Trooper laughed as I spent ages figuring out how to surmount one tree, only to find, upon rounding a switchback, the same culprit blocking that as well.

Access to this remote part of the world was difficult, but the forestry service had cleared a large area over many years, and the work was paying dividends. The workers had put in a mammoth effort. One huge sawn-off trunk revealed growth rings dating back to the Middle Ages and further.

Someone had marked notable dates on the rings, such as the world wars, Declaration of Independence and so forth.

Trooper had a metal mug strapped to his pack, which kept banging against the metal buckle. It was like being followed by a Swiss cow.

"You like your coffee in the morning, huh, Fozzie?" Trooper said, breaking a spell of contemplative walking.

"Coffee in the morning should be compulsory for everyone," I answered, smiling.

"I agree. But what is the fashion these days for putting other stuff in with it and ruining the whole drink?" "Like syrups?" I asked.

"Yep. Vanilla flavour, hazelnut, cream, sprinkles, hell, even the milk should go."

"Strong, thick and black, one sugar," I continued. "Just like motor oil."

"I've given up smoking and gambling but never, ever, coffee," he added.

"At least it's natural. I know it gets a bad rap sometimes, but there's nothing wrong with it."

"And Fozzie, you know when you've found a coffee shop with good coffee?"

"No?"

"They charge for refills. Free refills don't necessarily mean bad coffee, but if they're charging, it means it's the real thing."

I was contemplating a serious caffeine top-up in town when I approached the aptly named Deception Creek. It tumbled through a slice of mountain and, although not particularly wide, flowed quickly. The stepping stones looked slippery, and the first one meant leaping four feet. I eyed the route and crouched, ready to spring. Once there, I'd need a balancing act to jump to the next boulder, and then a final vault to the far bank. I reached the other side and, aware of Trooper's propensity to fall, I dropped my pack in case I needed to rescue him from the currents.

Trooper eyed the hardest boulder for an eternity. He kept making false starts and then backing down. I glanced around and waited patiently until I looked back to see him in mid-flight. His right foot landed on the boulder but didn't grip and he did the splits. A four-point plan rushed into my head. First, drag him out; second, dry him out; third, get him comfortable and warm; and fourth, run back to the two equestrians we had passed earlier and have them ride back and call mountain rescue. I rushed to the bank, where he'd managed to curtail his fall. His face suggested he was in pain. I gestured as though to grab him.

"No, Fozzie! I'm good, I can get over!"

Feet now wet, he cautiously made it to my side and rubbed his shin.

"All OK?" I asked hopefully.

"Yeah, I thought I'd broken something when I landed, but it feels fine."

We struggled through to Trap Lake and camped by the shore. We were taking a hammering. Exhaustion set in when we stopped in the evening. After getting into warm clothes, erecting shelters, building a fire and eating, all we were fit for was sleep. I watched the moon reflecting in the lake; a slight wind rippled the water's surface and blurred the reflection into a huge, curled serpent. The tops of the pine trees painted an irregular border to the night sky above them. The fire faded as the last weak wafts of smoke rose and disappeared as they left the orange embers.

We hit Highway 2 late morning and spent a frustrating hour trying to catch a ride. Roadworks spilled on to the hard shoulder, leaving nowhere for vehicles to pull over, so we walked for a mile and tried again. A young guy soon stopped, eager to show off his new silver Mustang. We reached Skykomish and collected our bounce boxes from the post office. An extra warmer top and gaiters had also arrived.

"You're late to be thru-hiking, aren't you?" came a voice from behind us. We turned around, and Trooper recognised Jerry Dinsmore from his previous hike.

"If you can wait until two o'clock, I can give you a ride when I finish work," Jerry continued. "Come to the school when you're ready."

We thanked him and sat outside the brilliant deli by the junction. It was a beautiful day, and we warmed ourselves on the deck while scoffing delicious, homemade breakfast muffins. So good were they that we each ordered the same again, washed down by their excellent coffee. The refills cost extra.

I'd not found much internet access in this remote stretch of Washington. I now had an iPod so sat expectantly outside the library; closed but the Wi-Fi was on, so I was able to rattle off a few emails and update my blog. There was no news from Rockets and, as usual, I had no cell reception on my phone with which to check on him.

The Dinsmores' home, River Haven, lay eight miles from Skykomish. Jerry, puffing on a cigar, gave us a brief description of how he ran things with his wife, Andrea. They'd converted a large garage for PCT hikers, and there was ample room. We were the only ones there. We did our laundry, fired up the stove and bought provisions from the store. Several hiker boxes brimmed with surplus food; if it were not for these, our cuisine for the section to Stehekin would have been limited.

"You're English, Fozzie, yes?" Andrea said when she came over to check if we were comfortable.

"Yes, I am."

"Two English guys passed through last week and stayed for a few days to help build the new deck."

"They did?" I exclaimed, wondering who it could have been. "What were their names?"

"Nick and Chris. They've been walking since the start but missed a section between Crater Lake and the Bridge of the Gods. They said they intended to return and finish it to complete their thru-hike."

I couldn't believe my luck and the coincidence was too good to pass up. Not only had they missed the same section as I had, but they were returning to walk it, and they were fellow countrymen. I emailed Rockets the news, saying I intended to catch them and that he should join us. I contacted Uncle Gary, who had walked for many weeks with them, and asked if he could forward their contact details.

We ate well at the café over the road and slept like fallen logs. We woke in darkness to pack our bags and prepare for the 99-mile section to Stehekin. After giving our thanks and farewells to the Dinsmores, we went back to the café for breakfast.

"Be careful!" Andrea called out after us. "The weather's turning for the worse. They say storms are rolling in."

Chapter 15
Monument 78

A hiker whose desires stray from the PCT becomes an empty vessel stumbling across beauty without ever touching it.
Jake Nead

We tucked into breakfast at the café and were lucky to catch a ride back to Skykomish with the deli owner. Seizing the opportunity to stock up on more fat, I promptly ordered four muffins wrapped in foil to go, figuring the cold would preserve them. I visited the library again to check on news from Rockets. There wasn't anything, so I emailed him our plans and returned to the deli. Trooper looked suitably pleased with himself as he introduced a local called Kathleen, who'd offered to take us back to Stevens Pass.

"I need to walk my dogs and would love to come with you for a few miles, if that's OK?" she said.

"No problem," Trooper replied. From his expression, he seemed a little smitten.

Kathleen walked with us for an hour, kissed us both on the cheek, and wished us good luck.

We had 99 miles to Stehekin. After some discussion, we

decided four days for the hike would be more achievable than three, bearing in mind the terrain and weather. Also, the Stehekin post office, where we had mail, was shut on Sunday. We adjusted our plan to knock out four 25-mile days, arrive Saturday afternoon, take a zero on Sunday, re-supply and collect our packages on Monday, then head off for the last stage.

The going was gruelling but beautiful. A pattern emerged – uphill, then flat, and downhill. At the summits we glimpsed the land and lakes below through breaks in the trees. I wondered who'd first discovered and named the waters. Some were obviously christened because of their shape – Heart Lake and Pear Lake, to name two. Others mimicked their appearance, such as Mirror Lake and Glass Lake. The origins of the more curious names kept me guessing: Lake Janus, Sally Ann, and Valhalla.

We reminisced about wrong turns we'd made and the time wasted as a result. I boasted I'd only slipped up once, with Brains and Rockets at Kings Creek. Feeling well pleased with my natural navigation skills, I soon found myself munching on humble pie as Trooper called out from behind, "Fozzie! You're going the wrong way! That's Cady Trail! The PCT is down here!"

I backtracked sheepishly and watched, amused, as Trooper swung his pack on to his back – and toppled unceremoniously backwards, caught off guard by its weight.

Surveying the land from Fire Creek Pass, we saw a huge storm front rolling in from the west. By the time we'd descended 200 feet, it had cleared the ridge line to our left, the clouds whipping ferociously. Tossed around like leaves in a storm, we sped off the pass towards Mica Creek, where we'd spotted flatter ground nestling in the forest. It was dark as we filtered water and camped, just in time for the rain to fall as another mist bank swallowed us.

The morning dawned dull although it wasn't raining. Trooper was just ahead but had disappeared into a foggy gloom. Passing Vista Creek, menacing skeletal trees appeared in the murk, huge Grim Reapers eyeing me. Occasionally, a sign reassured us of the right track. I pulled my jacket collar tighter and shivered, trying to fend off a chill that penetrated like a ghost. The mist created an eerie, oppressive environment, the opening sequence to a black and white horror movie.

I longed for warmth. We spent most of our time cold and damp, only warming around a camp fire or in our sleeping bags. Waking in the mornings, I stayed in my bag while boiling water for oats and coffee to stay warm as long as possible. Packing gear, I emerged only to stow my tent, and then we left, using movement to generate body heat. I battled the stationary chill monster, stay still long enough and the demon attacked, fleeing was the only weapon I had.

I started to fantasise about a back-up team. Amongst the attractive benefits such as an evening massage, mobile shower tent, and a personal chef, the thought of someone gently waking me in the morning with a cup of hot chocolate and cooked breakfast bordered on nirvana.

Descending 3,000 feet from Dolly Vista to the Suiattle River, we again clambered unceremoniously over and under fallen trees, emerging at a wide expanse of sand and rock either side of the river. Shielding our eyes from the sunlight, we scanned the opposite bank for a gap in the forest, any hint of the trail while following the occasional pile of stones left by others. Trooper said the bridge had washed away the last time he'd passed through. We hoped it had been rebuilt since but unfortunately, we were disappointed. We wandered along the water's edge, our feet sinking into the waterlogged soil, trying to cross. Eventually, a fallen tree offered a slippery crossing point, and I cringed as Trooper cautiously stepped across and then ran the last few feet to safety. One slip meant plunging into the raging, icy torrent below.

Energised, we raced up the incline as night fell, collecting water from Miners Creek. Reaching flatter ground in fading light, we turned on our head torches. For an hour we walked, sweeping the beams around the dense forest, hoping to spot a flat clearing for camp. We pulled up at the best option available, a meagre space battling for room with the trees, where we squeezed in our tents. We talked of making the 22 miles into Stehekin the following day, and looked forward to drying out.

Trooper had stumbled four times in as many days. We reached High Bridge mid-afternoon after good progress, but my ankle ached; after six months' hiking, I feared I was injured. We turned right after the bridge, hoping the Ranger station was occupied, for a possible ride into Stehekin. A padlocked door suggested otherwise, so we began an 11-mile plod to town.

After two hours a house appeared, with several buildings resembling holiday cabins. No one answered the door, and the cabins were locked, following the end of the season. Just as we walked away dejectedly, a car pulled in and stopped. The window lowered, and Martha stuck her head out.

"You doing the PCT?" she enquired. "You're late, aren't you?!"

I smiled.

"If I had a dollar for every time I'd heard that!" I said. "Yes, we are. We're looking for somewhere to stay. Are the cabins available, or do we have to carry on to Stehekin?"

Her husband, Martin, leaned over from the driver's side.

"Follow us, we can help you."

We trailed the car up to a beautiful log cabin set in grassy grounds with a vegetable patch to one side. Martin led us to a room above the wood store.

"You're welcome to stay here," he said. "Give me a minute to turn on the hot water. There's a shower next door, and I'll bring you more logs for the fire. Knock at the house in an hour and we'll feed you."

I looked at Trooper; he was speechless, as was I. We thanked Martin, and Trooper agreed to light a fire as I stood under a steaming shower for ten minutes, feeling the heat slowly penetrate my chilled bones.

As we walked to the house, Tip, a border collie, intercepted us and demanded I play ball, which I did gladly. We knocked on the back door and as it creaked open, Martha's kind face beckoned us in.

"Take a seat. Coffee?"

"Yes, please," we replied in unison.

As she placed popcorn and vegetable snacks on the table, her daughter, Misha, chatted. I thought how accommodating the Americans were, compared to us typically reserved English. There'd been few occasions back in my home country when I'd been offered somewhere to stay, a plate of hot food and good company. It's not that we English are unfriendly; we just don't take people in off the street and give them a bed. I'd experienced similar hospitality in other countries and always made a point of doing the same if I saw wet cycle tourists or hikers. I cannot fault the affability of our US friends.

Trooper, being vegetarian, winced as Martha placed a deer heart on the chopping board and cut it into bite-sized pieces.

"You both OK with deer heart?"

"Never eaten the heart from anything, but I'm willing to try it," I said, glancing at Trooper.

"I'm vegetarian," he said, shrugging his shoulders. "But by the look of that salad and rice you're making, I'll be fine."

She dusted the meat chunks with flour and carefully tipped them into a hot pan, the meat sizzling and spitting as it hit the oil. Having lit the fire and settled comfortably in a chair, Martin explained how he'd lived in the cabin all his life; his father had built the place years earlier.

The table groaned under the salad, heart, rice, vegetables and homemade bread. We wolfed it all down. The deer was excellent: not tough, as I'd feared; it melted in my mouth like a perfectly cooked steak. Martha didn't even let us help clear up. She then turned on the radio to contact friends.

"Martin can take you to town tomorrow," she said, turning to us. "I'm trying to arrange a ride back to the trailhead, and I can probably get the postmistress to open up for you as well. Come over at eight-thirty for breakfast; we'll leave after."

We thanked them profusely and returned to our cosy haven with full stomachs and warm limbs.

"Unbelievable!" Trooper exclaimed as we relaxed. "Incredible hospitality; I've never experienced anything like it."

"I know," I agreed. "If we hadn't walked up that drive, we'd be shivering in the woods again."

As Martha dished up homemade buttermilk and oat pancakes, maple syrup from their own trees, eggs and a fruit smoothie in the morning, I wondered about the whole karma thing. Believe what you will, but I feel that whether you offer someone shelter, such as we'd experienced here, work voluntarily, even buy a friend a coffee or hand your finished newspaper to someone, the goodwill, hopefully, returns. Those who give freely and thoughtfully are looked after.

The karma issue rolled around in my head further. How, I wondered, were our karma 'points' recorded? After all, to offer an extreme scenario, if I stood on a street corner for a week handing out £10 notes to everyone, invited them to dinner, offering to clean their houses and do their shopping, then surely, I'd rack up a fair-sized karma points balance? I'd never expect it to be directly returned; that would be missing the point. I realise that it may return in another form at another time if we're lucky. However, would my altruism on the street corner earn me points? 12 points for making someone dinner? 15 for cleaning their house? Who was keeping the records? Could I expect my balance to return in equal value? Martha's karma balance must be running into the thousands, I thought. Mother Teresa did well too, and all those who volunteer for good causes. I made a note to try harder in the future. What goes around comes around.

Martin drove us to Stehekin. We passed the famous bakery which, to our dismay was closed, while Lake Chelan sparkled and winked through the trees. He dropped us at the quayside, said he'd see us again as it was a small town, and we thanked him profusely. Checking in at a cabin overlooking the lake, we ventured to the post office which opened up as we approached. Inside one package was a cigar – or 'stogie', as they're called in the States – from Elk. He'd written a short note:

"Fozzie, three requests, please. Firstly, smoke this stogie at the Canadian border for me. Secondly, send me a postcard from Stehekin, and thirdly, sign the book at the monument for me. I was a dumbass and couldn't find it! Lastly, you are a savage badass, congrats on your accomplishment. Stay in touch, please – Elk."

I smiled. Despite last seeing him just weeks before, I felt nostalgic, as if it had been 20 years ago. I wrote him a postcard (he'd even left a stamp), tucked the stogie safely in my pack and went to do laundry.

Trooper was snoozing as I reached the cabin. I quietly made myself a cup of tea (an Englishman must have his tea), grabbed my journal and sat outside on the deck. A gaggle of geese glided effortlessly over the lake, and a solitary fisherman rowed out with his line in tow, creating arrow head ripples. I thought of the distance I'd come and the miles still ahead. Four or five days to Canada and three weeks in Oregon. Back in Packwood, I remembered reading an email from a friend. "Don't worry," she said. "You'll breeze the last section and soon it will all be a distant memory."

Still, I didn't want to finish; I cherished the memories, I didn't want them faded and distant. I was among only a handful of hikers still on trail. I'd come to the PCT to experience the adventure of a lifetime, a dream ten years in the making, and despite the hardships, I was still happy to be here, still marvelling at the craziness, still proud to be living it. I recalled a man in the launderette earlier who'd said, "Rain for the rest of the week, snow at higher elevations, ninety percent chance," and that Trooper had replied that the weather will do what it will – we couldn't change it – but we would succeed.

I remembered a quote from a book called Zorba the Greek. It proposed that when we're happy, often we fail to recognise it in the moment, and it's only when we look back that we fully realise how happy we'd been. Sitting on that deck in Stehekin, I was happy; but, more importantly, I was aware of my happiness.

My phone beeped with a message from Rockets: "Mucker, in Chelan, three hours' ferry ride from Stehekin. Will arrive late afternoon."

Trooper was awake, and I told him the news. After much discussion, we reluctantly agreed we couldn't wait. Time was now seriously against us, storms were forecast, and we had to get through the mountains. I replied to Rockets: "Mate, we have to move early. Heading for Rainy Pass at day's end, catch up; you always do."

I felt guilty, like a mountaineer abandoning his partner, but my goal was clear and I needed to move. I'd waited for Rockets too many times.

Journal entry:
I'm writing this from a cabin overlooking Lake Chelan at Stehekin, the last chance to re-supply before Canada.

I look at what lies above. There's a clear snow line at 4,000 feet; the mountains are stark white below clouds obscuring the upper elevations. Solitary spectres of mist float across the lake and geese call me to move. The greens of pines coat the hills, the uniformity broken by the occasional gold of a lost maple. It's eerily quiet save the leaves rustling as they play with a swirling breeze.

I think about how far I've come, and how far is left. My time with Trooper has been terrific; he's a fine companion. Tomorrow we leave at 7am for the final 89-mile stretch, whereupon he finishes his PCT thru-hike. Rockets has a confirmed case of E. coli and has been told by the doctor to get off trail. He is ignoring this, telling me, as usual, "You can't keep Pockets down."

We stumble in here on Saturday, October 23rd. Trooper has fallen four times today, a habit earning him the revised nickname of 'Tripper'. We're increasing our speed noticeably because the snow is worsening, and the route in Washington is a tough one through the North Cascades. A few miles from Stehekin, my ankle started aching, but I just put it down to over-exertion and figure rest will sort it out.

Martin and Martha offered to take us back to the High Bridge trailhead, and we met in the café. She returned my gaze as we entered, looking concerned.

"Fozzie, there's bad weather rolling in. Forecast says four feet of snow. Martin said nothing, but his expression mirrored her concern. They knew from experience how fruitless it was to warn stubborn thru-hikers.

"The weather will do what it will," Trooper said. "We have to move."

"We'll call you from Canada," I added. "If you don't hear from us within seven days, then we may be in trouble." I wanted to smile to lighten my comment, but it seemed inappropriate.

Martha did smile, but weakly. As we drove to the trailhead, I wiped the condensation from the window and peered at the mountains. It had snowed again.

If we knew then what the next few days had in store, I doubt we'd have even left.

During my PCT research, I watched a series of videos made by two brothers who'd hiked the trail some years earlier. One had been plagued by blisters and foot problems from the start, which never eased for the entire hike. They arrived at Rainy Pass; nothing more than a picnic area by the side of Highway 20, situated at mile 2,595, just 61 miles from the northern terminus. After several months hiking, and with only three days before completion, the guy quit, stuck out a thumb and got off trail. He'd simply reached breaking point, unable to go further.

I was dumbstruck, incredulous even. I sympathised but screamed at the TV in disbelief. Little did I realise how similar my experience would be.

The day started innocently enough. We made slow progress up the 3,500-foot climb to the pass. Rain fell constantly, the tracks awash with water. My skin felt like a sponge, soaking up ice, which penetrated deeper. We concentrated on our breathing and focused on our target. Hunting the best route through a shallow creek, I placed my right foot on the ground and came to a shuddering halt. Pain shot up from my ankle, my leg buckled in surrender, and I fell. Trooper, tucked into his jacket, hadn't heard, so I picked myself up and carefully placed my foot back down. My ankle screamed again.

"Trooper!" I cried.

He turned around, peering through his hood. "You OK? What's up?"

"My ankle. I've done something to my ankle."

We sat under a tree, shivering, eating lunch in the rain. I'd not experienced joint or muscle pain like it. I was convinced my ankle was broken, but then I remembered it aching approaching Stehekin. Trooper said little, letting me deal with it. We set off again, but as I put weight on it, pain seared like a hot iron. Trooper looked anxious, pausing and giving me time. I let the trekking pole take the strain and hobbled, fighting the urge to return to safety. The rain turned to snow as we climbed, covering our heads and packs in white powder. The temperature plummeted, and my body screamed.

Two miles from Rainy Pass, I decided to quit my thru-hike; I'd had enough. I thought about the brother who'd given up and suddenly I understood why; his patience, worn unendurably thin, had finally run out. He was empty, there was nothing more to give.

I'd started at Campo with a full bag of patience, courage, and stamina. Slowly, like my water bag had punctured on Hat Creek Rim, those traits had also leaked, dripping away slowly over 2500 miles until suddenly it was empty. Like Hat Creek, I'd nothing to refill that bag. It was over.

I said nothing to Trooper, but plodded on, looking up at the stark white landscape that lay between us and Canada. This was no mere dusting – it was deep snow. I'll come back next year and finish off this section, I reasoned. I can be in a warm motel in a couple of hours.

"Trooper, I'm quitting here."

"You're what?!" He swung around almost before I'd finished the sentence.

"My ankle is excruciating. I've had enough; I can't go on any more. I'm done"

"Fozzie, hold on!" He held out his hands, moving them gently up and down in a calming motion. "Give it time. Get in your tent, warm up, eat some food and think. Don't make a rash decision; you're four days from Canada and then there's Oregon, it'll be warmer there. Wait 'till the morning and then decide."

We smashed a frozen puddle and filtered the water. Snow continued falling as we made camp, inflated our mattresses and puffed up our sleeping bags. I checked my watch for the temperature – 20F. I slid, aching, into my bag with all the clothing I possessed, and cupped my hands round a mug of tea, idly observing a lump of powdered milk floating on the surface. Tapping the roof of the tent occasionally to remove the accumulated snow, I read until my eyes were heavy, zipped up my bag and drew the hood string tightly around my head.

Waking early, I called to Trooper.

"You awake, Troop?"

"My mind is, I'm just waiting for my body to catch up. Go in 30?"

"OK."

We hauled ourselves up to Cutthroat Pass at 7,000 feet. The snow deepened, at times to our knees. By some miracle, my ankle never even twinged during those four hours.

However, I grimaced at what greeted us at the top – the PCT had all but disappeared. The snow had settled on the trail, leaving a faint indentation. An ice-encased sign directed us onwards. I checked my map, picturing the contours of the terrain ahead. My navigation, normally sound, isn't great in the dark or poor conditions. Trooper asked if we should continue.

"I can get us through, but you'll have to bear with me and excuse the occasional error," I said, trying to sound confident. "I'm not good at navigation in these conditions, Troop, but you can pick out the trail occasionally." I showed him the map. "We have to keep this side of that ridge, about 200 feet down; look, you can just pick it out."

A faint trail cut through the hillside before fading.

"If we concentrate, keep an eye out and check the GPS occasionally, let's see how we go. We've got 25 miles to Harts Pass, there's a Ranger Station there and a road. I don't think we'll make it today but if we're struggling, then we have a get-out clause."

The weather cleared, and even the fickle mountain weather suggested storms were unlikely. Through ever-deepening snow, we pushed onwards, at times up to our waists. On the west-facing slopes, we guessed our way through drifts that had obliterated not only the trail but everything around it. My ankle continued to hold, the snow acting like a huge ice pack, numbing the pain and cushioning my stride. We warmed in our jackets, rubbing and blowing our hands, keeping them warm before quickly put our gloves back on. Sunlight bounced everywhere, blinding us as we fumbled for our sunglasses. We saw no one, there were no footprints, and at that point I realised, save Rockets, we were the last hikers on the PCT that year.

We carefully descended to Methow Creek, keeping back from the edge of the trail, which dropped away steeply. Pausing to take in water and calories, we cooled, shivering as our clothing struggled to keep in our body heat. Huge expanses opened out below us, green valleys dotted with forests as creeks tumbled over the hills.

I slept badly, curled in a foetal position wearing my hat and gloves, my bag wrapped tightly around me. Nine miles from Harts Pass, we progressed slowly. Constantly comparing the map to my field of view, I regularly checked the GPS and my compass. Somehow, we were still on the PCT.

At Harts Pass, we startled two hikers sitting in their car who looked as surprised to see us as we were to see them. We sat on the steps by the Ranger station, closed for the winter, and took stock. The hikers came over, and we told them our plans. Offering bananas, apples and cups of tea, they apologised for having eaten their chocolate brownies. They looked concerned for our welfare and insisted on providing their phone number, pleading us to call when we reached Canada. The weather, they advised, was a mixed bag; sunny at times but with fierce winds and low cloud.

There were picnic tables, fire pits, a latrine and enough firewood to last the evening. It was now 5pm and nearly dark; the wind had increased and the clouds were indeed hampering visibility. We had 31 miles until monument 78, three wooden pillars marking the end of the PCT, and then another six miles to Manning Park. Trooper was nearly a thru-hiker.

We dragged a log to the fire pit to sit on and spent time

stocking up the wood pile. As the flames came alive, my body responded, and we sat huddled with our palms facing the heat. I drank cups of tea and hot chocolate, ate my dinner and then cooked another to battle my endless hunger pangs. We agreed to start early next morning, and Trooper retired for the night; it would be a difficult day.

At 4am my alarm kicked me rudely into consciousness. I peered under the fly sheet into the darkness; snow fell and low clouds streamed past. Staying in my sleeping bag, I drank coffee and cooked an extra-large helping of oats. I heard Trooper stir as his spoon clinked a pot, the sound fading into the forest. We emerged, rubbed our eyes, smiled nervously, and packed our gear away.

Trouble hit straight away. Visibility was down to 50 feet, a merciless easterly wind slammed us and snow streaked across our faces, forcing us to turn our heads away and pull our hoods tighter. Clouds whipped past as we strained to spot a trail that was vanishing by the second. We could barely hear each other through the noise; just concentrating was exhausting. Trooper said he'd never have attempted it on his own and that it was my navigation that had got us this far. I put it more down to luck than skill and was glad of the company. Walking with him, he'd never complained, despite the battering we were taking.

It took forever for the sun to rise; at times I doubted it even would. We hiked at 7,000 feet, and as light slowly came, our surroundings materialised. I tried to record a video, but the batteries failed within seconds in the cold even though my camera was warm inside my jacket pocket.

We battled up hills, and I waited for Trooper at the summits while scanning the lay of the land, finding our position and route. He struggled, but I needed the time to navigate and rest myself. Simple tasks, such as reaching for my map or unwrapping a snack, were hampered by the cold that attacked our hands when we removed our gloves. Snow clung to our gaiters and boots, accumulating to blocks of ice. Whenever we stopped, the chill sank in further, so we kept moving, even strolling around when we ate to keep from seizing up. I felt like an engine low on oil, trying to turn over on a cold morning.

My snack rations depleted. I'd packed enough to see me to Canada, but my hunger ran deep, and my body craved sugar. I kept borrowing more than my allowance, so the next break or meal would be one or two candy bars short. Candy loans, as I called them, were becoming dangerous. At this rate, I thought, I'd be negotiating a food overdraft at breakfast.

"Trooper!" I called out through the wind.

"Yes, Fozzie."

"When we get through this, I'll buy you a beer!"

"I don't drink!"

"Oh, yeah, I forgot. OK, I'll treat you to a huge steak dinner then!"

"Fozzie, I'm vegetarian!"

We settled on a meat-free breakfast, the thought of which had me salivating for hours.

At mile 2,628 (for Trooper, at least), and cresting a summit getting icier by the minute, we saw a suitable flat spot to camp. I was fed up with the unremitting cold. My gloves were struggling, my hands cracked and bleeding. No matter what clothing I wore, the chill penetrated the layers and chipped away my resolve. The wood was too damp for a fire, so we sucked the heat from our food and drink, our bodies clinging to that warmth and portioning it to our needy extremities. I figured my mug of tea must have been the warmest thing for a twenty-mile radius. We scraped back the snow to solid ground to drive in our tent pegs and then made plans for Trooper's final day before attempting to sleep.

We had 12 miles to the finish and then eight miles further to Manning Park in Canada. Once we'd surmounted the imminent Devils Stairway, it was downhill to the border. The problem was one section called Lakeview. The hikers at Harts Pass had warned of a quarter-mile-long west-facing slope, renowned for accumulating snow. It was the last hurdle. As I rounded a corner, I realised they were right. A steep hill plunged menacingly, the trail was non-existent and we didn't have ice axes or crampons. The only saving grace was the soft snow, offering grip; if it had been frozen, we'd have the danger of an angled traverse, like walking on a slanting mirror. We took slow, deliberate steps across, the snow reaching our thighs, and cautiously glanced at the 1,500-foot drop to the rocks below. The wind intensified. Even the clouds lowered as if a higher power were trying every mean trick to make us quit at the last stretch.

We reached the top of the staircase and sat on our packs. Ice encased my boots. I looked at Trooper; he grinned, and for good reason. In eight miles he'd become a PCT thru-hiker, and it was all downhill now. After admitting he wasn't good in winter conditions, having never camped in them, I was initially worried about him. I couldn't have wished for a better companion through the toughest and most extreme conditions I'd ever hiked in. Upbeat to a fault, he'd made me smile in the direst of circumstances.

As we descended, the snow stopped, the temperature rose and we peeled off our jackets. Water dripped from the trees and we skidded on wet mud and rock.

"There it is!" Trooper said, stopping abruptly and pointing.

"There's what?"

"Monument 78. That's the finish of the PCT."

I moved my head from side to side, looking through the foliage. Trooper handed me his camera and asked me to film his moment. He sped up in anticipation, finally reaching a small clearing with three wooden pillars on one side. He let it all go.

"Yes!" he cried. "YES!"

Looking skywards, he raised his arms above his head.

"Well done, mate," I said.

"Thanks, Fozzie. Couldn't have done that without you."

"Nor I you."

We spent an hour relaxing. There was no border control here, simply a clear-cut line through the forest, stretching from one horizon to the other. I wondered if it was necessary to fell thousands of trees just to mark a boundary.

We found the trail register in a metal obelisk, and I signed my name as well as Elk's. Trooper scanned back through the pages to see who else had finished. I lit the ceremonial stogie Elk had given me. After his successful second attempt, and unsuccessful first, Trooper had hiked 5,300 miles for that moment. I could only admire his resolve and hoped mine would get me through the remaining 300 miles left in Oregon.

We followed forestry tracks for another two hours before

emerging at the highway. A mile further, we reached the most welcoming Manning Park Hotel. Eating a hearty dinner, Trooper bought me a celebratory meal and a bottle of wine. I chuckled as the waitress offered me water.

"Yes, please," I replied. "But no ice, I've had enough of that stuff to last a lifetime."

For the first time in days I was warm and well fed. I looked forward to Crater Lake and the final section in Oregon to earn my place as a Pacific Crest Trail thru-hiker. It had been the hardest week of my life in those violent conditions, with my ankle nearly ending my adventure; but I was proud to have persevered. I was on an immense high, buzzing with excitement.

I had no inkling then that the news I'd receive in the morning would send my world crashing down around me.

Chapter 16
A New Strength

How can we return to our normal lives and ever hope to achieve the high we've experienced out here?
Nick 'The Brit' De Bairacli Levy

I woke early and called my parents.

"Dad, I made it to Canada, just have to do that section in Oregon. Is Mum there?"

"She's at your nan's. Well done."

His voice sounded unusual and I dialled my nan's house. My mother answered but immediately broke down in tears as she handed the phone to my sister.

"Sis, what's going on? What's wrong?"

"Keith, Nan died this morning. She had a stroke two weeks ago and has been in hospital since. She couldn't really talk but understood what we were saying and nodded her answers. We didn't want to worry you with it, which is why we didn't call; we thought she'd be OK. We asked her if she wanted you to finish the walk for her and everyone. You'll probably miss the funeral, but she wants you to complete it – you should go for it."

My sister also cried and then I broke down too. My mum took the phone again.

"Keith, you must finish now for Nan. Do it for her."

I tried dealing with the news. My high had come down to earth with a thump, and it hurt bad.

"OK, I will," I said. "I'll do it for Nan."

Ending the call, I fought back more tears. I'd enough reasons of my own to finish the walk, but now I hiked for my nan's memory. After a couple of hours I'd calmed down and, strangely, felt uplifted, even managing to smile. The shock and grief abated, and a new strength surged. Before I'd left, we'd said our goodbyes.

"See you when I get back," I said as she kissed me on the cheek.

"Bye, Keify."

It felt like a broken promise, that I'd lied, but I took comfort in knowing she wouldn't have held that against me. Now her strength bolstered me, and I felt it. In a moment of clarity, I knew she'd be right there by my side as I finished the PCT.

We'd never shared an angry word. She'd struggled to bring up three children through a world war, scraping together enough money to live on. My walk paled in comparison to her toil, and I reminded myself that, if it were not for her, I wouldn't even be doing the PCT, let alone be on this planet. A new determination surged, an invigorating feeling. I took a deep breath and watched the snow float down outside.

"OK, Nan, let's go finish this bastard."

Apart from the usual thru-hike niggles such as expenses, cold and constant hunger, I'd had this additional anxiety:

what would I do if someone back home, especially immediate family, died? If I didn't get to them in time, my world would collapse. It concerns me when I leave and it troubles me when I walk. I hate saying goodbyes to loved ones for fear that it could be the last time.

Now I finally knew how it felt to lose someone and not be there to bid farewell.

Uncle Gary had emailed with the contact details of Nick Levy, who hiked with his mate, Chris Read; they were the only other Englishmen on the trail that year. I'd last seen them in Bridgeport. As I'd discovered from the Dinsmores in Skykomish, Nick and Chris had missed the same section as I had, and I hoped they were returning to finish it. I emailed Nick.

"Rumour has it you and Chris missed a section from Crater Lake to Cascade Locks. Me too and I'm looking to finish it. Fancy some company?"

He replied immediately.

"Fozzie! We're in Vancouver, heading to Seattle soon. Definitely doing the final stretch; come join us!"

Trooper and I caught the Greyhound to Vancouver, the nearest transport hub. I slept most of the way until we arrived mid-afternoon.

The city bustled as I ventured out looking for food, and downtown depressed me. Light rain fell and autumnal leaves carpeted the park like a giant Turkish rug. Concrete hemmed me in, traffic hooted, sirens blared, people shouted, dubious-looking characters lurked on street corners. I grabbed a sandwich and sought solace back in the park, sitting on a bench and trying to feel at home among the trees. Civilisation felt wrong after months in the woods. Smoking a cigarette outside the station, I broke wind out of habit, and smiled apologetically as people turned around in surprise.

"Sorry," I offered. "Been out of touch for a while."

The 7pm to Seattle hissed as it pulled up, and Trooper and I boarded. Water trickled down the windows, separating me from an alien world. I was way out of my depth and longed to be back on the PCT. Seattle, seemingly a more affable city, welcomed us both. It was Halloween and party season, so finding accommodations proved difficult. We walked into a well-known hotel and leant on the reception desk.

"Hi," Trooper said. "We need a room for one night; how much are you charging?"

The receptionist sneered and looked us up and down rudely.

"180 dollars for the night."

I interjected. "You're taking the piss, mate; don't judge people because of a rucksack."

We walked off and found a Best Western, both pleasantly surprised by the very reasonable room price. Trooper was leaving in the morning to return to California. I called Nick and agreed to meet him and Chris in two days for the early bus to Portland and then onward transport to Cascade Locks. I had a day to get organised, replace some gear from REI, clean myself up and perform some in-depth research of Seattle coffee houses.

"Fozzie, give me a call when you reach Crater Lake,"

Trooper said as he left in a taxi. "My sister lives in Oregon, and I plan on returning to visit in a couple of weeks. There's a good chance I can collect you from there."

It was a nice gesture on his part. Crater Lake was in the middle of nowhere, and the thought of trying to get a ride out had played on my mind.

"Trooper, it's been a blast. Thanks for the company."

I returned to the room and lay on the bed. My phone rang. 'Rockets' flashed up on the screen, I picked up.

"Mucker!" he said. "Where are you?"

"Seattle. Heading out tomorrow with Nick and Chris," I replied.

"Stay there! I'm coming down."

A block from the hotel, I stumbled across a great health food store, where I gorged on salads, beans, pulses, grains and fruit, drank loads of water and rested. I re-supplied, bought warmer gloves, socks and prepared for the final 330 miles.

Rockets arrived that afternoon and I laid out my plans. He seemed eager to join us but was lethargic, and clearly still ill from the E. coli. The familiar alarm bells tolled.

"I'm leaving tomorrow, mate," I said. "Come with us but I'm not hanging around. I've cut it fine as it is. I shouldn't have made it through Washington but somehow, I did; now I need to polish off Oregon before the winter strikes down there as well. Be absolutely clear, I'd love for you to come, but I'm not prepared to wait anymore, I'm sorry."

When I left in the morning, he wasn't ready. I shook his hand and walked to the Greyhound station with his familiar words ringing in my ears: "Go; I'll catch you up."

Despite my rucksack and typical thru-hiker appearance,

Nick and Chris passed straight by me in the waiting room, and I also failed to recognise them. We shook hands and briefly discussed our plans for the final section with renewed excitement.

They both lived near me, in West Sussex, south England. Nick, the more outgoing, always craved his next adventure. He was 33 and a carpenter by trade. A mohawk striped his head, two fat rings pierced his ears and countless tattoos adorned his stringy frame. Conventional this man was not; he looked like a cross between a benefits scrounger and the sort of bloke you wouldn't buy a used car from. Appearances are deceptive, however, and contrary to my snap and unfair character judgment, he turned out to be priceless. Born to a Jewish mother and Moroccan father, he nurtured a love and respect for the outdoors, and his intelligence shone. Nick wouldn't just have an opinion on any topic you cared to mention, he'd also reel off a string of facts and statistics to back his view up. Whether it was the cooking habits of ancient Greeks, how to repair fridges in the African bush, or where to rent a hedge trimmer in Mongolia, he knew something about it. His erudition showed up my comparative ignorance. Sometimes I thought he was just making stuff up, but he spoke with a confidence that suggested otherwise.

Chris had joined Nick for the adventure. He was younger, at 24, and less of a conversationalist than Nick (which wouldn't be difficult). He'd never even been for a day hike back home; the PCT was his first hike, and one hell of a baptism. He was stocky, but still slim, and his stomach tended to inflate alarmingly when he ate. And, boy, did he know how to eat!

After a series of bus journeys and local rides, we arrived

at Cascade Locks late that afternoon. It seemed warmer, and as I looked up, the snow hadn't yet fallen on the higher ground. We crammed in some last-minute calories at the supermarket, and I stocked up on candy for fear of running out again. Leaving the Bridge of the Gods southbound, we vanished into the woods and our final 330-mile section of the PCT. With darkness falling we hiked just a couple of miles and needing water, camped by the promisingly named 'Not Dry Creek'.

Nick and Chris made a well-oiled team, and I admired their organisational skills as they set about their respective camp tasks. Chris treated water while Nick prepared their food. Together they set up their two-man tent, and as a light rain fell, we all chipped in to start a fire. Campfires, I was to learn, were a regular staple for them. It took planning every evening, but I soon warmed, as it were, to the reward of a crackling fire. I thought I was an accomplished pyromaniac, but Nick was quite the expert. As we gently fed a smouldering pile of damp wood, the flames flickered before dying, with only a weak puff of smoke for our efforts. I would've given up after ten minutes, but they persisted, spurring me on, until eventually the fire burst into life. With the rain still falling, we sat near the warmth and I marvelled at Nick's persistence. Occasionally, he glanced over to check if it was still burning. He'd feed more fuel, blow a little life into it and generally nurse it as one would a sick relative. As the skies cleared, stars blinked, and despite our pitched tents, we decided to risk the elements and sleep cowboy-style.

At 3am the forest reverberated from a huge crash. We immediately sprung bolt upright like petrified Jack in the boxes.

"What the hell was that?" we cried in unison.

At first, I feared it was a bear, but as I came to, I realised no creature could make such a thundering noise. We shone our lights but, seeing nothing, cautiously fell back to sleep. I woke thinking I'd dreamt the whole event, but soon realised it was very real.

Walking around the camp, we found a freshly fallen tree that we'd not noticed the previous evening. We suspected a lightning strike, but the skies had been clear and storm-free. Maybe the tree's time had simply come. Nick, deepening the mystery, said he'd seen what looked like an asteroid, complete with blazing green tail, shortly after the event. We also recalled a crash in the adjacent valley just after the tree fell. Perhaps I'd read too much into it, but we agreed that something weird had happened that night. My time with Nick and Chris was off to an interesting start.

Over a few days we got to know each other, having gelled well from day one. We walked at the same pace, required similar periods between rest breaks and covered the distance easily. The weather held, and I looked forward to the evenings most of all – round a fire, relaxing.

We left Salvation Camp Spring, hoping to reach Timberline Lodge 20 miles away. The exterior of this huge hotel was used in The Shining movie, and it attracted many outdoors folk who hiked or skied in the area. It was also renowned for laying on one of the best breakfast buffets on the entire trail. However, our hopes of getting there by evening were dashed. Some days on the PCT, one can reel in 20 miles in no time. Other times the same distance takes an eternity. That day fell in the latter.

Mt Hood, with its near-perfect symmetry, dominated

the skyline. The contours on my map were regular until they reached the base of Hood, and then all hell broke loose. Ridges, ravines, glaciers and cols jostled for position amid a jumble of lines. It was a cartographer's nightmare.

Oregon had received two feet of snow three weeks before, but thankfully it was receding; the lower elevations seemed untouched. However, it made route finding difficult. We were exhausted, having hiked for ten hours, and our lethargy was reflected in our navigation. As night fell, we knew we were off course, albeit near the lodge. My journal at day's end simply said, 'Lost'.

We agreed to sleep and wait for sunrise to get a better fix on our position. However, even finding somewhere flat to sleep was a battle. The foothills of Mt Hood rose and fell all around us like a rumpled rug, but eventually we found a level area. Our spirits lifted momentarily before Nick brought them down again.

"Shit, we forgot to get water."

We hadn't seen water for miles, so we began melting snow over a fire. This is not as easy as it sounds; it needed to be collected away from overhanging branches, to avoid detritus from the trees such as bark pieces and pine resin. The surface collects environmental contaminants, so we dug down. Melting snow also requires a lot of fuel. Our stove alcohol was low, so we continued to gather wood, and before long we had enough water. It was strained to remove the last of the impurities and finally, we sat around the fire, warming ourselves and watching our dinners bubble.

My sleeping area was narrow, perched on a slim ledge. I had a natural pillow where the ground rose slightly, and my feet were also a little elevated. It was like lying in a hammock.

We packed quickly at sunrise, eager to reach breakfast nirvana. Following some ski lift cables, suddenly the lodge loomed into view. I'd spoken to Logic a few days earlier; she lived nearby and had asked me to call when we reached Timberline so she could join us. When she pulled into the car park, I barely recognised her in civilian clothes, but she greeted me with a welcome hug.

Retreating inside, we found the buffet that could feed an army, and I watched in amazement as Chris demonstrated his eating capabilities. He ladled a generous portion of batter into the waffle machine and, when cooked, spooned some fresh fruit on top and added a large dollop of cream. Having wolfed that down, he went back for more. And then another one. 'Dessert' followed: a huge portion of bacon, sausage, hash browns, scrambled eggs and toast. Then another one of those as well! I was struggling after one portion. Nick merely raised his eyebrows at the gluttony; he'd seen it before. Chris would've made a prime candidate for the Beaver Buster. Logic demanded we stay with her that night and agreed to meet us at Highway 26 a few miles further on.

As we lost altitude, the heat increased, and we stripped down to T-shirts. It was like summer again. Oregon was hitting us hard though. We'd been lulled into thinking this beautiful state was easier going, and sometimes it was, but other times it was punishing, especially through snow. I sensed a change in the air also; the temperature fluctuating. The days were a mixed bag of cool and warm, the nights cold. Winter was clearly imminent, and we played a dangerous game. Hikers enjoyed the last days before the snow, while conversely, skiers waited impatiently for the first powder.

Logic leant on her car, reading pages from her studies as we emerged from the forest.

"Slight problem," she announced. "I locked my keys inside!"

She'd called her boyfriend, Ben, but he couldn't make it for two hours, so we all scanned the area for pieces of discarded wire. Nick spent 30 minutes prodding, pushing and pulling, eventually earning his car thief wings. Driving to her house, she made us feel welcome. Logic only ever intended to complete a portion of the PCT and returned shortly after. Her house sat on a quiet road with beautiful views of the Oregon mountains.

I wonder how I'd have coped without trail angels. Whether simply providing a water cache or offering accommodation, they demonstrated overwhelming generosity. Logic had transitioned seamlessly from hiker to angel.

Trail angels were rare now the thru-hiker season was over. During the first months, water caches had been a regular sight. I'd topped up on calories many times from generous individuals taking time out to sit in the heat for a weekend, dishing out food. The Saufleys, Andersons, Heitmans, Dinsmores and others – all wonderful people offering hospitality for free, or a small donation, expecting nothing in return. I couldn't do it; if I had twenty hikers staying at my house every night, fond as I am of them, I'd go nuts.

Ben dropped us at the trailhead the following day and wished us luck. The clocks had gone back an hour, so darkness fell at 5.30pm, which meant stopping around 4.30pm to camp in the fading light. Compared with the height of the summer, when we walked till past 8pm, we now had four hours less to make any headway.

We passed a south-bounder packing enough gear to support all three of us, including a rifle. His pack, he said, weighed twice ours at a hefty 82 pounds. Most of it was food, mainly heavy army surplus packs. His rifle was for protection against bears, although they were preparing for hibernation. We chatted for five minutes, and I suggested politely that he could halve the load just by re-supplying weekly and losing the gun. I left him, wondering how the hell he was going to make the Sierras, let alone get over them in winter.

During the afternoon, it snowed as we climbed steadily to our target for the day, Skyline Road, where our maps showed a shelter symbol. We eventually located it: a simple, three-sided hut with a fire pit on the exposed entrance. Piles of wood scattered the ground, and a lonely picnic table squeezed inside. We set about making a fire and restoring some life into our numb feet.

Four inches of snow covered the ground, and it continued falling. The following day we had a 6,500-foot ascent. Normally, this wasn't daunting, but we were concerned about the conditions. If it was snowing now, what lay in wait higher up?

I rose early, despite the cold, and took a stroll. More snow had fallen, and Oregon appeared white, crisp and frozen. I had to break through icy puddles to access water. Breitenbush Lake had frozen over, and Campbell Butte reached skyward from the far shore. Animal tracks littered the white crust in a maze of crisscrossing lines, and all was silent.

I was back in similar territory and conditions that I'd

experienced in Washington with Trooper. We didn't know what lay above, but the situation was not likely to improve with altitude. Again, I scolded myself for leaving my hike so late. Discussing the timings of our adventure, Nick and Chris put forward the intriguing notion that we'd come to experience the PCT and live in the woods for a few months – everyone else had finished, but we were still out here, so in a way we were the winners.

But to win, we had to finish. And to finish, we had to beat the winter and hike 217 miles.

We left at 7am. Three miles in, winning seemed rather distant. As we climbed, the snow deepened and continued falling. Snowdrifts met our thighs, we lost the trail numerous times and those three miles took three hours. We put our packs down and evaluated. This wasn't like Washington. There was far more snow, the temperature had plummeted, and we were still climbing. At this point, a mile an hour would be good going, and we faced long, tiring days with minimal progress.

Not only that but the PCT had disappeared, even though I took regular GPS readings to find it. We unanimously agreed to return and re-group at the hut, where we built another roaring fire and ate, restoring some morale. With plenty of concentration, map reading, GPS checks and observation, we might have been able to cover nine miles a day. However, it was almost mid-November, and at that rate we'd be walking until the middle of December – assuming conditions remained the same, which they wouldn't.

"We could road walk it?" Chris said.

"How do you mean?" we replied in unison.

"There's a track leading to this campsite for vehicles," he

continued. "That track must, at some point, meet a road; once we get our bearings, we can road walk all the way to Crater Lake. OK, so it's not the PCT; but as far as I'm concerned, it still means hiking from Mexico to Canada. We won't have to worry about navigation; the elevation will be lower so it should be snow-free. The surface will be harsher, but serious mileage will be easy. We'll be passing plenty of places to eat, which means carrying less food, there'll be more motels and, of course, more chances to drink coffee." He sat back like a confident lawyer having defended his client.

We looked at each other, waiting for expression changes to hint emotions. Nick scratched his beard and I raised his eyebrows. Slowly, we smiled.

"Road walk!" I piped up, and Nick nodded in agreement. It was agreed!

I'd become fond of these guys. Some hikers would've given up and gone home by now; indeed, many had. We were still there though: the last PCTers of the year. It made me proud to be English, proud of my stubbornness and proud to be walking with two like-minded fellow countrymen. Either that, or we were bloody idiots.

As I got to know them, I developed a strong respect for Nick and Chris. Living with other hikers for twenty-four hours a day isn't easy, requiring patience, diplomacy and forgiveness. Not a single bad word passed between us. It was an English team effort – the British bulldog fighting spirit.

I'd become familiar with their quirks and habits. Nick

was used to hardship on adventures. In previous travels, he'd survived winters and existed on budgets so meagre that I wouldn't have even attempted the journey. He was the talker. I joked that he held records not just for long-distance walking, but also long-distance talking. I often enjoyed solitary, silent walking, but after a few days of being with Nick, that became a distant memory. We took things easy, with regular cigarette and snack breaks, sometimes talking for an hour. We didn't know when we'd get to Crater Lake, but we knew we would.

The first obstacle was finding the actual road to even attempt the route. We hiked down the track, and as we lost altitude, snow merged to rain, the surface thawed and we donned waterproofs. The guys had jackets and trousers that were excellent at shedding water, but none too durable. Over time, their gear had snagged on bushes and the seats had worn, with hilarious results. Chris's trousers had so many rips and tears that, as he strode forward, one leg emerged completely and a second or so later, the material caught up. Nick's jacket was in no better state, sliced and slit as though he'd been mugged by someone with a sharp knife. Various pieces of yellow duct tape were unsuccessfully trying to hold the garments together, and as I walked behind I laughed at the strips of material flapping aimlessly in the wind. The guys were also wearing running shoes – ideal for the drier, hotter sections, but now they'd permanently cold and wet feet. I'd had my waterproof boots for a while, and even they were struggling to keep out the damp.

Nick's violent phase, as I called it, kicked in around 2pm.

"He does it every day, sometimes several times," Chris commented.

Nick craved constant mental stimulation, and if he didn't get it, frustration kicked in. To vent his irritation, he'd suddenly lash out with his trekking pole at innocent foliage that he'd taken an irrational dislike to. In between blows, he'd chase imaginary gazelles with his pole as a spear in the African bush. The whole display lasted several minutes.

Sometimes he'd speed off to dissipate some excess energy, so Chris and I spent many an hour chatting. Chris never appeared stressed, took each day at a time and just did what needed to be done. He walked a solid and steady pace, had good stamina and didn't complain about anything. He was so laid back I figured he'd end up as a monk.

After two hours descending the track, we intersected a country road but had no idea which way to go. Following the compass, we continued south through pouring rain. Though we moaned about the snow, at least it merely settled on our bodies, whereas the constant downpour soaked us with a mighty chill.

A sign stated the town of Detroit was 18 miles away, which lifted our damp moods. The thought of drying out at a motel and eating some decent food edged our speed up. A truck passed and stopped, and two rangers got out to chat. They confirmed the mileage to Detroit, offered us a ride, which we declined, and described the place. A good motel, a couple of nice eateries and a store, they said. We also learnt that it was on the main road to Crater Lake, with a few towns en route. We continued, cowering from the spray of passing vehicles.

Signs constantly reminded us of the remaining mileage. On those flat roads, we knew our average speed, and it was easy to calculate our arrival time. As we reached the highway, Detroit appeared through the rain and mist, and we huddled under the store awning. A hot dog and coffee solved the immediate hunger and caffeine crisis as we lit cigarettes and discussed the next move. The motel, we were assured by the cashier, had recently been refurbished and was excellent. The bar was friendly and served basic but filling grub, and he also recommended the café. We didn't need persuading to get a room, dry out and warm up so checked in.

"Could you please turn on any item capable of producing heat and leave it at maximum?" I asked.

Chris laughed as the owner nodded in acknowledgement, and by the time we entered the room, it was toasty. As we took off our wet items of gear and hung them on anything resembling a hook, the windows rapidly steamed up. I collapsed into a hot bath and slowly felt the warmth penetrate my limbs and drive out a stubborn chill. After days outdoors in the winter, we were tiptoeing around on the floor complaining about the cold tiles!

Spirits restored, we ventured out to revive them further with that marvel of pick-me-ups, alcohol. A row of 15 guys lined the bar, and Nick had to squeeze politely between them to order drinks.

"You doing the PCT?" asked Brad, one of the locals. "You're late, aren't you?"

The eight blokes to Nick's left shifted along, and the other seven to his right did the same. Brad grabbed three stools and we jostled in. The bartender placed a pitcher of beer in front of us.

"On the house," he said, smiling.

We chatted to everyone that evening, and I have fond

memories of the occasion. Ensconced in classic American hospitality, the stresses of the previous days melted away in a sea of Pale Ale. We felt like minor celebrities amid the compliments and encouragement from the patrons.

"I take my hat off to you," said Brad. "I live here and I'm lucky if I get one day a month to go for a walk. You guys come to my country and experience the woods for six months, something I'll probably never be able to do. It makes me proud to be American when people travel huge distances not just to get here, but to hike. Best of luck to you; I'm truly inspired."

People left, and others arrived. The cook dished up an admirable burger and fries as the whole focus of attention centred on us and our hike. We staggered back to the motel, half expecting to sign autographs.

Our gear was still wet the following day, and a depressed newsreader informed Oregon to expect a washout. We decided to zero. Returning to Cedars Bar once more, we were fed an excellent breakfast. Oliver, the owner, offered to take our laundry away to wash. I must admit I didn't envy him opening the contents of that bag.

A lazy day ensued, checking emails, keeping warm (something of a novelty at that point), eating and sleeping. The weather forecast changed from 'occasional rain' to the slightly perkier 'random showers'.

Journal entry:
Wet! Resting in the Lodge Motel in Detroit. Been thrown out of the mountains! Too much snow to carry on. We discussed the options, settling on a road walk to Crater Lake, and then a little further to where we left the trail at Mazama

Village. There's no other option really. We now have 157 miles on tarmac, which means only one thing: blisters. I know this from my experience on previous road detours. I'm looking forward to it, though. I think it will be a novelty not to worry about navigation, and we'll pass plenty of places that serve real food.

Nick and Chris are good company. We laugh, and we must to maintain morale; the weather is either wet or cold. I think about, among other things, the desert; it was brutal at the time, but now I yearn for the warmth and have fond memories of those days in a T-shirt. The sun rose early and set late. The spring flowers bloomed before retreating underground for another year. It reminded me of my hike; it was never intended to be a race against the weather, but it became one. I remember that hummingbird hovering before me; it seems so long ago.

My friends have finished their hike. They are back in their normal lives, and I hope they're planning their next adventure. I miss them, in particular Stumbling Norwegian, Sugar Moma, Hojo, Logic, Burnie, Your Mom, Pony, Pigpen, Evo, Gabe; really, everyone I shared time with. The messages I receive from them and family back home are encouraging – they spur me on. Only a few more days and we can call ourselves thru-hikers.

Chapter 17

Crater Lake

It's more than just hiking. There's a whole culture that goes along with the people. You know how you want the world to be? It's like that on the Pacific Crest Trail. Everyone helps each other.
Monty 'Warner Springs Monty' Tam

We set off on Highway 22 south-bound. Checking the map, we needed to stick on the 22 until it merged with the 20, then the 97 for most of the way before a small side road led to Crater Lake. A few towns dotted the route such as Sisters, Bend, La Pine and Chemult. They were evenly spaced, making ideal two-day targets. We hoped to reach Sisters, 58 miles away, the following day by crushing two 29-milers. We lightened our packs by taking less food, hoping to supply en route.

Morale was high. We knew our target was close and the effort over the previous months would pay off. Very soon we'd be thru-hikers. The rain cleared and we walked in sunshine. An occasional cloud wandered past harmlessly, the air was lush with the smell of fallen leaves, and steam rose from the tarmac, catching chinks of sunlight filtering through the trees.

We warmed up, peeled off a layer, donned sunglasses and accustomed ourselves to our new environment. The road wasn't busy, but we had to pay attention to the traffic. It was easy to become blasé, a dangerous attitude when road walking. Every few seconds we'd check oncoming vehicles in case we needed to squeeze to the verge. The bitumen started playing games. Sometimes we walked on a softer, gritty surface to the side, which cushioned our feet and crunched satisfyingly. More often than not, it was hard asphalt, as grit was in short supply. Crash barriers protected vehicles from drops or bridges, hemming us between the steel and passing traffic, so we'd size up the approach and run past quickly. White lines became mesmerising and I'd slip into a trance, just letting them flash one by one across my field of vision.

Bends were uncommon. Often, we faced long stretches of road disappearing over the next horizon, which never seemed to get closer until finally we hit it, crested the hill and saw more of the same. Trees dripped water on our heads, and we splashed through occasional puddles. At last we stopped for a coffee in Idanha.

"What are you guys up to?" asked the waitress.

"Walking the Pacific Crest Trail," Chris said. "We're on the road to Crater Lake because of too much snow up there." He nodded towards the hills.

"Awesome!" she replied, scratching her head and nodding. I could tell she had absolutely no idea what we were talking about.

Quick progress on tarmac isn't difficult as roads are built as flat as possible, following easier terrain. We skirted mountains rather than climbing them, walked over bridges as opposed to descending into valleys. We'd no need for maps; road signs calculated distances, and the smooth surface meant we could enjoy the views without concentrating on foot placement.

However, it soon became monotonous. Pleading for even a morsel of stimulation, I resorted to old tricks like catching a speedy glimpse of passing drivers to guess their life story. I regularly smiled and awarded myself bonus points for a reciprocated grin. I endeavoured to look mischievous when the police approached, just so I might be questioned. If I was struggling mentally, Nick had reached breaking point: his violent phase kicked in earlier and lasted a little longer.

Our speed varied all the time, and we stretched out, changing positions. Whenever Chris reached the brow of a hill half a mile ahead of me, or Nick disappeared around a corner, I wondered if my pace was too slow. Equally, if I led, perhaps I was too quick, or they'd slowed down. The person up front dictated breaks so the other two could catch up, but we generally walked for two hours, covering six to eight miles, and then rested. During one section, five miles passed in no time and I felt I'd glided along with no effort whatsoever. Had I reached walking enlightenment?

Trying to make our situation more interesting, Nick connected his iPod to a speaker, strapped to the top of his pack. We sang to various artists, two favourites being Kate Bush and Nick Cave, our voices occasionally drowned out by passing trucks. His other trick of postponing madness involved the sport of trekking pole balancing. He pulled this off admirably, even in the forest, but on the smoother and uninterrupted roads with no obstacles, he flew. The challenge required balancing the tip of the pole on one finger and keeping it upright for as long as possible while still walking. He'd developed many ingenious tactics, which Chris and I borrowed: keep the eye focused on one section of the pole (I stuck duct tape below the handle for the purpose) and block out your surrounding field of vision. Dangerous as this may be, the risk of colliding with a vehicle was deemed acceptable in the continued pursuit of records.

A couple of hours usually elapsed before the first event began. Nick steadied an outstretched arm, delicately balancing the pole, often for several minutes. Occasionally, he'd lose concentration or a breeze would throw him off balance – and then the fun started. At times he'd stop dead in his tracks or hit reverse to prevent it from tipping back. Or his speed increased to catch up as it toppled forward. I lost count of the times Chris and I observed, hysterically, Nick breaking into a sprint, disappearing down the road, trying in vain to postpone defeat. A sideways pole tilt was our favourite, catching him off guard as he negotiated a scrubby embankment to one side and vanished into the forest. All went quiet for a minute amongst the pines before a simple "Bollocks" floated out, confirming game over.

I reflected on the last 202 days. The initial excitement, meeting my fellow hikers at the kick-off party, those blazing desert afternoons or standing on top of the world. Fondly remembering those characters I'd met, I wondered where they were now. Hojo, Stumbling Norwegian, Your Mom, Burnie, Elk and others had sent texts saying they'd finished. I caught up with others through their blogs or email.

We drifted up hills and walked through occasional shallow snow before descending to wet, shiny roads again.

With fading light, we donned head torches, the last in line shining his behind to warn vehicles, just in case, as we searched for somewhere to sleep. Dense forest lined both sides of the highway, dropping to dank darkness. We passed a closed campsite, and hiked further, taking a side track to escape the traffic noise. Fallen trees and leaves hampered the search, but eventually we found a suitable spot. I pitched my tent between two logs and, on opening the vestibule, a bright orange fungus with a patterned dome that looked like a face winked at me; and studied me all evening. Tyres hissed from the road, and the traffic slowly faded.

We'd done well the first day, pulling in 28 miles. This left 31 miles to Sisters, a long haul but achievable despite shortening daylight. However, by 3pm a miserly 17 miles had passed under our boots. We ate a late lunch sitting on a solitary bench overlooking the mountains. Occasionally, a car pulled in and the occupants spilled out with cameras to admire the view. Some eyed us warily; others ventured closer and made conversation or tentatively offered food as though we were wild animals. One elderly couple spent a good 15 minutes chatting, showing genuine interest. As they walked off, I overheard the wife ask, "What are they doing?"

"I have absolutely no idea," her husband replied.

Lights blinked ahead on the approach to Sisters, but it took an hour to reach town. Traffic slowed, pedestrians appeared and houses dotted the roadside. In a restaurant, we took advantage of the 'buy one, get one free' menu, warming our backs against a radiator as we tore brutally into our burgers.

Our feet were on fire. Walk to work every day on concrete and it wouldn't bother you. Do it for ten hours and it's a different story. Despite all our conditioning over hundreds of miles, the humble blister was making an unwelcome comeback and we grimaced, stretching out sore limbs. It was like being back at the start. Calves, tendons and thighs all ached and pain shot up into our backs. Thank God for ibuprofen.

Reginald at nerve centre HQ, having dealt with constant temperature fluctuations, eye grit removal, and mild constipation worked his way through a long string of messages from Angela, down at feet level.

"He must be hiking on tarmac," she began. "Maybe it's temporary, but I'm experiencing impact problems, blisters and the soles are tender again. Anything you can give me down here?"

"They're road walking," Reginald answered, "and we've got another few days of it as well. Don't worry; the diet is better. He's just consumed burgers so take some protein, and whatever else you need from the nutrients cupboard."

Sisters Inn and Suites sat next to the supermarket, so we checked in for the night. We re-supplied, and Nick and Chris prepared meals for the coming section. They concocted their own recipes from staples such as rice or couscous, adding spices such as garlic powder, cumin, and turmeric. At camp the addition of cured meat or canned fish bulked out the protein. Nick filled five Ziploc bags, carefully dispensing the same amount of each ingredient, while Chris sat on the bed chopping various additions, occasionally handing over more for each bag. They offered to do the same for me but I declined as I enjoyed my cooking ritual.

I took an evening stroll around Sisters, a place well regarded by thru-hikers. Towards the town centre, I came upon historic buildings, an assortment of restaurants and curious little shops. Christmas lights twinkled and tinsel hung from window displays already. Holidaymakers strolled, and chatter spilled from bars. I reached the end of town and looked south, hoping to see the mountains near Crater Lake, but they hid 127 miles distant beneath an orange horizon.

The temperature rose as we left Sisters to cover the 23 miles to Bend, also held in high hiker esteem. We wore T-shirts through flat, agricultural land, the fields dotted with cows or horses, and a dry pale-yellow grass bordered the roadside. Cars honked and motorists stopped, asking if we needed anything.

"My sister met you at the motel back in Sisters and told me what you're doing. That's amazing!" said one excited woman.

Word had circulated that three mad Englishman were road walking to Crater Lake. We entered a bar for lunch.

"You're the three Englishman! Come in, sit down, you must be starving!" the waitress cried. She flapped like a worried mother hen looking after her brood. We lapped it up; if nothing else, we were famous along a slim ribbon of tarmac in Oregon.

At another roadside café, the waiter showed us to a table as customers nudged each other, nodding our way, and returned our smiles.

"You're doing what?" exclaimed one guy as we brought him up to speed, a section of rump steak hanging from his startled mouth. "What, er, how, why, no, wait, you've walked from Mexico? That's impossible!"

Most of the clientele busily discussed our plans, the road

options and the weather outlook. The waiter placed the bill on the table. Red ink streaked across it, with the words 'paid' underneath.

"Guys, it's your lucky day. Your bill's been settled."

We abruptly stopped eating our apple pies.

"Huh?" Chris said.

"One of the locals listened to your story. He used to hike but doesn't anymore because of a bad injury. He asked me to say it was his pleasure listening to you and he'd be honoured if you'd allow him to meet your bill. He's left; he didn't want to be known."

I wished I'd ordered the steak. I sat back in my chair, feeling a little humbled, and emotional. 'He can't hike any more' echoed in my mind over and over again, and I realised how lucky we were. Fortuitous to have a pair of legs that worked.

We thanked the waiter and left in a grateful, contemplative silence.

We'd received good reports about Bend from other hikers, but as we entered the outskirts, we failed to see why. A nondescript collection of garages, stores and fast food outlets – hardly enough to justify the claim of one of the best trail towns. Stopping at an intersection, not knowing which way to head, a woman appeared, waiting for the lights to change so she could cross. It was a rarity to see a pedestrian; most people didn't venture out without their cars.

"Do you know where the centre is?" asked Nick.

"Yes, it's about a mile, I can show you if you like."

We followed her for a short distance and she directed us left at another intersection.

"You can't miss it," she said. "Go straight down there."

The out-of-town shopping areas slowly dwindled, to be replaced by attractive houses. The Deschutes River curled up to the road and turned back to run along the town's edge. The ugly duckling merged into a swan as our expectations of Bend changed.

Nick stopped to chat with a local, Kelly, who immediately offered us a place to sleep and get cleaned up. I needed to write and email a magazine article about El Camino de Santiago in Spain, a walk I'd completed some years earlier. Kelly insisted we stay with him, so we all bundled in the back of his van.

"Don't worry, Fozzie," he said. "There's a great café with internet just around the corner."

He showed us his home, which backed on to the Deschutes. We sat drinking beer on the jetty, watching the sun set. Kelly went out but left a key and told us to make ourselves comfortable.

We ate at the café where the owners took a keen interest in our adventure, and I managed to write the magazine article amid the cacophony of rowdy drinkers. The barman even asked everyone to quieten down.

"There's an English writer in here trying to work!" he cried. "Keep the noise down a little, guys!"

Returning to Kelly's, I joined Nick and Chris on the jetty for more beer and we idled away an hour just watching the river drift past.

We never did see Kelly again, as he returned in the early hours, but we left him a thank-you note. Oregon hospitality still proved priceless. Word of our adventure had spread, and more cars hooted as we raised our trekking poles in recognition.

I detained the guys in Bend the following morning chasing my coffee habit and the proliferation of establishments serving an excellent espresso; I think I stopped at three of them, much to the guy's bemusement. We scrambled up a steep embankment by the railway to reach Highway 97 and continue our road walk. A long, boring line of asphalt disappeared over the horizon miles distant, but the 97 consoled in other ways. There was less traffic and a soft soil stretched right up to the verge, making for easy walking.

The amount of litter and discarded items was astonishing. Nick's fascination with trash meant regular stops to examine objects; frankly, I struggled to see the appeal. We found endless lighters (most of them working), food scraps, old cell phones, CDs and quite a few plastic bottles filled with what we assumed was urine. Passing roadworks, the construction team stopped to chat and offered us hot drinks from their flasks.

Abandoned buildings also sparked Nick's curiosity. If he spotted something in the forest that appeared manmade, he'd disappear to investigate. If this happened near day's end, I'd groan because I knew he'd want to sleep in it. I reckon his fondness for such structures stemmed from his budget, travelling days without a shelter, so anything with a roof meant shelter and a dry night's rest. We often queried why he held these structures, with animal corpses or excrement sitting in the corner, in such esteem when he could pitch his tent. I guessed old habits die hard.

We had 50 miles left to Mazama Village, Crater Lake and the end of our hike. Word had reached us of an approaching storm. The trail by the lake itself topped out at 7,700 feet, so we knew if it rained on us, then it would be snowing up there. We hoped to reach our finishing point before the weather turned further. A cold wind blew down from the mountains, but the peaks were clear. Fresh from my triumph against the elements in Washington, I'd begun to regard myself as invincible. I wasn't bothered by snow anymore; I didn't particularly enjoy it, but I dealt with it.

After a brief cigarette and M&M'S break, we continued. Nick and Chris were up front as I took a cursory glance behind to check for incoming trucks, and noticed a Sheriff's car tailing us as a bear dashed across the road. At least the drivers had some entertainment, I thought. Those coming from the opposite direction would have first seen three scruffy English guys with backpacks, followed by a police escort and a bear scampering into the trees. When the Sheriff caught my eye, he accelerated past and pulled in a few yards ahead of Nick. He stopped, got out and talked to them. I arrived a minute later.

"What's going on?" I enquired.

"Apparently," Nick explained, "we've had an altercation with a gentleman back down the road."

I looked at him, then at Chris. I don't know who seemed more perplexed; even the sheriff mirrored our puzzlement.

"Huh?" was all I could think of saying, but then added, "We haven't seen anyone for at least an hour."

The sheriff attempted to shed some light on the situation. "We received a call from a gentleman saying you'd shouted abuse at him two miles back. Do you know anything about this? His dog went crazy."

"Oh, the dog!" I said, realisation suddenly dawning. "We passed a house and a dog peered through the gate at us, so we whistled at it, but not out of aggression. You know? You see a dog in the park and you sometimes whistle at it. We didn't even notice anyone else."

The sheriff scribbled on a pad and had a quick conversation with someone on the radio.

"What are you guys doing anyway?"

"Hiking the Pacific Crest Trail, but we got snowed out of the mountains above Detroit, so we're finishing it by road, walking the section down to Crater Lake," Chris explained.

"You know there's a storm blowing in? Snow higher up."

We confirmed we'd heard.

"Our phone call," he said, "was obviously a misunderstanding; I'll go back and tell him to stop wasting our time. Guys, good luck, I wish you well."

Generally, I don't get on with those in authority, but I do enjoy encounters with the American police. There's the odd officer who thinks he rules the world, but generally they're a reasonable bunch, and this guy was no exception.

We made better progress than expected, and suddenly La Pine looked within reach if we could pull in a 30-miler. We put our heads down, forgoing breaks, and cracked out nine miles in two-and-a-half hours.

La Pine was basically a trucker stop. An old-fashioned motel in a rather fetching shade of pink bordered the highway, and Gordy's restaurant looked like it might serve up a decent dinner. Nick charmed the woman at the motel's reception into a healthy discount for cash, and we holed up in our art déco-styled accommodation as a frost crept up the front door. The push-button TV needed several minutes to reach optimal operating temperature, but there were gallons of steaming hot water with which to have a bath.

A solitary drinker propped up Gordy's bar, and an empty dining room didn't bode too well. Stuffed animals hung on the walls and I wondered if someone had a penchant for taxidermy more than cooking. As I perused the menu, an elk eyed me cautiously, two raccoons sized me up and an imposing black bear held his paws above his head as if surrendering. It seemed a touch creepy. Thankfully, the owner was a good cook and we tucked into a great dinner.

We'd calculated just 44 miles to Mazama Village, achievable in two days providing the weather held. However, after checking on the map, I announced my maths needed adjusting and in fact the figure neared 68. Highway 97 carried on a further 33 miles to an intersection, where we turned right on to the 138. 15 miles up there was the entrance to Crater Lake, and from there a further 15 miles led to Mazama Village. Two days suddenly seemed a little ambitious, even with easy walking; moreover, once we hit the Crater Lake National Park turn-off, it could be covered in snow. The road plough, said one local, only clears the highway, not the park roads, which had closed for the season.

The junction at the 138 also housed a motel and restaurant. Although the finances were taking a battering, our stomachs were full and we stayed warm at night. Sleeping in a tent in freezing temperatures, however, does condition you to the cold. Snuggling up under blankets in toasty rooms doesn't. As we emerged from our haven, we shivered and jumped up and down. Ice covered the car windows and dusted long blades of grass, making them curl downwards like white talons. Postponing our exercise in warming up to operating temperature, we ducked into

Gordy's again for breakfast.

The adventure I'd hoped for didn't consist of road walking, but sometimes plans alter to fit circumstances. In an ideal world, my hike would've been in total wilderness, all re-supply conveniences and motels would be clustered near the road every week and then I'd be back in the hills. My dream would have started at Mexico and weaved north to Canada in one, unbroken line. Skipping a section to return and complete it wasn't part of the plan either. I'd wanted a pure hike, start at Mexico and finish at Canada with no diversions, and the guys shared the same dream. We'd rather have followed the natural course of the PCT and not been snowed off. Yet, aware that a small proportion of our hike was off trail, we never once considered reaching Mazama and not calling ourselves PCT thru-hikers.

Although Highway 97 hadn't crossed my mind before, I didn't begrudge her company. She looked after us, we were warm at night with full stomachs. By now we'd become known on the highway, and people waved, beeped, gave thumbs-up out of windows, fed us for free, didn't charge for coffee and offered a roof for the night. It wasn't the wilderness, but it was pure entertainment.

After finally emerging from Gordy's, we crunched along on ice and grit. It had turned much colder, perhaps signalling the imminent storm. Cloud blocked out any hope of warmth, the wind increased and leaves flew across the road as if trying to escape.

After a disappointing 17 miles that seemed to last an eternity, we reached Chemult, essentially a garage and a drive-through coffee shop. I walked up to the window in search of an espresso and startled the woman inside.

"You're supposed to be in a car!" she joked.

"I wish," I replied.

"What are you guys doing?"

After relaying the shortened version, she handed us each a coffee, gave me a hand-crocheted beanie and called her husband.

"Wait five minutes and you two can have beanies as well," she added, pointing to Nick and Chris.

We'd managed just three miles by the time we reached the turn-off for Highway 138 and the Whispering Pines Motel. 'Whispering' was a bit weak; 'howling' seemed more appropriate. We checked in, relaxed and battled the gale to the diner opposite. Although about to shut up shop, the owner cooked us a quick burger and chips.

According to the owners at the motel, this was the forecast storm; and snow was certain overnight. The road to Crater Lake, we assumed, must already be covered. We got our heads down for an early start and the final 30 miles to our finish.

At 4.45am, Nick hesitantly drew the curtain back and pressed his nose to the glass.

"Raining," he announced with little of the emotion it deserved.

As I also looked, a solitary street light illuminated the road junction as the rain came in waves and water trickled down the cold window. An occasional car speeding past sent a fine spray skywards. We harboured mixed feelings: anticipation at finishing together with hesitation about going out in the rain and probably snow. My stomach fluttered with butterflies. We wrapped up in waterproofs and gingerly stepped out. It was still dark and noticeably colder. We had 15 miles before the turn-off for Crater Lake Park, all uphill. I pulled the draw cord on my hood tighter and slapped my arms to warm up.

Gradually, the slick, shiny black bitumen changed. Rain slowly merged to snow, settling on our shoulders. The moisture froze on my jacket and I found myself encased in ice, which cracked as I bent my arm. The splashing of feet turned to crunching as black faded to white. The higher we ventured, the colder and whiter it became until everything sparkled virgin silver. In the space of an hour, we'd walked into deep winter. Ice crystals formed on my beard, and flakes rested on my eyelashes.

Tyre tracks vanished as a plough suddenly approached, sending huge arcs of snow onto the verge. It was barely light, but he saw us and graciously stopped until we'd passed, puzzlement and curiosity etched into his face.

Reaching the Crater Lake Park entrance, our ploughed road ceased, and we encountered a strip of pure white powder stretching through the trees. A solitary latrine offered shelter as we ate snacks and smoked cigarettes. Cringing, we drank our partially frozen water. It was already painfully cold, and we'd further to climb.

We focused our attention on the road. Our map lacked detail, so we clung to this fast-disappearing safe haven. Where it cut through sheltering trees, we could see it well enough, but once we emerged it took all our concentration to pick out the narrow white ribbon that wound up to Crater Lake. The snow drifted, and our only clue of tarmac came from tufts of grass and vegetation poking through the surface at the roadside. It deepened to a foot as the clouds merged into a grey mist, cloaking the forest tops. Nick's knee began troubling him; he'd taken a week out at the start to rest it and it hadn't bothered him since. Now, though, having to pull his legs out of the snow with every step, it was painful, and he lagged behind.

Finally, we reached Crater Lake, and it took our breath away. A giant caldera six miles wide, flanked by peaks and filled with the purest turquoise water, glittered and sparkled. The blue receded as an ice sheet spread. Below us, the conical symmetry of Wizard Island broke the surface. We sat on the cold, hard ground for an age and just looked, speechless, a hint of a smile cracking our frozen faces. There was no need for words, nor could I have found the right ones to describe the sight that I'd been dreaming about for months. We were nearly at the end. Nearly.

The last few miles down to Mazama Village couldn't be that difficult, we thought. The western side of the lake, however, had received the full brunt of the elements. Only the occasional morsel of open road peeped out of the drifts, which reached our waists. We constantly checked ahead to catch glimpses of black poking through white.

Nick was having a rough time. He spent most of the afternoon hobbling in between fairly frequent stops to rest his knee. Either Chris or I shadowed him as the other walked ahead and pushed through a route. He didn't complain, just updated us and got on with it, albeit slowly. Several months of solid hiking and then his legs quit on the last day! He had no choice but to struggle on or be left out in the freeze. It was painful progress, and we were all exhausted. You don't walk through snow, you plough through. Most of the time we were knee to waist deep. We'd step forward, guessing whether the snow would hold or whether we'd sink further, as invariably we did. Drag the trailing leg out of the hole, keep it bent to clear the surface, place it down and repeat the whole process. We were near the edge of energy reserves, dangerously cold, disheartened and on the verge of calling it a day. The only solace was the hope of seeing Trooper again at Mazama after I'd arranged for him to meet us. The guys were worried whether he'd turn up.

"Trooper will be there," I told them.

We knew Mazama Village would be a ghost town; it closes out of season, so there'd be no chance of food or board. After 30 miles in these conditions, our only reward would be sleeping out in them.

Gradually we descended, too tired to even rest and eat, and slowly the road cleared. We stamped our feet to dislodge ice encrusted on our boots, brushed the snow off our shoulders and somehow staggered the last few miles to a small cluster of buildings. Darkness fell as we stood by the intersection where I'd been with Rockets weeks earlier. I was startled at how everything had changed. Before, I'd sweated in shorts and a T-shirt. Now I wore most of my clothes. Trooper was nowhere to be seen as it hit 9pm. A few tyre tracks ribboned and swirled around, and then a ranger pulled up.

"Are you Fozzie?"

I raised my eyebrows in surprise and smiled. "Yes!"

"Guy called Trooper wants you to know that he waited for you. He said he'll come back at nine tomorrow. Where you guys going to sleep? Will you be OK?"

"We'll be fine," I replied. "Thanks for the message."

In better spirits, we pitched our shelters, fluffed up our bags and blew up our mattresses for the last time that year.

Before long, we huddled in our tents, watching steam rise from our stoves as I had done way back on the first morning in the desert chill. Cupping my mug, I sipped delicately at the hot chocolate. There'd been no celebration. We were so tired that finishing had been completely forgotten.

Chapter 18
The Original Question

Days like today I'm a half step from putting on my pack and wrapping my hands around those trekking poles. I just want to go back to what makes sense to me. Back to where I'm happy. Back to where I'm the best me I've ever known.

Dave 'Upchuck' Ferber

I woke up grinning. After completely forgetting to celebrate our finish, the realisation dawned; I was now a Pacific Crest Trail thru-hiker. I poked my head out of the tent to bright sunlight bouncing off glittering snow. I'd stopped worrying about the cold, the exhaustion or the hunger; I'd beaten all the odds. California couldn't stop me, Washington didn't hold me back and Oregon tried but failed. I felt like a seven-year-old waking up on Christmas day, eager to get out of bed and open my presents.

The guys were already up, and after breakfast, we broke camp and strolled down to the road junction where I needed to organise a quick task before Trooper arrived.

At the beginning of my hike I'd continued to playfully pester Chris McMaster, the proprietor at ÜLA, for pack sponsorship. I knew it was a futile exercise; just a bit of a joke between us. Attached to the last email he'd sent was a photo of a woman carrying one of his packs. It was taken from behind and she was naked. The message was simple: "She gets one, you don't."

Occasionally, during my hike, I'd smiled as that email flashed into my mind; walking 2,640 miles also provided ample time to plot my revenge. The guys agreed with my plan. After setting Nick's camera up on his tripod, we set the timer, stood in line with our backs to the lens and dropped our trousers. We checked the photo: it was perfect. Three guys wearing ÜLA packs, and three pairs of butt cheeks. A few days later I sent this to Chris, again asking for a free pack. I heard nothing for a week, so I emailed again.

"Yes, Fozzie, I received your message," he replied. "I've just got out of therapy and no, you still don't get a freebie."

It would be remiss of me if I didn't mention that a year later, Chris finally crumbled and sponsored me with a gorgeous red and black Ohm 2 pack. He even stitched my name on it.

True to his promise, Trooper came sliding down the road and skidded to a halt in front of us, beaming.

"I said you'd make it!" he cried. "You must have been through hell and back!"

"I think hell would have been somewhat warmer," I replied with a satisfied grin.

I introduced him to Nick and Chris, and we bundled in, heading to Ashland, the nearest transport hub, from where we could continue our journeys. In south England we don't know how to drive in snow because we rarely get any. Trooper took off down the hill as if on a rally stage while I grasped the door firmly and looked skywards for help.

The guys were heading south, Chris to Los Angeles and Nick to San Diego for different reasons, but sun and warmth was a major factor. I had to get to San Jose, collect my belongings from my relatives, wind down for a couple of days and fly back to the UK. We stopped at the first diner and ate like wolves, treating Trooper to his meal, as he wouldn't accept any money for fuel. Chris needed a different bus station than us and, as Trooper agreed to take him, it was time to say our farewells. Chris lived near me back home – as did Nick – so I knew I'd see him again. I gave heartfelt thanks to Trooper. Nick and I boarded our bus to Sacramento where we would go our separate ways.

Too tired to talk but not enough to sleep, I gazed out of the bus window as darkness fell and city lights appeared. While Nick slept, I answered voicemails from friends demanding news and watched the world flash by. Sacramento was uninspiring, especially in the middle of the night; and after an hour's waiting, Nick boarded his onward connection, smiling with a thumbs-up. Before I knew it, I was back at San Jose, booking a flight to the UK.

Journal entry:
Nearly four weeks back in England now. I still sleep with my head torch by the bed. I'm way too hot in the house and have to open the windows, even in November. I wake thinking I have to walk 25 miles and feel strange when I'm not wearing my trail gear.

KEITH FOSKETT

It's great not to be cold for days on end. I love my bed, now free of sleeping bag restrictions. I can have a coffee whenever I want and I don't have to filter my water. When I walk in my local woods, I continue to note the water sources and find myself sussing out suitable camping spots. Unencumbered by pack weight, I hike quickly and have to remind myself to slow down, that I'm in no rush.

The transition back to 'normal' life is relatively smooth. I don't appear to suffer from the post-travel depression that usually dogs me when I return from adventures. However, I do miss the trail. Being out in the wilds has left a mark. Leaving my humdrum existence behind was easy. OK, sometimes I yearned for civilisation, but in the main, I relished being lucky enough to have witnessed the wilderness at its best.

I'm more patient now. Few things stress me, and after a trip of this kind I realise that most situations are not as bad as they appear. Spending time outside is nurturing; it seizes hold and lures you towards contentment. The logistics of the PCT can be complex, but once there, it's worth the effort.

So, what now? I'm back decorating, which is bearable, but I daydream between brush strokes. I think about the next hike: where, when, and for how long? All the British national trails in one attempt? A walk around the coast of my home country maybe? Or how about all 3,200 miles of the classic European E1 hike from Italy to Norway? There're also many other long-distance paths in Europe I have my eye on. My thoughts return to America; the Appalachian Trail and the Continental Divide Trail beckon, along with the prospect of becoming a Triple Crowner. I dream about the Himalayas, the Far East, Scotland. Each has its own unique perspective, and each should be experienced. This isn't a competition though; it's an education. I may not be walking at the moment, but life's good when I'm planning adventures; the anticipation is intoxicating.

The transition back to 'normal' life is smooth for some hikers. However, many struggle with it. Flyboxer told me what happened to him:

"In some ways, I felt my post-PCT experience was more interesting than my actual hike.

I finished on November 3rd after south-bounding from Idyllwild to Campo. I'd hiked from Idyllwild to Manning Park from May 22nd to October 13th. I thought I'd budgeted my trip well. I tried to keep zeros to a minimum, didn't waste time in town and limited my motel stays. However, I had a couple of unforeseen expenses that basically wiped out the money I'd saved for my post-hike transition. I found myself unemployed, almost broke and homeless in San Diego. A good friend of mine lived there, but I didn't want to crash at his place while I was looking for work. I got the vibe that I wasn't welcome anyhow, so I decided to live in my car.

I missed how the trail seemed to consume my day, physically, mentally and emotionally. I found this gaping hole screaming to be filled. I felt lost in San Diego initially. I spent most of my time walking all over the city because I still wanted and needed to walk. I felt more akin to the homeless than my working peers, and frequented places where they were. In parks, near the water and on benches. I was still in survival mode, and my eyes were constantly looking for natural shelters to sleep in. It felt strange, something I'd never done before. I kept my beard, didn't have access to a regular shower and people began talking to me who never used to before, mostly homeless folks."

I felt lucky when I first read Flyboxer's experience – at least I had somewhere to live. He continued:

"I knew I needed structure, so I set up a daily routine. My day revolved around the toilet. It's amazing what a person can take for granted when they have a place to live. On the trail, I stayed hydrated, almost over-hydrated; it didn't matter. You stop and pee wherever you want. Now I found myself restricting my liquids because I got tired of searching for public toilets. The park restrooms were always filled with creeps, and weird stuff seemed to be taking place in them all the time, which was very disheartening.

I started drawing. I'd hang out in the park and draw for hours; it was therapeutic and gave me something tangible when the day finished. My computer was in storage in Los Angeles, so I searched for employment on the library computers. They felt more like mental institutions than libraries.

My car's brakes were shot, so I had to spend $600 fixing them, just so I could drive up to LA, get my laptop and look for jobs. The trip up there and back would cost another $100. Driving helped me feel normal, but I had to keep it to a minimum. For a start, gas was expensive. Also, having found a good parking spot where I felt relatively safe to sleep at night, I didn't want to lose it and have to find another. I kept an eagle eye on my savings, watching the numbers fall. I was in a race against my bank account.

I attended daily Mass at the Catholic church in Little Italy. It forced me to wake up early, and the predictability provided a sense of normality. After one morning Mass, I watched a homeless man exit, using a door no-one else used. Why did he leave there? I wondered. I did the same and discovered a sparklingly clean private restroom in the courtyard. Hallelujah!

Once I got my computer back, I frequented the café every day, where I took advantage of the free Wi-Fi to look for jobs. My life fell into a routine. I went to Mass in the morning, then drew in the park for a couple of hours. I looked for work, walked around the city, visited a different café in the afternoon, allowing myself a cup of coffee or two, searched for jobs again or wasted time online, then walked in the evening before sleep. It was amazing how hard it was to fill my day. I craved normality.

Often, I'd walk by the waterfront at night and look at people eating in the restaurants. It was a life that appeared unattainable. My heart ached, wondering what I'd become. I saw my peers going to work and having lunch. That too seemed out of reach. Paradoxically, I carried this fire within, this wholly satisfying feeling of accomplishment, knowing I'd completed the PCT. It was pure 1984-style doublethink: carrying two contradictory notions in my mind at the same time.

Having lived in my car for a month in San Diego, I experienced a new low when a homeless man actually gave me a dollar. I couldn't believe it. What was happening? It was almost comical. I tried to refuse it, but he had collected $45 that day, begging down by the waterfront, and was going to sleep in a hotel room for the night.

'I have everything I need for today,' he said. 'Take the buck.'

A few days afterwards, I got a job offer. Although I wanted to live in San Diego, the position was in northern California. Unable to wait any longer, I took it. By the time I left, picked up the rest of my belongings in LA and arrived, I was down to my last few hundred bucks. I was in a completely new town, didn't know a soul, and for the first couple of weeks was unbelievably lonely. I tried to keep my situation to myself. I put my things in storage, joined a gym to access the showers and opened a PO box. My monthly expenses were $80. I started the job immediately, worked out and showered at the gym in the morning, went to work during the day and ate at a café at night. I didn't have enough money to rent a room, so I continued to live in my car. When my first paycheck arrived, I cried with relief and a sense of achievement. Now my routine became solid, like hiking the trail, but naturally different in many ways. The PCT had given me the knowledge and confidence to survive, the patience to focus on a goal and the determination to face difficult circumstances.

Four months later, I was finally able to get out of my car and back under a proper roof. I'll never forget how it felt to sleep in my own room again, to use my own toilet and shower, to cook on a gas stove! It was all luxury to me – anything other than a meal and shelter was sheer indulgence.

Despite it all, I'm hoping to hike another long trail soon and am currently planning an attempt on the CDT. Hopefully, this time, I will be in a better place financially afterwards."

Most hikers' post-trail experience is not as difficult as

Flyboxer's. I'd given up my rented house, my possessions were scattered amongst friend's garages and I had a little money, though not enough to rent anywhere, so I moved back with my parents. My decorating jobs picked up quickly and, despite the fears that my business might have suffered after leaving it for seven months, I enjoyed a busy year.

The problem with this successful period of work was I wasn't thru-hiking. Putting away trip funds is a necessary evil unless you're rich or have financial sponsors. To save funds, you must work: it's a terribly unfair arrangement. I often wonder who invented money, and what idiot thought up the notion of exchanging it for goods and services. Did they have the remotest idea what they were getting us into?

It's a common pattern among hikers. Go long-distance hiking, live free (in spirit) for a few months, forget about your worries and then return. Realise how many useless possessions you own, find somewhere to live, get a job and then the process starts over again. I don't dislike my life in town; I would just rather be up in the hills. Post-trail depression is also intensified by the weather, as most hikes take place in the summer, bringing you back to the comfortless gloom of autumn or winter. Daylight recedes, the cold sets in and you're not where you want to be, geographically or emotionally.

We still cook our meals in one pot over one burner, the heating gets turned off and the bedroom window stays open; being warm just isn't right. Except for the reunion with a favourite pair of jeans, we still wear our hiking clothes because they're comfortable. We shower when the smell is strong enough and wash our clothes when they look grubby. Rising in the morning, we try reluctantly to come to terms with the fact that there's no trail waiting for us.

It's a long, slow transition, or perhaps more of a reluctant acceptance, until gradually we return to the nine-to-five and settle grudgingly back into society.

"What changed me most is that I'm way simpler than I ever was, although I was pretty simple to begin with!" Sugar Moma explains.

"I can live off 200 to 300 bucks a month, and I sleep in my sleeping bag almost every night. I shower no more than three times a week. I still cook and eat out of one pot. I long to hike, and when I'm in the city, I walk everywhere. My dog, Kharma, doesn't have many car rides anymore.

My feelings after getting off the trail? Oh my God, so mixed. Sad because it's over, happy not to have to get up every day and plan my miles, missing my hiker friends a lot (they're the ones who know how I'm really feeling), confused about what to do next, where to go, do I want a real job with a home or should I gypsy everywhere and continue adventuring?

I love the outdoors and what Mother Nature provides. I respect it more now and appreciate every moment I have with her; rain, snow, sunshine. I try and smile always, even when I'm sad or angry. It not only makes me feel better, it lifts everyone around me too.

Did I learn anything on the trail? So many things: be creative with your food, drink lots of water, smile despite the aches and pains, stop and smell the roses, don't sweat the small stuff, be grateful for the big stuff, which is usually little anyway. Relish the moments you have simple things that most people don't appreciate: a soft bed, long hot showers, a real meal that someone else cooked! The company of people you haven't seen in a while, transport, a chair to sit on, pretty dresses, heating when it's cold out, fresh clean laundry – shall I go on?

Leaving the PCT made it difficult for me to return to the city and be a part of society again. Those who haven't thru-hiked just don't understand. I've been called lazy, a runaway from the real world. I look at it differently. I hiked 2,640 miles, with everything I needed on my back – that's hardly lazy. It took a lot of planning, configuring and mental drainage, not to mention the physical aspect of walking and carrying my gear. Sleeping in the rain and the snow, worrying about bears and mountain lions, finding scorpions in my tent, dealing with sore feet and running out of important items, knowing I still had 50 miles to the next town. I've learnt to appreciate every day as it comes. I'd rather be in the mountains, with nothing but necessities, than in the city with the hustle and bustle. People too busy to stop and notice what's around them, too stressed to notice the beautiful flowers growing right in their yard or the homeless sleeping on the sidewalk. Things I didn't see before, I do now. I notice all of it."

It's interesting that Sugar Moma picks up on others calling her lazy and a runaway from society. Adventuring confuses people who don't understand it, and can even make them bitter. We seem to be brainwashed into thinking there's an acceptable way of living, and anyone who moves off that path or makes their own choices against the grain is not normal. Few like straying from convention.

I've experienced it myself. Despite most of my family and friends having accepted my wanderings and encouraging them, nearly all of them struggled at first. I, too, was often called lazy and accused of running away from my problems. As Sugar Moma says, the one thing you cannot accuse a thru-hiker of is being lazy. Months of planning, logistics, securing sponsorship, saying goodbye to people you love and then walking 2,640 miles with everything strapped to your back? This is not laziness, it's pushing mind and body as far as possible.

I suspect that underneath the accusations lie the difficulties many have in grasping the notion of leaving their everyday lives to go and do something they really want to do. OK, so hiking isn't to everyone's taste, but we all have passions, loves, fixations and pastimes that need feeding, whether it's mountaineering, fishing, yoga, cooking or riding a horse.

I fully appreciate that most people who are happy in their careers, bringing up children, paying the mortgage have no desire to go anywhere for several months, regardless of the reasons. I have no argument with this choice (I'm actually a little envious) and equally I understand that some of us can't leave because of these commitments. I'm not married, don't have kids or a mortgage and I'm my own boss. These weren't conscience decisions (perhaps they were subconscious), but they worked out perfectly.

Elk summed his hike up from a different angle:

"After the PCT, I returned to Utah and tried re-joining a wilderness therapy program, where I'd worked before. My old boss strung me along for a few months until I realised it wasn't going to happen.

I had a little money left over, so I scrounged and saved while putting resumes together to try for other jobs. After nearly a hundred attempts, I was successful.

However, while unemployed, I had some realisations about my old job, my life and the period I took off for the PCT. It sounds basic but I understood, finally, that it doesn't matter how much energy you put into something, the return you want isn't guaranteed. It's important to be proactive but, even then, one needs to understand that it's how you react to certain situations that counts. This is sometimes even more important than not reacting at all.

In short, I finally realised the importance of making a timely decision and not allowing my emotions to make my choices.

Now I'm working in the commercial fishing industry as an oceanic observer. I have short hair and I shaved my beard. In other words, I'm really lame but no longer hungry. I can't begin to describe how great the trail was for me."

Elk, Sugar Moma, Flyboxer and most of the others I met realise where their hearts belong: out in the wild. We work for a while until the bug hits again (if, indeed, it ever leaves) and we set off on another hike. When our knees give out, we'll call it a day and reflect, proud at what we've achieved. No sitting in that rocking chair and regretting what we didn't do.

I, too, began resenting my life back in town. When I decided to tackle the PCT, one of my goals was to be completely open to circumstance. Let me elaborate. We're not truly free, nor will we ever be. We only attain steps towards freedom; some of us get closer than others. We stick to familiar patterns: wake up, have breakfast, go to work, get back, chill out, then sleep. Imagine getting out of bed, looking out the window, to be met with a beautiful day and deciding to discard your normal pattern and simply follow whatever course you want – just for one day, just to see what happens.

Perhaps take a stroll in the park? You see an old man sitting on a bench looking sad. Instead of walking by because he seems unapproachable, you sit and try cheering him up. You chat for a while and leave him smiling, feeling better about the day. He mentioned a path leading into the woods that you don't remember being there. You take it. It leads to a stream winding through a copse bursting to life in the early spring. Flowers poke through the soil, you smell onions and then discover a huge swath of wild garlic. Picking a few leaves, you decide to cook some soup with them later. And so it carries on...

I wanted to nurture that freedom, take advantage of random events, delve into unpredictability, escape familiarity and for the most part I did, making as few plans as possible. Even then, of course, I wasn't completely free. I was entertaining one big overall plan, after all; to walk from Mexico to Canada. But in between those two points, I tried to pander to serendipity. Walking the PCT, I came as close as I ever will to being truly free, and I do on every long-distance hike.

I'll leave the last post-hike word to Hojo:

"I returned to my folks feeling like a zombie. I was exhausted physically, mentally, emotionally, and I slept for a full day. It took a while to recover, and when I did, the enormity of what I'd accomplished began to set in. I got up at 5.30am every morning for months, feeling like I had to break camp, make breakfast and put some miles in!

When I see a map of the United States these days, it makes me smile. I've always been patriotic, but I have more national pride now. Having walked both coasts of this great nation (I did the Appalachian Trail in 1998), I know it's an amazing place filled with incredible people and spectacular scenery.

I'm grateful for the opportunity to pursue my dream of hiking the Pacific Crest Trail. Sharing the experience with family and friends (I hiked three days and 33 miles with my father near Lake Tahoe) and meeting new people along the journey remains a highlight of my thru-hike. It's an incredible accomplishment, made extra special by the fact that I'm a cancer survivor.

Since finishing the PCT, I've been fortunate enough to give a presentation on my adventure and lead a college-level backpacking course in West Virginia.

As I write this, I'm sitting in my ski patrol dispatch building. It's 35 degrees and raining outside (essentially, the weather I walked through Oregon in). I didn't particularly like it then and I don't care for it now. It remains my least favourite weather to hike in!"

Hojo, Sugar Moma, Elk, Flyboxer and 99 per cent of the people I met on trail will be friends for the rest of my life. Most of them live in the States, so I won't get to see them regularly, but we share a common connection. They were all there for different reasons, apart from walking the PCT, but I felt as close to them after a day in their company as I am to friends I've known for years. Hiking makes for the strongest bond I know.

I'm asked many times why I hike. People wait for my answer with an expectant look on their face as if they think I've discovered the meaning of life. Of course, I haven't; if only it were that simple. However, spending so much time in the wild does change a person. It doesn't matter if the challenge is the Pacific Crest Trail, the Appalachian Trail, sailing around the world, climbing Everest or crossing the Sahara on a camel – adventuring for extended periods opens one's eyes. When we look back as an outsider to the lives we left, we can act as an impartial observer and see how we're actually living that life. Call it a reality check if you like. We are aware of how we can change our life, but when we are actually embroiled in it, changes are difficult to make. An escape to nature is a perfect time to take one step back and study the situation we have left. Invariably, we return as enlightened individuals with passionate ideas on how to be better people.

So, let's go back to the beginning of this book where I made you a promise. I said I'd answer, as best I can, that original question: why?

Because you can:

- Be free
- Eat as much as you like
- Get super-fit
- Meet like-minded people
- Meet some idiots
- Give up alcohol on trail
- Experience pristine wilderness
- Make up for lack of alcohol in town
- Live rent-free
- Appreciate people more

- Avoid losers
- Live by what you carry
- Ditch the alarm clock
- Forget about TV
- Leave your phone turned off for days
- Sleep under the stars every night
- Sleep under the sun during the day
- Answer the critics who say, "You can't do that!"
- Bathe in a lake
- Lie under the night sky at and fall away into infinity
- Lose weight
- Gain muscle
- Confuse town folk by telling them what you're doing
- Actually figure out what you want to do in life
- Have the guts to go and do it
- Make up stupid names for other people
- Have others make up stupid names for you
- Cleanse your body by drinking loads of water
- Accept and be at one with your stink
- Realise how bad town people stink
- Learn perseverance
- Learn stubbornness
- Learn how to never, ever, ever give up
- Implore others to never, ever, ever give up
- Actually enjoy a McDonald's
- Wear one set of clothes for a week
- Style your hair without products
- Be amazed at the hospitality of others
- Be a shoulder to cry on
- Find a shoulder to cry on

- Be a shrink
- Be a superhuman, indestructible hiking machine
- Have time to think and use it wisely
- Cook a filling meal for $1
- Be at one with and learn to respect wildlife
- Scare yourself shitless by meeting a bear
- Be the furthest you've ever been from anyone
- Make genuine friends for life
- Become mildly famous
- Gain respect
- Sleep outside more times in a year than you sleep indoors
- Become hypnotised by camp fires
- Breathe clean air
- Become speechless by a view
- Sit in a public place having not washed for nine days and observe other people's reactions
- Get asked to leave public places
- Go a week without checking your inbox
- Try to catch up with your inbox after a week
- Wear tights
- Wear a kilt
- Wear tights and a kilt at the same time
- Become an oats expert
- Avoid relationship commitments for months
- Meet the person of your dreams
- Pinpoint who has chocolate and quickly make friends with them
- Discover wild food
- Repair anything with nothing
- Realise what it's like to be homeless

- Understand why the love of money is the root of all evil
- Escape work for months
- Have the time to read your camera manual
- Sing at the top of your voice
- Read loads of books
- Discover the pleasures of dark chocolate-covered almonds
- Learn to accept ramen noodles
- Escape from ramen noodles
- Have a genuine excuse to video yourself
- Accept being cold
- Accept being wet
- Accept being too hot
- Moan at how cold, wet or hot you are
- Sleep outside at well below freezing
- Drink two litres of water in one go and still be thirsty
- Escape from the media
- Believe in conspiracy theories
- Accept anything offered to you
- Give freely
- Hug people and mean it
- Be hugged and know they mean it
- Invent disgusting new recipes based on the food you carry
- Have others confirm how disgusting your recipes are and try theirs
- Feel alive in a forest with the wind around you
- Realise the outdoors is where you are supposed to be
- Miss your favourite beer and discover new ones
- Learn how to really push yourself

- Make your dreams come true
- Have others appreciate and accept you for who you are
- Be as free as you could ever hope for

Any questions?

Chapter 19

What the Hell Happened to Rockets?

It is not so much our friends' help that helps us as the
confident knowledge that they will help us.
Epicurus

After I wrote this book, I realised that I'd overlooked something important. A month after publication I received the first of hundreds of emails asking the same question. The subject line varied but went something like this:

What the hell happened to Rockets?

Initially it confused me, but when I read the last chapters, I realised I'd left him stranded in the middle of nowhere – both narratively and geographically.

The emails kept coming until, finally, I decided to write an extra chapter. I'll now hand you over to the man himself to fill you in.

I took a bus to Chelan, on the southern edge of Lake Chelan, where a ferry service ran to Stehekin. I arrived late, resupplied, and got a room for the night. The weather reports forecast severe storms and the local rangers suggested I'd be foolish to carry on. In particular, the higher elevations between 6,500 and 7,100 feet would get hit hard.

Well, as I always say, you can't keep Pockets down!

I knew I could make it. Having honed my winter skills over several years, I was confident and never contemplated quitting. I had just 70 miles to finish the trail and become a PCT thru-hiker. Dropping out never entered my mind.

The ferry dropped me off in Stehekin the following morning, and I was hiking by 11am. A few miles in and I hit snow. Although I'd expected this, I wasn't looking forward to the harsher conditions, but snow did have one advantage: I found what looked like Fozzie's footprints, and what I guessed were Trooper's as well. Those prints guided me, spurring me on. Alas, fresh snowfall had covered them by the time I hit Rainy Pass.

I took a break under a restroom awning, figuring out my next move while eating a snack. Everything above me was white, and the conditions were worsening. I watched two guys on snowshoes approach.

"You hiking the PCT?" one said.

"Yup," I replied. "What's it like up there?"

"Brutal," the other said. "You shouldn't carry on, there's way too much snow."

"I haven't hiked 2,579 miles to quit now. Did you see any footprints? Any other thru-hikers?"

"No, there's nobody up there," came the adamant reply. "No prints, fresh snow, and it's still falling."

I trudged on through wet, heavy snow for a further two hours, covering just two miles, way off my normal pace. It was cold, and I needed to warm up. I found a flat spot, cleared the snow and pitched my tent, then crawled inside my bag until slowly my core temperature rose.

I got up at five the following morning. It was darker than a tunnel, and the chill hit me after a warm night in my bag. I packed my gear away, turned on my head torch and peered out. Sparkles of snow cascaded down. A fierce wind howled, ripping across the mountains. The storm had arrived.

It took six long, difficult days to reach the northern terminus. Under normal circumstances it would need a mammoth effort, and my condition was far from normal – I was sick and deteriorating, but I had to finish. What's the point of getting off trail a few days before finishing? It made no sense. Just six days, six more days.

Sometimes I managed no more than a mile every hour because of the snow. At the end of that hour, exhausted, I had to stop, pull out my ground cloth to sit on, and rest. I sobbed more times than I care to admit. I cried at the pain and battled the desire to quit; but, after I reached halfway, I had the same distance ahead as behind, which made the decision to push on easy. I'd never hiked in harsher conditions, and probably won't again.

Perhaps in reward, the conditions improved as, finally, I descended to monument 78, the northern terminus of the PCT, and the end of my thru-hike. I collapsed in a heap of exhausted emotions, my body hurting so much because I'd asked too much of it. As far as I know, I was the last thru-hiker that year.

The last American!

After the PCT, I lived in Washington DC for a brief time but grew sick of city life. Months in the woods teach you that cities are not nice places to be. DC was claustrophobic, noisy, and smelly. Everyone thought I was weird because I didn't have a high-powered job and my beard was too big. If those around me judged me by my beard, then it was time to leave. I needed to return to the outdoors, or at least find somewhere to live near it.

I flipped a quarter; heads Idaho, tails Washington State. I packed my car and a few days later landed in Victor, Idaho, right on the backside of the incredible Teton mountain range. The first time I saw them I couldn't believe it: towering rock pillars screaming from the plains below, talk about making a show!

It felt like home, the fresh start I needed, but then my symptoms returned. I kept losing fluids and masses of blood, and I didn't know why. I decided to sit it out for a few months in the foolish hope it would sort itself. It didn't. I got weaker until I couldn't stand for more than a couple of seconds without passing out. My weight plummeted to 130 pounds.

One day I managed to go out, and bumped into a friend. She looked at me in disbelief. Stubborn to a fault, I refused to acknowledge my condition, despite my clothes hanging off my stringy frame. She screamed at me to see a doctor, and, aware of my stubbornness, she then called my parents.

Next thing I knew my mom arrived in Idaho and drove me to Michigan to get help. I think if I'd left it any longer I would've died.

The hospital admitted me straight away. I thought of asking how bad things were, but the look on the doctor's face told me everything. They kept me in for a month running test after test. Eventually they diagnosed severe / extreme ulcerative colitis, an inflammation of the colon and the rectum. Since then, I've had multiple flare-ups and hospitalisations, but have been in remission for over a year. I have an infusion of Remicade every six weeks, which controls it, but I'm battling the insurance company who want to drop me. The treatment costs $14,000 every time.

Now I'm back in Victor, Idaho. It's 25 miles from where I work as a photographic guide and instructor in the Grand Teton National Park; I also work in Yellowstone National Park, and all over the world specialising in wildlife and landscape. My skills as a professional photographer are still in demand by many news sources, magazines, books, and companies.

I have a wonderful and supportive girlfriend, Kristi, and a daughter, Emerson, born three years ago. She's a new and beautiful challenge in my life. We live in the country with stunning views of the Teton Range.

Am I done hiking? Heck no! I've finished the AT and the PCT, and I plan on getting my Triple Crown by doing the CDT as well.

You can't keep Pockets down!

Taking a moment to review this book helps me as an indie author, and I'd appreciate it. Thank you.

Feel free to visit my website at
www.keithfoskett.com